The Growth
and Reform
of English
Local
Government

READINGS IN POLITICS AND SOCIETY

GENERAL EDITOR: Bernard Crick

Head of the Department of Politics and Sociology, Birkbeck College, University of London

ALREADY PUBLISHED

W. L. Guttsman, *The English Ruling Class*.
A. J. Beattie, *English Party Politics* (two volumes).
Frank Bealey, *The Social and Political Thought of the British Labour Party*.
Krishan Kumar, *Revolution*.
Edmund Ions, *Modern American Social and Political Thought*.

Forthcoming Titles

J. P. Poole and Kay Andrews, *The Government of Science in Britain*.
N. D. Deakin, *Race in British Politics*.
Maurice Bruce, *The Rise of the Welfare State*.

Previously published in this series by Routledge & Kegan Paul.

David Nicolls, *Church and State in Britain Since 1821*

The Growth and Reform of English Local Government

Edited and introduced by

W. THORNHILL

Senior Lecturer in Political Theory and Institutions, University of Sheffield

WEIDENFELD AND NICOLSON
5 *Winsley Street London W1*

ISBN 0 297 00402 6   Cased
ISBN 0 297 00403 4   Paperback
Printed by C. Tinling & Co. Ltd, London and Prescot.

Contents

General
Editor's
Introduction

The purpose of this series is to introduce students of society to a number of important problems through the study of sources and contemporary documents. It should be part of every student's education to have some contact with the materials from which the judgements of authors of secondary works are reached, or the grounds of social action determined. Students may actually find this more interesting than relying exclusively on the pre-digested diet of textbooks. The readings will be drawn from as great a variety of documents as is possible within each book: Royal Commission reports, Parliamentary debates, letters to the Press, newspaper editorials, letters and diaries both published and unpublished, sermons and literary sources, etc., will all be drawn upon. For the aim is both to introduce the student to carefully selected extracts from the principal books and documents on a subject (the things he always hears about but never reads), and to show him the great range of subsidiary and secondary source materials available (the memorials of actors in the actual events).

The prejudice of this series is that the social sciences need to be taught and developed in an historical context. Those of us who wish to be relevant and topical (and this is no bad wish) sometimes need reminding that the most usual explanation of why a thing is as it is, is that things happened in the past to make it so. These things might not have happened. They might have happened differently. And nothing in the present is, strictly speaking, *determined* from the past; but everything is limited by what went before. Every present problem, whether of understanding or of action, will always have a variety of relevant antecedent factors, all of which must be understood before it is sensible to commit ourselves to an explanatory theory or to some course of practical action. No present problem is completely novel and there is never any single cause for it, but always a variety of conditioning factors, arising through time, whose relative importance is a matter of critical judgement as well as of objective knowledge.

The aim of this series is, then, to give the student the opportunity to examine with care an avowedly selective body of source materials. The topics have been chosen both because they are of contemporary importance and because they cut across established pedagogic boundaries between the various disciplines and between courses of professional instruction. We hope that these books will supplement, not replace, other forms of introductory reading; so both the length and the character of the Introductions will vary according to whether the particular editor has already written on the subject or not. Some Introductions will summarise what is already to be found elsewhere at greater length, but some will be original contributions to knowledge or even, on occasions, reasoned advocacies. Above all, however, I hope that this series will help to develop a method of introductory teaching that can show how and from where we come to reach the judgements that are to be found in secondary accounts and textbooks.

Bernard Crick

Foreword

This collection of documents which illustrate the growth and reform of local government aims at providing the student of local government history, as well as the general reader, with an acquaintance with the major documents of the subject. In this way it is hoped to kindle an interest which will lead to a deeper understanding of, and a greater respect for, one of the most pervasive influences on the development of modern life. The lengthening of the span of life, the improved state of health of the living, the fight against filth and squalor and the general amelioration of the conditions of the great mass of the people all owe much to the activities of local authorities in the last century-and-a-half. An institution which has contributed so much to the avoidance of human misery is deserving of our attention and understanding.

My thanks are due to my former colleague, Professor Bernard Crick, for his editorial help and guidance, to Kenneth Carter and Regina Kibel of the Education Department of the National and Local Government Officers' Association for their help in locating a number of rare documents, and to the staff of the Sheffield University Library, especially Mrs J. Crane, for the efficient and prompt manner in which the copying of the extracts was undertaken.

Sheffield *September 1970*   W. Thornhill

Acknowledgements

The author and the publishers would like to thank the following for permission to quote from published material: *The Times* for 'Law Report', 9 December 1942; the County Councils Association for *County Councils Gazette*, December 1969; the National and Local Government Officers Association for *The Reform of Local Government*; the Labour Party for *The Future of Local Government*; the Rating and Valuation Association for *The Whitstable Survey of Site Values*; The London School of Economics for Sidney Webb, *The London Programme*, and Beatrice Webb, *Our Partnership*; Staples and Staples Limited for E. Cannan, *History of Local Rates in England*; Cambridge University Press for Hicks et al., *The Problem of Valuation for Rating*; George Allen & Unwin for RIPA Study Group, *New Sources of Local Revenue*, and T. E. Headrick, *The Town Clerk in English Local Government*; The Society of Authors, for the Bernard Shaw Estate, for Shaw, *The Commonsense of Municipal Trading*; Macmillan for D. Knoop, *Principles and Methods of Municipal Trading* and Redlich and Hirst, *Local Government in England*; David Higham Associates Ltd for G. D. H. Cole, *The Future of Local Government*, published by Cassel; and Basil Blackwell for C. H. Wilson (ed.), *Essays in Local Government*.

Acknowledgments

The author and the publishers would like to thank the following for permission to quote from published material: The Press for Carthusians, D Directories; The Controller, HMSO (Appendix);

List of Documentary Sources

1 The Structure of Local Government

4   Exchequer Grants

4.1   *Hansard*, 5 February 1856.
4.2   *Hansard*, 3 April 1871.
4.3   *The Economist*, 19 April 1890.
4.4   *Local Taxation (Customs and Excise) Act*, 1890.
4.5   *The Economist*, 11 October 1890.
4.6   Local Taxation Return, 1892/3.
4.7   *Local Government Act*, 1929.
4.8   Ministry of Health, *Financial Memorandum to the Local Government Bill*, 1947.
4.9   *Hansard*, 18 November 1947.
4.10 Ministry of Housing and Local Government, *Local Government Finance (England and Wales)*, 1957.

5   District Audit

5.1   B. Webb, *Our Partnership*, 1948.
5.2   Ministry of Housing and Local Government, *Report for 1958.*

6   Municipal Trading

6.1   *Tramways Act*, 1870.
6.2   Bernard Shaw, *The Commonsense of Municipal Trading*, 1908.
6.3   D. Knoop, *Principles and Methods of Municipal Trading*, 1912.
6.4   *Local Government Financial Statistics*, 1967–8.

7   Staff and Organisation

7.1   J. Redlich and F. W. Hurst, *Local Government in England*, 1903.
7.2   *The Local Government Officer*, September 1906.
7.3   Final Report from the Royal Commission on Local Government, 1929.
7.4   *Report from the Departmental Committee (Hadow) on the Qualifications, Recruitment, Training and Promotion of Local Government Officers.*
7.5   The 'Bolton' Case: *The Times* Law Report, 1942.
7.6   T. E. Headrick, *The Town Clerk in English Local Government*, 1962.
7.7   *Report from the Committee (Mallaby) on Staffing in Local Government*, 1967.

Introduction

Why is local government so often looked upon as a boring subject when it has the most continuous and immediate effect upon the daily lives of all citizens? The welfare state has claimed an interest in us from 'the cradle to the grave', yet local government can in all honesty express its interest in the homophonic, if somewhat bawdier, equivalent 'from womb to tomb'. National government is politically more exciting, and in modern times has come to direct vast enterprises which add to the quality of life. Local government is regarded as the poor relation, a view which has been supported by the extent to which the central government has amassed control and influence over what local authorities do. But it would be wrong to regard the two kinds of institutions as separate and different species. There never has been a golden age of local government in which the national power was less important or less active than the local institutions. Historically, our local government grew out of the local agencies of the royal power. Politically and administratively, the two have never been separate and independent institutions.

It has never been possible to separate local from national government – constitutionally because for over nine hundred years England (and later the United Kingdom) has been a unitary state; politically because the Crown has been the source of all government, even though its agencies have multiplied. It has never been possible to understand national government without regard to local government, simply because the local institutions have been the means whereby many communal activities have been accomplished. This has never been more true than in the twentieth century, when the notion of 'partnership' between national and local institutions in the execution of major public services has become a very sophisticated complex of political and administrative relations. From the heyday of the sheriff of the county, as the legend of

Robin Hood so romantically portrays, the local agencies have always had the opportunity to bend the central directives to local advantage; and there have been occasions when local government authorities have been able to exert great influence over the activites of the central power. Moreover, the peculiar nature of the English democracy depends on the fusion of the national and local institutions. They are not competitors for the allegiance of the people, but are the twin supports on which rests our extensive element of public influence over what government does.

Local government in England is usually regarded as an institution with ancient roots, but the old names of parish, borough and county obscure the almost total change of methods which took place in the nineteenth century. The original purposes of these old institutions were often lost, their procedures heavily veiled in judicial forms, whilst their restricted membership, especially in the case of the municipal corporations, was frequently a cloak for corruption and peculation on a grand scale.

By 1830 the parish and the borough were no longer administrative organs capable of carrying out their existing limited functions. The Reform Act of 1832 took away the sole *raison d'être* of many ancient corporations, and began a long process of enfranchisement which inevitably spread to the subordinate institutions of government. The middle decades of the nineteenth century were the years of struggle for more extensive services and wider opportunities for the participation of citizens in their administration. Whilst the landed gentry fought to retain their influence in the counties and the borough councils slumbered in their newly enforced efficiency, new institutions were invented to meet the challenges of urban life and to provide for the rising hopes of the new generation.

Though the political power of the old guard was eventually overwhelmed in 1884, they retained enough influence to ensure that the new institutions of the latter part of the century continued some of the ancient characteristics, particularly those of boundary and area. The new force of paid officials saw their future tied to the authorities they served – not to the central government as in some countries, and this was another factor which augmented the pressures of historical apathy against further moves to a more radical structure.

The hundred years from 1832 to 1932 was a century of reorganisation in local government – reorganisation, not revolution. This hundred years saw the ancient poor law institutions first reformed, and then abolished. It saw the growth of a system of representative, multi-purpose authorities. Yet this was achieved only after a long period in which the ancient but ineffective organs were by-passed by a wide range of *ad hoc* authorities based on the concept of service and efficiency. The reformers were indeed the leading statesmen of the period who, judging by the proposals they introduced into Parliament in the middle decades of the nineteenth century, would have given us a local government system fit to meet the challenge of the late twentieth century. As it was, they were constantly defeated by the die-hards of both county and borough who, for the most part concerned to protect their pockets, resisted all attempts to provide more services and more efficient institutions to manage them.

The multi-purpose authorities, though a great step forward from the *ad hoc* authorities of the previous decades, were doomed to failure. They were established within the areas of the ancient boroughs and counties, there was little prospect of change to larger and more viable units. As a consequence we are, within the century, still trying to find a more acceptable and efficient system.

The Structure of Local Government

In 1830 local government in England and Wales was carried on by three kinds of bodies. The borough councils existed in the towns incorporated by royal charter. Elsewhere, the county magistrates had been entrusted over the centuries with a variety of duties of an administrative nature. And finally, there were the parishes whose inhabitants were statutorily bound to elect officials for the relief of destitution (the Overseers of the Poor), the maintenance of the peace (the Parish Constable) and the upkeep of highways (the Surveyor of Highways). All these institutions were suffering strain, and their deficiencies were the cause of much protest.

The Reform Act of 1832 began the process of local government reform by removing the parliamentary franchise from the boroughs for whom it was their main *raison d'être*. The Royal Commission on Municipal Corporations proposed new machinery of local government for those places where the continued existence of a borough council was justified [1.1] – hardly true of places like Old Sarum which were no longer inhabited. The Municipal Corporations Act of 1835 gave effect to the reforms proposed by the Royal Commission and provided a system of administration which gave some safeguards against the worst forms of slackness and corruption in municipal affairs.

An early attempt was made, by the County Finance Boards Bill of 1836, to set up in the counties a form of representative government similar to that established for the boroughs [1.2]. This was defeated by the county gentry, as were many other similar attempts in the following half-century. The country gentlemen, who continued to be heavily over-represented in Parliament until there had been further reforms in the parliamentary franchise, were largely concerned to protect their pockets. They were the main ratepayers in the county areas and they feared the financial effects of allowing others to have a say in local affairs. This was elegantly explained in the report of the Select Committee on the County Rates and Expenditure Bill in 1850 [1.3]. Whilst they could confine local expenditure to the relief of destitution, the upkeep of county bridges and the expenses of the judicial system, their pockets were unlikely to be depleted [1.4]. The turnpike trusts had relieved them of the worst burdens of highway expenditure and the new railways were beginning to provide a mode of transport which made no calls on the county rates.

Whilst the squirearchy was thus fighting its long defence, other developments were taking place which were destined to add to the pressure for institutional reform at the local level. The parochial institutions were outmoded, and their services were abominable. The parochial officers of Surveyor of Highways and Parish Constable had ceased, almost everywhere, to exercise any effective function. The relief of destitution was ineffective, inhuman and often downright corrupt – but it was also expensive and was rapidly degenerating into a general public subsidy to wages. The euphoria about reform in the early 1830s extended to the Poor Law, and there was thrust into the midst of the debate a young man who was destined to play a large part in the construction of our local government system – Edwin Chadwick, the protégé of Jeremy Bentham. Chadwick became a member of the Royal Commission on the Poor Laws whose Report was the precursor of the Poor Law Amendment Act, 1834, which combined the parishes into unions and laid down a new and stricter code for poor law administration.

Chadwick was appointed Secretary to the Poor Law Commissioners – later the Poor Law Board – who were established to supervise the work of the Poor Law Guardians in the unions, but his relations with the Commissioners were fractious and it was with some mutual relief that he was seconded to the Royal Commission on the Police in 1837. This commission tried to find ways of improving the efficiency of the police outside the boroughs and the metropolitan area, but it did not get beyond an interim report since Chadwick was whisked off to another enquiry.

The Poor Law Commissioners had included in their annual reports for 1838 and 1839 some comments on the prevalence of certain diseases in parts of London, and had said that they arose from the insanitary conditions of the areas. It was felt that if these conditions could be improved, the diseases would be less prevalent and fewer people would sink into destitution on account of ill health. The Home Secretary, Lord John Russell, asked the Commissioners to enquire how far similar conditions existed elsewhere in the country. Chadwick was given the task of conducting this enquiry, and from it emerged his famous Report on the Sanitary Condition of the Labouring Population of Great Britain, dated 9 July 1842 [1.5]. By this time Chadwick's relations with the Poor Law Board were so bad that the members would have nothing to do with the report, merely passing it on to the Home Secretary as 'Mr Chadwick's Report'.

This enquiry was the beginning of a long campaign by Chadwick and others – he gave support to the Health of Towns Association – for public health measures. He advanced his own ideas from the narrow field of the improvement of dwelling houses to the wider one of environmental improvements to sanitation and drainage, and he wanted the various powers concentrated in the hands of a single authority [1.6] – a point of view which he succeeded in getting upheld in Parliament by Viscount Morpeth [1.7]. The outcome was the Public Health Act of 1848 [1.8] which created the General Board of Health and empowered it to establish Local Boards of Health. Chadwick was appointed to the General Board – the only full-time member at first – and his activities on behalf of the Board created much opposition; he was accused of setting up Local Boards of Health in many areas against weighty opposition, and in addition the General Board was accused of acting in a very paternal manner towards the local boards. The concept of centralisation, put forward by Chadwick as the basis of sound administration, soon became a cry of derision by his opponents, of whom the most learned was undoubtedly J. Toulmin Smith [1.9]. Though the opposition to Chadwick's methods was successful in bringing the General Board of Health to an end in 1858, the local boards carried on, but newly created boards were known as local government boards – perhaps a better name in view of their extensive functions beyond the field of environmental health.

The attempts to replace the parochial surveyor of highways by a more efficient medium of highway administration began with the creation of the turnpike trusts from the middle of the seventeenth century onwards. The trusts were seriously damaged by the Highway Act of 1835 which abolished the ancient system of statute labour and the system of money payments in substitution for this labour, to both of which the trusts had acquired the right. This loss of revenue (estimated in 1839 to be at the rate of £200,000 per annum) and labour coincided with the birth of the railways, which pushed the turnpikes into further decline as the nineteenth century wore on. The trusts began to disappear, simply by allowing their authorising statutes to lapse – and the last remaining trusts had disappeared by 1895.

The borough councils, with their reformed constitution and powers after 1835, were able to look after their own highways and streets as efficiently as they wished – and of that there could be room for doubt. For other places, an attempt was made in Parliament in 1839 to combine parishes into districts coextensive with the poor law unions, with the Board of Guardians as the highway authority, but the Bill was lost. A further attempt in 1848 to set up a County Roads Board was also defeated, but that year did see an important achievement. The local boards of health created by the Public Health Act were given responsibility for the management of streets and highways, other than turnpikes, and were to exercise the functions of the Surveyor of Highways in their area. Where a local health district was created for a borough, the borough council was the local board of health – in this way the highway functions of the boroughs were confirmed, if not extended.

The connection between good, well kept streets and highways and public health in populated areas had been recognised by Chadwick, and had been echoed in Parliament by Viscount Morpeth, the chief parliamentary supporter of the public health legislation. Notwithstanding the energetic efforts of Chadwick in establishing local health boards, there remained many parishes without any effective highway administration, and in 1862 another Highways Act sought to fill the gaps. This Act empowered the county magistrates to combine parishes into highway districts, with a partially elected board and paid officials. This, of course, followed the pattern of the poor law reform thirty years earlier, but certain places were excluded from the operation of the Act. They were principally the boroughs and places where public health and local government boards had been created. Moreover, the Act allowed a parish which subsequently adopted the Local Government Act 1858 to opt out of the highway district into which it had been merged. As a result there was a rush of small parishes to get local government boards for their areas to prevent their forcible merger into highway districts. Within the space of about a year over 900 small townships and villages achieved this; Chadwick's tally was only a fraction of this figure in five years. So great was the rush that an Amending Act had to be passed in 1863 to limit the creation of local government boards to places with a population of not less than 3,000. Even so, the rot had set in and the future growth of our local government system was destined to be deformed by a rash of small units which we are still trying to abate.

It is important to see how this came about. As a result of the measures so far described, the types of institution concerned with local administration had grown. There were still the county magistrates and the borough councils, but they had been joined by the boards of guardians for the poor law unions, the local boards of health, the local government boards and the highway boards; and there still remained some Improvement Commissioners and the like operating under local Acts. The attempt to remove the lingering influences of Chadwick, which resulted in the demise of the General Board of Health in 1858, also resulted in a dichotomy in the administration and development of public health functions, though there was no dearth of legislation conferring new and wider powers – all of which produced a chaotic situation.

So in 1868 the Government appointed the Royal Sanitary Commission to investigate this confused state of affairs. The Commission took the view that public health was 'part of the larger subject of the entire system of local government' and laid down some principles. Of the Commission's thirty-eight recommendations two were the key to further developments [1.10]. In the course of the parliamentary discussions which followed, Mr Goschen made that famous remark about chaos [1.11] which has provided so many examination questions over the past century. In addition to creating the Local Government Board to bring the supervision of public health, the relief of the poor, and local

7

government into one Department, the Government proceeded in 1872 with a Bill to provide for more efficient local administration [1.12]. The resulting Public Health Act divided England outside the metropolis into urban and rural sanitary districts, each with a local sanitary authority. The urban districts were defined as the boroughs and the areas which had local boards. The rural sanitary districts were the areas of the rural poor law unions except such parts of them as were included in the urban sanitary districts, i.e. those with an existing local board. Thus the division into urban and rural was made on an administrative basis, not on social characteristics, and the large number of units of the 1860s was preserved [1.13]. It is important to remember that these eventually became the urban and rural district councils in 1895, and from this has stemmed one of the inherent weaknesses – too many small authorities – of the present local government system. Equally important to remember is that this development of *ad hoc* authorities in the middle decades of the century was primarily due to the demand for efficient authorities for local services. But also it is obvious from the constant allusions to the desirability of concentrating the various powers in the hands of a single authority that much opinion saw the inefficiencies of a range of *ad hoc* bodies. There were some attempts to convert the Poor Law Guardians into compendious authorities, but the continual failure of the reformists to establish some form of representative county authority led to the continuance of the vast array of *ad hoc* bodies.

Two points may be made in passing. The chain of events just described provided a strong connection between public health and the local government system which persisted into the middle of the present century. When the county councils were required to review their county districts in the 1930s, the ability to provide the basic sanitary services without special financial aid was taken as the measure of viability. The all-embracing nature of public health also gave rise to a number of other local authority services which have become separate activities in their own right – housing and town planning in particular. The other point is that the problem of highway administration as such has never been solved. This ancient parochial function which was inefficiently carried out in 1830 has been reformed in a piecemeal manner. The county councils eventually inherited responsibility for the former turnpike roads, and after a rough partnership between the Ministry of Transport and the counties and county boroughs in regard to classified roads, progress towards a national road network has been so cautious that even now its achievement lies in the future.

The systematisation of the sanitary authorities in 1872 did nothing to abate the demand for representative institutions in the counties. The landowners constituted the largest contingent in Parliament up to 1880, and were able to defeat all measures for the reform of county administration, in spite of the fact that many of the bills brought forward in the sixties and seventies were supported by members of the Government. Success of a kind was achieved in the eighties, though the Local Government Act of 1888 which set up the County Councils and the County Borough Councils was an emaciated version of the Government's intentions [1.14]. The qualification required of boroughs seeking county borough status was reduced during the passage of the bill from 100,000 population to 50,000 and this created a tension in the structure because it produced antagonism between the county councils and the larger number of boroughs which could seek enhanced status. Neither were all the enacted provisions of the statute carried into effect; the intention to give the county councils powers of control over the boroughs and districts [1.15] was thwarted in Parliament in 1889, with the result that a rigid two-tier system emerged in the counties – to produce another series of problems [1.16].

This two-tier system was given firmer foundations by the Local Government Act of 1894 which created the Urban and Rural District Councils to take over the activities of the sanitary authorities and the local government and highway boards. As a consequence, the lower tier authorities were given a broadly-based representative direction, and this added to the lack of control and supervision by the county councils, gave rise to the notion that they were separate and autonomous authorities – a concept of 'separation' which was bound to have adverse effects on the efficient development of services. The 1894 Act also refurbished the parish as an institution of civil government.

The system so created was not a static one, but changes were both one-sided and were difficult to reverse. The provision in the 1888 Act which enabled Boroughs reaching a population of 50,000 to seek county borough status was used vigorously by all places which could gain by it; but of more serious effect on the administrative counties, was the concurrent process of expansion by existing County Boroughs. There was a kind of ladder of social dignity up which urban areas could climb: a rural parish could first be conferred with urban powers as a result of development, it would later seek to become an urban district, and in due course ask for a charter of incorporation as a municipal borough; and finally it would ascend the pinnacle of county borough status when its population reached 50,000. This was a one-sided process because it was at the expense of the administrative counties, and it was one way because there was no means of demoting an area if it failed to work effectively or to maintain its population at the higher level. As a consequence of the fears expressed by the counties at this trend, a Royal Commission on Local Government was established in 1923. Its First Report [1.17] led to the Local Government (County Boroughs and Adjustments) Act, 1926 which altered the procedure for contested creations and extensions of county boroughs and raised the population qualification for county borough status to 75,000.

Although the 1888 Act contained provision for the division or amalgamation of counties, the only use made of it was the division of the county of Southampton in 1890 to create a separate county council for the Isle of Wight. Hardly any use was made of the power to adjust county boundaries until after 1929, when some changes were made in connection with the review of county districts. The 1888 Act allowed changes in the area of county districts, but most of the changes that were accomplished were either the consequence of county borough extensions or the result of local initiative. The Second Report [1.18] of the Royal Commission recommended that each county council should make a regular review of its county districts, and the Local Government Act, 1929, imposed this as a decennial duty of all county councils.

The outbreak of war in 1939 led to a moratorium on all changes in local government structure, but after the war there was a lot of debate [1.19] about what should be done to create a more efficient local government system. There was little measure of agreement amongst the various advocates of reform, however, and this was recognised by the Government in its White Paper of 1945 [1.20].

The Local Government Boundary Commission, set up in 1945, was short-lived and unproductive. Its Report for 1947 [1.21] proposing a new scheme which was beyond its terms of reference, was destined to become of academic interest, but it produced one cliché which was eventually forgotten by those who gave the Redcliffe-Maud Commission its terms of reference. This was the assertion that it was no use talking about areas without talking about functions. The abolition of the Boundary Commission in 1949 was followed by a period in which the only attempts at reform appeared to be the annual bills promoted by a number of boroughs with over 100,000 population to acquire county borough status. These were regularly rejected by Parliament at the suggestion of the Government, largely because of the discussions being conducted by the Ministry of Housing and Local Government about further proposals for reform. As always, agreement amongst the local authority associations was hard to come by, and a further White Paper in 1956 [1.22] represented the greatest measure of agreement that could be achieved.

The Local Government Act, 1958 [1.23] established two Commissions, one for England and one for Wales, to review the areas of the counties and county boroughs. The English Commission had the additional task of making proposals for local government in the five major conurbations outside London, and for these areas the Commission was free to suggest whatever structure might seem most appropriate for each area. But the Commissions were essentially investigatory and initiatory bodies, making *proposals* for reorganisation to the Minister of Housing and Local Government. Any interested body could then lay objections and, after a public inquiry, the Minister could accept, reject or modify the proposals as he thought fit before laying an Order before Parliament to give effect to them. This procedure was both long drawn out (and indeterminate in a few cases) and ineffective. It failed to get rid of even the smallest county, Rutland; the proposals of the Commission, no matter how rationally drawn, were put in jeopardy by every objector, no matter how obtuse he might be; delay could be caused by legal action over jurisdiction and procedure, as it was in the case of the proposals for the West Midlands conurbation; and, as in the case of the Tyneside proposals, even the Minister could show dissatisfaction with what the Commission proposed and with what local opinion preferred.

The energetic Richard Crossman, who became Minister of Housing and Local Government in 1964, saw the deficiencies of this system. He proposed its abolition in favour of something more radical and more effective. In the event, though the achievement was less than his first promise, he established the Royal Commission on Local Government under the chairmanship of Lord Redcliffe-Maud and brought the earlier Commission and its processes to an end. The Royal Commission presented its Report, with a long dissenting memorandum from one of its members, in June 1969 [1.24]. Both made proposals for radical changes in the existing system, but what can be achieved still lies in the future [1.25].

One final structural change needs to be noted: the beginning of separate systems of local government for England and for Wales. Up to the 1958 Act, England and Wales had a common system. The creation of a separate Commission for Wales by that Act was the first separatist development. This Commission's proposals [1.26] proved unacceptable to most Welsh opinion. The Welsh Commission was formally abolished in 1966 along with the one for England, and the task of formulating a new system for Wales was assumed by the newly-created Secretary of State for Wales. His proposals [1.27] eventually attained a guarded acceptance, but remained unimplemented when the Royal Commission for England published its Report. The immediate reaction was to produce a fresh clamour in Wales for further thoughts.

London Government

In 1830, the government of the metropolis was in the hands of the Corporations of London and Southwark, and numerous parish vestries which, unlike their counterparts in the rest of the country, had continued to be active in civic affairs. Though the two Corporations were investigated by the Royal Commission set up in 1833, the 1835 Act did not apply to them, partly because the Royal Commission's Second Report which dealt with these two bodies did not appear until 1837, but largely because the City Corporation fought hard to retain its ancient privileges and customs.

There were two main obstacles to reform in addition to the recalcitrant attitude of the City. These were the large number of special bodies created for particular purposes (Commissioners of Sewers, Paving, Lighting, and Cleansing Boards, and Boards of Guardians) and the large extent of the built-up area of the metropolis. The latter led a later Royal Commission [2.1] to suggest that 'a single municipal corporation' on the principles of 1835 would be impracticable. Instead, the Commission recommended the creation of a Metropolitan Board of Works, which was achieved by the Metropolis Management Act, 1855. This new Board was the authority for the drainage, paving, cleansing, lighting and improvement of an area of 75,000 acres with a population of 2,800,000. It later acquired powers to control the embankment of the Thames, flood prevention, and many of the Thames bridges; and in 1866 it took over the fire services of the fire insurance companies in London.

Other authorities were established for the metropolitan area, such as the Metropolitan Asylums Board in 1867, the London School Board in 1870, and the Port of London Sanitary Authority in 1872. And throughout this period the vestries and district boards continued to be responsible for many minor services.

In spite of fears by the Conservative Party and obstruction by the City, the Local Government Act, 1888 provided that the area of the Metropolitan Board of Works should be an administrative county and that the Board should be replaced by the London County Council. The main advantage of the Council was largely one of composition; whereas the Board of Works was composed of forty-five members elected by the vestries and district boards (with a paid chairman), the Council consisted of 124 members elected by the ratepayers and twenty aldermen elected by the councillors. The elections to the Council were soon fought on party lines [2.2 and 2.4].

The London County Council replaced the Board of Works only; the various other bodies continued to exist. There was much dissatisfaction with the vestries [2.3] and their out-moded methods of election, and this was crystallised in 1897 by the attempts of two parishes, Kensington and Westminster, to secure incorporation as municipal boroughs [2.5]. In due course, the London Government Act, 1899, created twenty-eight metropolitan borough councils [2.6] to replace the mass of vestries and district boards.

It soon became obvious that the metropolitan area could not be contained within the boundaries of the administrative county of London. Whilst the population within the county area began to decline after 1901, that of the surrounding areas was growing. The problem of Greater London, and its transport, was becoming urgent. After the 1914–18 war, a Royal Commission on London Government was set up in 1921 [2.7] to consider the problem posed by the claims, made by the London County Council and by a Committee on Unhealthy Areas appointed by the Ministry of Health, that many activities such as public health, town planning, housing and transport could only be effectively handled by a single authority operating over a more extensive area than the administrative county. But agreement on how to combine different services within a single authority was difficult to achieve, and the only substantial attainment of the inter-war period was the creation of the London Passenger Transport Board in 1933, to which the London County Council lost its public transport services.

The continued inadequacies of the local government structure in Greater London, which were a reflection of those of central London sixty years earlier, were highlighted by the increasing pressure for effective planning, which culminated in the Report of the Royal Commission on the Distribution of the Industrial Population. The physical destruction arising from air raids during the 1939–45 war gave a sudden practical impetus to planning as a preliminary to the post-war reconstruction. This was a very special problem in London and was the main reason why the counties of London and Middlesex were excluded from the terms of reference of the Local Government Boundary Commission in 1945. A committee under the chairmanship of Lord Reading was appointed to consider the problems of greater London but it was disbanded without reaching any recommendations.

The proposals for reviewing the structure of local government in England and Wales which were incorporated into the Local Government Act, 1958, were accompanied by the establishment of a Royal Commission on Local Government in Greater London, and the metropolitan area consigned to this Commission's enquiry was excluded by the 1958 Act from the jurisdiction of the Local Government Commission for England. The London Commission reported in 1960 [2.8] and the scheme enacted by the London Government Act, 1963, followed the principles laid down by the Commission; however, its detailed recommendations were not followed in some significant respects, e.g. in the number of London Boroughs and in the administration of education in the area formerly under the jurisdiction of the London County Council.

Rates and Rating

The rating system is probably the most distinctive feature of our local government. It is certainly older than any of the existing institutions, and it is the one aspect of local government which is most familiar to the general public. First used to any great extent by the Statute of Sewers of 1429, rates were made of general application throughout the land by the Poor Relief Act of 1601. Their use, as a means of financing local activities was further extended in the latter half of the seventeenth century when money payments could be substituted for statute labour on the highways. By 1830, local rates were the recognised method of sharing out among the local inhabitants the costs of their local collective endeavours.

In the first half of the nineteenth century, there were two significant problems. The first was the determination of the kind of property which gave rise to rating liability. Fixed property, i.e. land and structures on or in land, was not in dispute, but an earlier judicial decision had extended liability to personal property, chiefly stock-in-trade. The issue was finally decided by the Poor Rate Exemption Act, 1840 [3.1], as a result of which liability to rates was confined to the occupancy of fixed property. The second problem was the multiplicity of bodies which could meet their expenses by levying a rate [3.2], though most had to collect their money through the agency of the boards of guardians or the county magistrates. In the municipal areas, of course, the borough council also had rating powers; and the fact that the borough council was often endowed with the powers of a statutory board, such as a local board of health, meant that it could levy a number of rates for different purposes. In the county areas, the arrangements were usually far more complex since the different levying authorities did not always have areas which coincided with one another.

Many of the attempts which were made after 1835 to establish representative government in the counties were often as much concerned with the management of the county rates as with the creation of a new agency for the administration of services. Much of the opposition put up by landowners against the creation of representative government in the counties was concerned with the protection of their pockets as the main ratepayers in the counties.

However, the struggle to establish acceptable machinery to control the spending of money collected from the rates still left untouched the technical problems of the rating system itself. These continued to excite controversy long after the publication of the classic work on the subject, Edwin Cannan's *The History of Local Rates in England* [3.3]. There were three elements in this controversy. The first concerned the method of determining the base on which rates were levied; this is the problem of valuation for rating. The second was the multiplicity of authorities able to levy rates, and the difficulties of managing a system shared by so many different bodies. The third, which is probably the most important aspect of the rating problem which exists today, is the relative burden of rates on different classes of property and the associated difficulty of applying to all the types of property in the modern age a taxation principle which was designed centuries ago when 'property' was a simpler and cruder phenomenon than it is today.

In the latter part of the nineteenth century the major problem was to get rating assessments to bear some relationship to rents [3.4], rents having been used since Elizabethan times as the measure of liability. Most of the attempts were unsuccessful. Further proposals for reform were made after the turn of the century, first by the Royal Commission on Local Taxation 1899–1901 [3.5, 3.6, 3.7], and secondly by the Kempe Committee on Local Taxation 1914 [3.8] – this was, incidentally, the last *general* review of the rating system. The improvement in valuation methods sought by these two bodies had to wait until the Rating and Valuation Act, 1925 provided for quinquennial revaluations and regularised the method of computing rateable values. The development of housing policy since 1914, and the particularly acute problems of the post-1945 period, created further difficulties for the valuation of domestic property. The application of rent control in the two wars, the growth of owner-occupation, and the provision of an increasing number of houses by local authorities which were let at non-market rents, combined to make the rental basis of valuation for domestic property more and more of a myth. The Local Government Act of 1948 attempted to establish a different basis for fixing rateable values for domestic property, but the idea proved unworkable. Pre-war rentals were resorted to in the Rating and Valuation Act, 1955, and current rentals in the Rating and Valuation Act, 1961. The dearth of domestic properties actually let at rents recognisable for rating purposes was finally conceded in 1969, when the Government produced a Bill to allow valuation officers to establish comparable rents by reference to houses and flats anywhere in the country.

The various attempts to reduce the number of authorities levying rates suffered the same fate as those to improve the level of valuations. The effects of the 1914–18 war on price levels, combined with the increased expenditure by local authorities on education and health services, created pressure for more uniform levels of valuation, particularly within county areas. The government produced proposals in 1923 which eventually led to the Rating and Valuation Act, 1925 [3.9] whose most important provisions created a consolidated rate in every area and considerably reduced the number of assessment and collecting authorities from 15,546 to 1708 – thus fulfilling Goschen's ambition of over half a century before. A further development occurred when the Local Government Act, 1948, transferred responsibility for making assessments to the Inland Revenue, thus achieving the centralised system of valuation recommended by the Kempe Committee in 1914.

The burden of rates on different classes of property has often been the cause of complaint but there has been hardly any attempt to provide a broadly-based solution. Successive governments have succumbed to the blandishments of particular groups of ratepayers and as a result there has been a series of provisions to give preferential treatment to particular classes. There was the partial derating of agricultural land and buildings in 1896 and 1923, and their final exemption in 1929 [3.10]; the partial derating of industrial and freight transport hereditaments from 1929 to 1962; the post-war valuation of domestic premises on pre-war rents; the temporary reduction of shop and commercial property valuations after the 1956 revaluation; and finally the rebate on rates on domestic properties brought into the Rate Support Grant in 1965. All these brought anomalies into the rating system: they were all attempts to limit the impact of rates on particular types of property. Taken together, they contribute to the destruction of the rating system as an effective source of local revenue. Of a different order was the introduction of rate rebates in 1966, which reduced the sums of money paid by low income groups without affecting the level of valuation of the property.

Various attempts have been made to replace or supplement rates. The hardy annual has been the rating of site values [3.11, 3.12], but other sources of revenue have been canvassed from time to time. These were succinctly brought together by the Royal Institute of Public Administration in its 1956 study of new sources of revenue [3.13].

Exchequer Grants

The first Exchequer grant to local authorities was made in 1835 to meet the cost of removing prisoners from local prisons to the convict depots, but the first grant of any significance was that of one quarter of the pay and uniform costs of the police, introduced by the County and Borough Police Act, 1856 [4.1]. This provided the means of marrying the claims of the boroughs and the county magistrates for some compensation for the additional costs they would incur from the Act, with the desire of the Home Office to ensure that police forces were efficient. The simple device of providing for the withholding of the grant in cases of inefficiency was the basis of the union, and formed the foundation for a century's development of control over local services by central departments.

By 1888 the number of grants had grown quite considerably. (Their development was summarised in a report to Parliament in 1893 [4.6].) A number of the grants were replaced by the share of Probate Duty which was transferred to the county and county borough councils by the Local Government Act, 1888. This was the first of Goschen's 'assigned revenues' [4.2] and it was complemented by the additional duties on beer and on spirits which were imposed for the benefit of local authorities by the Customs and Inland Revenue Act, 1890 [4.3]. The portion of these duties attributable to England was applied by the Local Taxation (Customs and Excise) Act, 1890 [4.4], as to £300,000 for police superannuation, and the residue to the county and county borough councils – who were empowered to use any sums so received to defray the expenses incurred by them in carrying out duties in relation to technical education.

Goschen's 'assigned revenues' were his second attempt to relieve the burdens of the ratepayers. His first attempt, in 1871, failed, but the principle was the same in both cases – that part of the growing yield of nationally levied and collected taxes should be made over each year to the local authorities [4.5]. The assignment of national revenues was conceived as the answer to the growing needs of the local authorities and the inability of the rates to expand sufficiently to meet those needs. Yet, within a generation, the assigned revenues of 1889–90 had fallen foul of the rapaciousness of a line of Chancellors of the Exchequer who, from 1908 onwards, sought to limit the amount being transferred out of the Exchequer. As a consequence, the assigned revenues were no more beneficial than an ordinary annual Exchequer grant and they were eventually brought to an end in 1929.

The failure of the assigned revenues was aggravated by developments in national policy arising from the war-time growth of services and the beginning of the disintegration of the poor law. A number of local authority services were developed with the aid of specific grants; to the police and education grants, dating from the nineteenth century, were added grants for classified roads, housing, and for numerous health services. In addition to these developments, there was national concern in the early twenties for economy in public expenditure, and in 1922 the Committee on National Expenditure called for a review of the grant system and of the burdens of local expenditure on agriculture and industry. Out of all this controversy, there emerged the financial settlement embodied in the Local Government Act, 1929 [4.7].

This Act abolished the assigned revenues, the grants under the Agricultural Rates Acts, 1896 and 1923, the percentage grants for tuberculosis, maternity and child welfare, blind welfare, venereal diseases and mental deficiency, and the grants for Class I and II roads in London and in county boroughs and for the maintenance of scheduled roads in county districts. These were replaced by an element in the new system, known as the General Exchequer Contribution, which the Act introduced and which continued until 1948 to be the main form of general subvention to local authorities. A second element in the new system was compensation for the loss of rates from the derating of agricultural and industrial properties, whilst a third element was what was described as 'new money'. Like the assigned revenues, the new system of Exchequer aid aimed at providing the local government system with a gradually increasing amount of money from national taxation, but whereas the amount of the assigned revenues was determined by the yield of the national taxes concerned, the amount of the General Exchequer Contribution was fixed in relation to the growing expenditure of local authorities. The new system also aimed at distributing the total amount made available to local authorities on a formula which was weighted to favour those areas with higher demands or lower resources than average. The scheme was wrecked by the financial consequences of the 1939–45 war, and after the end of the war it soon ceased to have any great relevance to the new circumstances of local government.

The abolition of the poor law and the transfer of hospitals to the State in July, 1948, removed from local government its two most expensive services; whilst the basic figures used for resources in the formula were recognised as unrealistic. The Local Government Act, 1948, abolished the General Exchequer Contribution and replaced it by the Exchequer Equalisation Grant, which was based on a formula more relevant to the contemporary circumstances of local government, and designed to have a more discriminatory distributive effect [4.8, 4.9]. This was achieved by the simple expedient of providing assistance only to those authorities shown by the formula to have less than the national average of resources per head of (weighted) population.

Ten years later, the equalisation grant was renamed the Rate Deficiency Grant and its manner of computation was tightened. In addition the major specific grants, those for education, health, fire services and child care, and some minor grants were replaced by a new General Grant. This was the Government's answer [4.10] to the arguments for new sources of revenue and for less 'nannying' by the central departments. In 1965 these two systems became, with a few changes, the basic elements in a comprehensive grant system with the grandiose title of Rate Support Grants. A third element in this new scheme, called the domestic element, is designed to provide an annually increasing reduction in the poundage of rates levied on domestic property. The domestic element is probably the most pernicious of any kind of Exchequer aid ever provided; its *reductio ad absurdum* is the eventual extinction of rates on domestic property. Far from releasing the local government system from bondage to the central Exchequer, it must inevitably proceed to the destruction of the rating system as the sole independent base of local government finance. And if it should be abandoned before it reaches that state of utter despair, the consequences will be so great – because of the great gap which will have to be filled – that the local government system will be shaken to its foundations.

The District Audit

No account of the growth of the English system of local government would be complete without some attention being paid to the District Audit. This was one of the controlling devices invented with the reform of the poor law in 1834, and although it was not applied to the reformed boroughs in 1835 it was extended to most of the other bodies created in the nineteenth century. But the boroughs did not remain entirely free; over the years the District Audit has been applied to some of their accounts, and since 1933 those boroughs which wish to do so have been free to adopt the District Audit for all their accounts.

The most distinctive feature of the District Audit is the ability of the auditor to demand repayment to the funds of a local authority of any money which has been improperly spent or not properly accounted for; and the persons responsible must restore the money out of their personal pockets. There have been a number of celebrated judicial decisions about the powers and functions of the district auditor. The most famous is that of Roberts *v.* Hopwood, decided in 1925, which confirmed the district auditor's power to disallow expenditure on grounds of its being unreasonable even though for a lawful object. It has also been held that the district auditor can surcharge an officer in respect of expenditure incurred directly as a consequence of his negligent performance of his duties -- as a school caretaker recently found when he had not taken enough care to ensure that the amount of fuel delivered to his school corresponded with the weight shown on the delivery ticket. In another case, it was decided that the power of surcharge extended to third parties who had business with a local authority and who conducted their transactions in such a way as to secure from the authority payments beyond the amount properly due. In this way we can see how the audit augments the popular control over local authority spending which is exercised by the members of an authority [5.1, 5.2].

Municipal Trading

If there is any aspect of local government to which the epithet 'failure' can be applied, it is municipal trading. The earliest activity to which the concept of trading – i.e. the charging of fees or tolls for individual items of service with the aim of securing a surplus over costs – could be applied in the municipal field was that of markets and fairs. The nineteenth century was the boom period in the development of municipal trading, bringing first gas works, and then electric lighting and passenger transport (tramways) to the general field. The early Fabians promoted the ideas of 'municipalisation' as one of the strongest planks in their platform, and thereby earned the nick-name of 'gas and water socialists'.

The concern of successive Parliaments in the nineteenth century, in this field as in that of the railways, was how best to confer and regulate the monopolist powers of the undertakers who were granted the right to operate these new utility undertakings. And where private companies were endowed with powers to operate gas, electricity or tramway undertakings, the enabling legislation usually allowed the local authority of the area served by the undertaking to acquire it after a limited period of private operation [6.1], and on terms which were highly favourable to the acquiring authority.

In the hectic developments of the last two decades of the nineteenth century, the politicians were anxious to avoid the nuisances and wastefulness of competition as well as the vices of monopoly. With their ensuing concern to regulate the activities of the franchise holders, whether municipal authority or private company, the politicians failed to see the wood for the trees. This sometimes appeared as a failure to grasp the imminent prospects of technological development, as in the case of the electricity legislation. But more generally they failed to ensure adequate management procedures for the municipal enterprises.

The Fabian arch-priest of municipal trading was Bernard Shaw [6.2] whose views about the benificence of municipal managers were wildly optimistic. A more sober and, as events were to prove, a more accurate view was presented by Douglas Knoop [6.3]. Though the restriction on the transfer of profits from electricity undertakings to the relief of rates was an official concession to the danger that city-fathers might raid or rig the finances of their trading undertakings for the benefit of the rate fund, the ultimate failure of municipal trading to provide the cornucopia prophesied by the Fabians was due to the ravages of competition and obsolescence. Later, especially in the case of electricity and gas, and to a lesser extent in the case of passenger transport, the arguments for nationalisation overtook those for municipal control. The electricity undertakings of 326 local authorities in England and Wales were taken over by the British Electricity Authority and its area boards on 1 April 1948; and the gas undertakings of 269 authorities went to the area gas boards on 1 May 1949. Although the provisions of the Transport Act, 1947, for the transfer of municipal passenger transport undertakings to the British Transport Commission proved abortive, the Passenger Transport Authorities created for the large urban areas under the Transport Act, 1968, have made considerable inroads into municipal passenger transport.

The most important groups of trading undertakings, if we exclude housing from this category, are crematoria, slaughterhouses, and wholesale markets and cold storage facilities [6.4]. All these have a long history, but post-war developments in public health and in techniques of food distribution have been giving these activities a new lease of life.

There are still a few optimistic observers who point to individual municipal enterprises which bear an apparent air of success: the telephone system at Kingston-upon-Hull, the Savings Bank at Birmingham, the airport at Manchester, and the racecourse at Doncaster are the favourite examples. These are quoted as enterprises which other local authorities might emulate, but also they are most likely to remain unique. Successful as individual ventures, they are the accidental scatterings of the seeds of wider fields of municipal enterprise. Hull retains its telephone only by grace of the Post Office, whilst the Birmingham bank is as much a monument to a momentary lapse of the Treasury as to the enterprise of Birmingham's city-fathers.

Staff and Organisation

The old parochial and county authorities had to rely on the compulsory unpaid service of the local citizens, but in the nineteenth century the employment of full-time paid executive officers became the general practice. This is probably the most distinctive development in the local government system after 1835.

By the end of the century, Josef Redlich [7.1] was able to record the growth of the body of paid officials with which we are so familiar, and he was perceptive enough to outline the problems thrown up by a non-collegiate body of chief officials and the peculiarities of the position of town clerk. The county councils, which had been created only a few years before Redlich wrote, had inherited the Clerk of the Peace as their chief officer, an indignity which they had to continue to endure until 1929.

Redlich also commented on the labyrinthine growth of committees, which even in his day threatened the virtues of the multi-purpose authority, still in its infancy. The creation of the urban and rural district councils by the Local Government Act, 1894, was the formal death sentence on the *ad hoc* authorities, though the school boards lasted until 1902 and the boards of guardians until 1930. Yet, within the multipurpose authorities, the growth of separate committees, paralleled by independent departments headed by professionally-qualified officers jealous of their independence of their fellows, effectively thwarted the potential advantages of the multipurpose authority. This process of frag-

23

mentation was supported and enhanced by the phoney doctrine, called local democracy, which proclaimed that elected members in committee directed, supervised and controlled the work of the paid officials. As a result the committees became so important and did so much in relation to their services, that there was hardly anything left to the council to do.

The long-term consequences were two. First, the loss of control by the council assemblies; they became rubber stamps, approving or disapproving the proposals of committees; rarely giving something of their own, such as the adumbration of policy or the determination of priorities. Secondly, because in theory the elected members did all the thinking and gave the staff their instructions, no one recognised the need to ensure that the staff got essential training.

The creation of a complete system of multipurpose authorities, backed by the abolition of the school boards in 1902, led to the emergency of a mass consciousness amongst the paid officials of the large number of bodies embraced by the single title of local authorities. The staffs of the boards of guardians enjoyed the generic name of poor law officers, and had gained the statutory right to superannuation on retirement by the Asylum and Poor Law Officers Superannuation Act, 1892. The staffs of the local authorities, the local government officers, saw no reason for this differentiation, especially as the asylum officers had become employees of the County Councils when the latter were established in 1889. Largely as a result of local initative in Liverpool, a movement to establish a national organisation for local government officers gained speedy support and in 1905 the National Association of Local Government Officers was formed [7.2]. The Association soon established two basic aims: to gain the right for local government officers to be superannuated on retirement; and to secure proper training for its members so that the local government service could become a fully-trained profession.

Superannuation rights were basically achieved by the Local Government Superannuation Act, 1922, which allowed but did not require local authorities to establish superannuation schemes for their officers, and by a further Act of 1937 which made the superannuation of officers compulsory, and allowed authorities to make schemes to cover their manual workers. Meanwhile, many authorities had gone beyond the basic requirements by schemes authorised by Local Acts.

In spite of Nalgo's efforts, the defects recognised by Redlich remained. These were brought to the attention of the Onslow Commission [7.3], and they eventually formed the basis for a full-scale inquiry by the Hadow Committee [7.4]. Nalgo was now beginning to force the pace. Its Education Department, following the example set by the poor law officers (who became local government officers in 1930 when the poor law functions of the boards of guardians were transferred to the county and county borough councils), had established its own examination. More important, it began to encourage the universities to provide some training for public servants generally, and local government officers in particular. From this encouragement there sprang the Diplomas in Public Administration offered by most of the civic universities from about 1930 onwards. (This was to have an unexpected and important side effect for most of the universities, because after 1945 the teaching of public administration was the base on which they built their larger and wider-ranging departments of politics.)

The Hadow Report was destined to be a pious hope, until it was largely regurgitated a generation later by the Mallaby Committee on Staffing in Local Government. The local authorities received the recommendations of the Hadow Committee at a time when they were just emerging from a period of enforced constraint on their expenditure. In the middle thirties the emphasis was placed on expenditure which could generate employment in the community, such as house building and slum clearance. The late thirties were overshadowed by the threat of war and by expenditure on air raid precautions. In all this, expenditure on staff and staff training got scant consideration.

But Nalgo was working on a broader front, pushing the idea of Whitleyism in local government. Little headway was made, except in the north-west, until the effort was given a sudden boost by the war-time emphasis on good industrial relations, including joint consultation. In 1942, in the 'Bolton Case' [7.5], Nalgo had established its right to use the war-time procedure of compulsory arbitration in disputes with employing authorities, and this emphasised the significance of adequate negotiating machinery.

As a result of continued pressure from Nalgo, aided by a benevolent Government attitude, the local authority associations eventually agreed to the creation of the National Joint Council for Local Authorities' Administrative, Professional Technical and Clerical Services in 1943. (A number of other joint councils were also established for special groups of local authority employees.) Two great achievements quickly followed. The first was the creation of a national scheme of conditions of service and salaries, the 'Charter', which came into force on 1 April 1946. The second was the creation of the Local Government Examinations Board in 1946 to provide a scheme of promotion examinations suitable for the local government service and to approve such independent qualifications as were relevant to promotion in local government.

The 1950s and 1960s were a difficult time for the local government service; a dearth of suitable applicants for general administrative and specialist posts; intense competition from other forms of employment; and changed public attitudes, especially on the part of younger people, which relegated public employment to a low place in their preference scale. In the sixties, there has been increased emphasis on in-service training and on modern management devices as essential for the efficient use of manpower [7.6].

This new climate led to uncommon unity amongst the local authority associations. At their request, the Ministry of Housing and Local Government established two committees to investigate the twin problems of staffing and management. The Mallaby Committee [7.7] on Staffing in Local Government and the Maud Committee [7.8] on Management in Local Government (it was really concerned with internal organisation) reported in 1967. Their reports provoked much speculation especially the latter, which suggested a more effective form of internal organisation and a redistribution of functions between members and officers, but action on the lines recommended has been slow.

The Local Government Training Board superseded the Examinations Board at the end of 1967, its conception having been blessed by the Mallaby Committee. Its main aim is to promote wider schemes of training on a cost-sharing basis through its system of levies and grants. Much remains to be done, and it is by no means certain that the Training Board has secured a permanent place in the local government system. The probable reorganisation of the structure of local government into larger but fewer authorities will inevitably improve the opportunities for staff management and internal reorganisation. At the same time, the new larger authorities will need less help from external agencies such as the Training Board, especially if regional groupings lead to more effective use of manpower and training facilities by combined effort. But the idea of a national local government service, parallel to the civil service, appears utopian.

Public Health

The growth of the modern local government system since 1835 has been inextricably mixed with the development of public health services. The powers to pave and cleanse streets and to provide other sanitary services were bestowed on the reformed municipal corporations in 1835. The Public Health Act, 1848, empowered the creation of local boards of health, which became urban sanitary authorities by the Public Health Act, 1872, and urban district councils by the Local Government Act, 1894. The 1872 Act also provided for the rural boards of guardians to act as sanitary authorities in their areas, whilst the 1894 Act replaced them by rural district councils. There is, therefore, a direct connection between the public health service and the structure of local government, especially as the county councils soon gathered some public health powers.

But public health has been important in the growth of local government in two other ways. First, the activities embraced by this function are extremely numerous. The Act of 1848 was drawn very widely, and there has been a whole succession of statutes, too numerous even to list here, which have considerably extended the scope of public health activity. Secondly, within the original concept of environmental health other local government services have been nurtured until they now operate as separate activities in their own right. Many of the existing personal health services embraced by the National Health Service Acts, such as maternity and child welfare, midwifery, health visiting and vaccination and immunisation services, began as aspects of public health. So did the infectious diseases hospitals; whilst under the Public Health Act, 1936, all counties and county borough councils were given the duty of ensuring that their areas had adequate hospitals for the treatment of the sick.

Housing was another service brought up under the general guidance of public health. It was an easy step from the early Chadwickian concern with the sanitary condition of houses, to the provision of new houses to replace those found inadequate. Though the first tentative housing legislation was enacted in the middle of the nineteenth century, the Housing Act, 1890, was the first effective step; but it was only a small one, and local authority housing did not really get into its stride until after the 1914–18 war. Even in the inter-war period, many local authorities had no separate housing department or staff; the medical officer of health, the surveyor or architect, and the treasurer jointly handled the housing activities in such authorities. Adequate housing is still basically a problem of environmental health: the certificate of the medical officer of health is necessary to initiate a clearance area programme, particularly if it involves a large number of sub-standard houses.

Town and country planning also had its roots in public health. It developed as part of the concern for the creation of healthier communities as a reaction against nineteenth-century industrial towns. The idealism of Ebenezer Howard for garden cities spilled over in a limited practical way to some kind of concern that large-scale housing development by local authorities should display an elementary social conscience; the relationship of housing to town planning was rather vaguely implied by the Housing, Town Planning, &c. Act, 1909, but later developments in the twentieth century have taken town planning through a basic concern with land use to a more esoteric and questionable mixture of aesthetics and community development. 'Environment' is now a concept lively in politics if ill-defined in law.

The Literature of Local Government

Though much has been written on local government, most books are either descriptive and historical [8.4] or expository legal works. There is very little of what might be termed the fundamental literature, which makes a contribution to thought about the subject. This is partly because local government has not excited any great constitutional writers, and partly because most of the developments in structure and finance have been fought for at close quarters over long periods. The great visions, such as those of Bentham in the 1830s and Goschen in the 1870s, have met every obstacle that vested interests and apathetic governments could muster.

Whilst local government has produced few writers [8.1, 8.3, 8.5, 8.6] who could rise beyond the descriptive minutiae of routine processes and problems, the few who were competent to do so had their noses too close to the grindstone to be able to see the true nature of the system and to relate it to the wider aspects of the government of the State. On the other hand, some have declared

John Stuart Mill exhausted the subject in his chapter on local government in *Representative Government* [8.2], and certainly no academic has matched Mill in general perception. The Webbs could only record; William Robson has spent half a century fulminating about the deficiencies of the system, but little change has been achieved, whilst the Redcliffe-Maud Commission of 1966–9 was prevented by its terms of reference from considering the place of local government in our modern society. The best we have of modern thought on this subject was that provided by the Royal Commission on Local Government in Greater London [8.7] which did, at least, have a quick glance beyond the pinnacles of Westminster.

What, then, is the place of local government in our modern society? There is a danger that it will be seen in terms of the services that it carries, or could carry, out. The Royal Commission on Local Government 1966–9 could hardly get away from such a position; the majority report resolved the list of functions into 'the substance of what it does . . . an all-round responsibility for the safety, health and well-being both material and cultural, of people in different localities, in so far as these objectives can be achieved by local action and local initiative, within a framework of national policies.' Mr Senior, in his dissent, starts from an idealised and mythical view of the historical primacy of local government, but then takes a more expansive view than his colleagues of the role of local government:

> Local government has a general responsibility for the well-being of the communities it represents: its concern is not confined to the discharge of the duties imposed on it by Parliament. It must seek to promote community well-being in all its aspects – economic as well as social, cultural as well as physical – whether or not it has a statutory duty in relation to any particular aspect. And in discharging its statutory duties it must put the general well-being of the local community before the sectional interest of the central government department that is nationally responsible for the functions concerned.

In fact, the role of local government can never be expressed in terms of services carried out, simply because the range of services at any given moment derives from technological and administrative possibilities not from any inherent or constitutional 'right'. Neither can the role be defined in terms of a peculiar kind of democracy, 'local democracy', to which so many councillors make obeisance. There is no sensible way in which the national and local governments can be categorised on democratic gradings. Democracy is a characteristic of the state as a whole, derived from the cohesion and inter-relation of its constituent elements, not from the mechanical addition of the supposed values of its individual institutions.

The true role of local government lies in its political potential rather than in its technological and administrative accomplishments. There is no special case for local administration *per se*, especially with modern communications and management techniques. The functions of local government are largely a matter of convenience – derived primarily on the basis of giving an institution, which derives its true value from other principles, a range of useful tasks to perform; 'useful' in the sense that they allow a meaningful exercise of its real purpose. The value of local government is political; it is to be seen in the contribution it makes to the character of our political life as a whole.

Local authorities in England enjoy, if only in a limited manner, a 'will' of their own which is derived from the elected element in their personnel. This 'will', which may be constrained but can never be suppressed entirely by legal prescriptions or the over-bearance of national politicians, is the essence of free institutions – providing at one time a simple alternative to central decisions, at others acting as a counterweight to centralised power, and may be on some occasions lending support to the centre. This sort of balancing mechanism is only a part of the political role of local government. It also provides a means whereby there can be associated with the affairs of government a much larger number of citizens than would otherwise be the case. The opportunities for citizen involvement are not only more numerous, but are also more varied, so that citizens can choose the extent and kind of their public commitment – thus helping to widen the range of interests and abilities brought to bear on the affairs of state. Whatever criticisms there may be of political life as such, particularly as a result of the growth of mass political parties with their tendency to the marshalling of their members, there is no doubt that the opportunities for political expression and service which are provided by a viable and effective local government system have given to the English democracy the element of stability and resilience for which it has for so long been admired.

1 The Structure of
Local Government

1.1 From the First General Report of the Commission appointed to inquire into the Municipal Corporations in England and Wales', *HCP* (1835), Vol. XXIII, pp. 17, 34 and 49.

This Report marks the beginning of local government reform in the nineteenth century. It was really a consequence of the reform of the parliamentary franchise in 1832, and these extracts show (i) how the two subjects were connected, and (ii) the generally notorious state of municipal administration as the Commissioners found it.

13. The greater number of the governing charters of Corporations was granted between the reign of Henry VIII and the Revolution; the general characteristic of these documents is, that they were calculated to take away power from the community, and to render the governing class independent of the main body of the burgesses. Almost all the councils, named in these charters, are established on the principles of self-election. The criminal jurisdiction of the boroughs received still further enlargement; and numerous instances occur in which a recorder was created, which office had been before that time confined to some of the larger boroughs. There is little reason to doubt that the form given to the governing classes, as well as the limitation of the burgess-ship, during this period, was adopted for the purpose of influencing the choice, or nomination, of Members of Parliament. At this time the honorary office of High Steward was created in many boroughs, by which the borough became connected with the aristocracy or with the Crown. Some of these charters contain clauses by which the right of electing Members of the House of Commons is limited to the select bodies which they created.

14. During the reigns of Charles II and James II many corporate towns were induced to surrender their charters, and to accept new

ones, containing clauses giving power to the Crown, to remove or nominate their principal officers. After the proclamation by James II, dated 17 October 1688, the greater number of these towns returned to their former charters. The charters which have been granted since the Revolution are framed nearly on the model of those of the preceding era; they show a disregard of any settled or consistent plan for the improvement of municipal policy, corresponding with the progress of society. The charters of George III do not differ in this respect from those granted in the worst period of the history of these boroughs. It has become customary not to rely on the Municipal Corporations for exercising the powers incident to good municipal government. The powers granted by Local Acts of Parliament for various purposes, have been from time to time conferred, not upon the municipal officers, but upon trustees or commissioners, distinct from them; so that often the Corporations have hardly any duties to perform. They have the nominal government of the town; but the efficient duties, and the responsibility, have been transferred to other hands. . . .

73. The importance which the privilege of electing Members of Parliament has conferred upon Corporate Towns, or rather upon the governing bodies there, and the rewards for political services, which are brought within the reach of the ruling corporators, have caused this function to be considered in many places as the sole object of their institution. In some Boroughs this right has survived all other traces of municipal authority. The custom of keeping the number of corporators as low as possible may be referred to this cause, rather than to the desire of monopolising the municipal authority, which has been coveted only as the means of securing the other and more highly prized privilege.

Hence a great number of Corporations have been preserved solely as political engines, and the towns to which they belong derive no benefit, but often much injury, from their existence. To maintain the political ascendancy of a party, or the political influence of a family, has been the one end and object for which the powers intrusted to a numerous class of these bodies have been exercised. This object has been systematically pursued in the admission of freemen, resident or non-resident; in the selection of municipal functionaries for the council and the magistracy; in the appointment of subordinate officers and the local police; in the administration of charities entrusted to the municipal authorities; in the expenditure of the corporate revenues, and in the management of the corporate property. The most flagrant abuses have arisen from this perversion of municipal privileges to political objects. The Commissioners have generally found that those Corporations which have not possessed the Parliamentary franchise, have most faithfully discharged the duties of town government, and have acquired, more than others, the confidence and good-will of the communities to which they belong. This has been the case in some, even where the ruling bodies are strictly self-elected, and where the general character of their constitution is open to the objections common to the great majority of Corporations. Very few large corporate towns were without Members of Parliament, even before the Reform Act, so that many instances cannot be given from among them. The Corporations of Leeds, Lynn and Doncaster may be cited as turning their attention to their municipal duties more sedulously than the majority. Among small towns, deserving the same character, we refer to the Corporations of Louth, Bideford, Maidenhead, Beccles, South Molton and Stratford-upon-Avon. . . .

In conclusion, we report to YOUR MAJESTY that there prevails amongst the inhabitants of a great majority of the incorporated towns a general, and, in our opinion, a just dissatisfaction with their Municipal Institutions; a distrust of the self-elected Municipal Councils, whose powers are subject to no popular control, and whose acts and proceedings being secret, are unchecked by the influence of public opinion; a distrust of the Municipal Magistracy, tainting with suspicion the local administration of justice, and often accompanied with contempt of the persons by whom the law is administered; a discontent under the burthens of Local Taxation, while revenues that ought to be applied for the public advantage are diverted from their legitimate use, and are sometimes wastefully bestowed for the benefit of individuals, sometimes squandered for purposes injurious to the character and morals of the people. We therefore feel it to be our duty to represent to YOUR MAJESTY that the existing Municipal Corporations of England and Wales neither possess nor deserve the confidence or respect of YOUR MAJESTY's subjects, and that a thorough reform must be effected, before they can become, what we humbly submit to YOUR MAJESTY they ought to be, useful and efficient instruments of local government.

1.2 From a 'Bill for the establishment of a Council and Auditors in every county in England and Wales, for the better management of County Rates, and for amending the laws relating thereto', *HCP* (1836), Vol. III, p. 117.

This Bill was the first of many which sought to establish elected institutions for the counties, but it is also of interest for its proposal to establish an Executive Committee – which in a way was an early idea of the management board proposed by the Maud Committee on Management one hundred and thirty years later.

And whereas in the several counties of England and Wales the County Rates have been assessed, levied and expended by the Justices of the Peace of the respective counties, and have not been subject to the control of those who contribute the rates: And whereas great inequality in the assessment of the County Rates have long prevailed: And whereas the levying, collecting and expending of County Rates would be rendered more certain, speedy, economical and secure if the several powers and authorities for levying, collecting and expending the same, and the penalties, allowances, compensations and other expenses relating or incident thereto or to the assessing thereof by the said several Acts of Parliament vested in the Justices of the Peace, High Constables and other persons of the several hundreds, divisions and liberties within the several counties of England and Wales, were transferred to and vested in a Council for each county to be elected by the rate payers. . . .

And be it further Enacted, That the Councillors elected under the authority of this Act, and their successors, *One-third* part of the whole number of the Councillors being present, from time to time and at all times hereafter, shall be and they are hereby con-stituted, named and styled 'The County Council', and at their first meeting the Sheriff shall preside as Chairman . . . and at such first meeting and from time to time as occasion shall require, the Council shall elect a Councillor to be the Chairman of the Council, and such election shall be finally determined by the majority of votes of the Councillors then present, and if such votes shall be equal, the Sheriff presiding at such meeting shall have the casting vote, and immediately such Chairman shall have been elected, the Sheriff shall then cease to act as such, and shall take no further part in the proceedings of the Council. . . .

And be it further Enacted, That a Special Council shall be held within *One* calender month next after the first day of meeting as aforesaid, of which *Ten* Days' notice shall be given to each Councillor, and from that time and ever afterwards a Special Council shall be held in every *Twelfth* succeeding month in every year, and like notices shall be then given; and at such Special Councils or adjournment thereof, the Councillors then present shall proceed to elect by the majority of votes, *Five* Councillors to constitute an Executive Committee to manage and conduct such matters and affairs as may be directed by the Council from time to time between and during the intervals of the sittings of the Council, and such Committee when elected, shall continue in office during the period of *Twelve* Months and until others shall be chosen in their stead, unless the Council, at a Special Council to be held for the purpose, choose other Councillors in their place, before the expiration of the *Twelve* Months, and the Executive Committee for the time being shall have full power and authority to meet and adjourn from time to time, and from place to place, and also at any time to call a Council for any purposes they may think proper, and to appoint the time and place of holding the same, and at all meetings of the Executive Committee one of the members present shall be appointed Chairman, and all questions which shall be proposed, discussed or considered at such meetings shall be determined by the majority of the Committee then present (the whole number present not being less than *Three*) and such Committee shall have full power and authority to direct and manage all the affairs from time to time committed to their charge by the Council, and such Committee shall from time to time make reports of their proceedings, and be subject to the examination and control of the Council, and shall act according to all such orders and directions, and not otherwise, in and about the affairs referred to them, as shall from time to time be made by the Council; such orders and directions not being contrary to any express directions or provisions in this Act contained, and the Clerk of the Council shall attend such Committee and keep regular minutes and entries of their proceedings. . . .

And be it further Enacted, That from and after the first meeting of the Councillors under the provisions of this Act in any county, the Justices of the Peace of such county, whether assembled at their General, Special, Quarter or Petty Sessions, or any adjournment thereof, or at any other meeting whatsoever, or otherwise, shall not have any power to order or direct any County Rate to be made for any purpose whatsoever, nor to assess or tax any property within any parish, township or place, whether parochial or otherwise, nor to have or exercise any control, power or authority for the raising, assessing, levying or collecting any County Rate, nor to issue any precept or other order by themselves or any of them, or by their Chairman, or by the Clerk of the Peace under the authority of the said Justices or any of them, to the High Constable, Petty Constable, Churchwardens, Overseers of the Poor, Assessors or Collectors respectively, or to any other person or persons whomsoever, to make returns of the amount of the annual or other value of the property within the parish, township or place, whether parochial or otherwise, to which they respectively belong, nor otherwise by any ways or means, directly or indirectly, to interfere with the raising, levying, collecting, assessing or expending the County Rates; and that all jurisdiction, powers, authorities and control whatsoever heretofore vested in or exercised by the said Justices in, over or concerning the finances of the county, or any officers, persons, matters or things connected with such finances or paid thereout, shall as to such Justices thenceforth absolutely cease and determine, any letters patent, commission, grant, charter, custom or any general or local Act of Parliament to the contrary notwithstanding. . . .

And be it further Enacted, That it shall be lawful for the Council from time to time and as occasion shall require, to nominate and appoint, to be removable at their pleasure, any fit or proper persons, not being a Councillor, to be their Clerk, Treasurer, Collector, and such other Officers and servants as they shall think necessary for carrying into execution the various powers and duties vested in the Council or Executive Committee by virtue of this Act, and shall and may from time to time, as they in their discretion shall see fit, discontinue the appointment of such Officers and servants, and shall and may take such security for the due execution of the respective duties of any Clerk, Treasurer or other Officers and servants as the Council shall think proper, and shall order to be paid to the Clerk and Treasurer and to every other Officer and servant as aforesaid such salary or allowance as the Council shall think reasonable and proper.

1.3 From the 'Report from the Select Committee on the County Rates and Expenditure Bill', 20 June 1850, *HCP* (1850), Vol. XIII, p. 1.

Select Committees were used frequently in the nineteenth century to investigate the aims and content of bills, particularly those relating to local government and public utilities. They were the means whereby a wide circle of supporters and opponents of a measure could be consulted before a final decision was taken in Parliament. This extract shows how pressures from outside Parliament could make their effects felt in official statements of opinion.

(4) That the effect of the Bill would be to exclude a numerous body of gentlemen in every county in England, from the transaction of Financial business in which, as Magistrates and Proprietors, they have an immediate and extensive interest, and which, under the authority of successive statutes, they and their predecessors have conducted for a long period of time to the advantage, and generally to the satisfaction of the public, and to substitute for them a small and fluctuating body of men, who would in many cases be less fitted for the discharge of such duties, and who would individually have a much less degree of pecuniary interest in the counties in which they live.

1.4 From *Hansard*, 3rd Series, Vol. 141 (25 April 1856), Cols 1574-6.
The ingenuity with which the county representatives defended their interests in Parliament is seen in this extract from the speech of Mr Beckett Denison in opposition to the Police (Counties and Boroughs) Bill.

Mr Beckett Denison said, his first anxiety was to show that the allegation made on a former occasion by the right hon. Baronet, the Secretary of State for the Home Department, 'that the West Riding was in a most discreditable state', had no good foundation in fact. The West Riding magistrates, consisting of 300 gentlemen, had met and discussed the proposition to adopt the Constabulary Act three times; and on each occasion the proposition had been negatived by very considerable majorities. The magistrates were of opinion that a rural police were wholly unnecessary in the West Riding. . . . He found that in Yorkshire pauperism and crime were as low as in any part of the kingdom, and that was the reason why he had always opposed the introduction of a rural police, believing it unnecessary. Indeed, crime in Yorkshire was below the average of the other counties in the kingdom – less than Lancashire, with its police; less than Durham, with its police; and less than Nottinghamshire, with its police. Those were the counties which bordered on Yorkshire, and it might be supposed that they drove all their thieves into it. The returns which he had quoted showed that Yorkshire had still less than any other county in England. The noble Lord (Lord Lovaine) might say that in Yorkshire we did not catch all the thieves, but that was easier said than proved; for it was his (Mr B. Denison's) belief that they were generally caught, as they all made their way into the large towns, in which there were strong bodies of police, and where they were sure to be apprehended. He confessed he saw no necessity for an alteration in the present Act, under which the county magistrates had abundant power of adopting a rural police, if they thought such a force requisite. There were in Yorkshire 320 magistrates, and they had on every occasion on which the subject had been brought before them rejected it, which they would not have done had they thought that the population was of a character to require such supervision.

1.5 From the *Report of the Poor Law Commissioners to the Secretary of State on an inquiry into the sanitary condition of the labouring population of Great Britain* (9 July 1842), pp. 338-9 and footnote.

Chadwick's opponents made great play with the centralising features of his schemes, first for the poor law and then for public health. He felt that the true nature of these central bodies was misunderstood, and in this report he restates his own definition.

In 1838, I was examined before a committee of the House of Commons on their resolution, 'That it is expedient that the parishes, townships, and extra-parochial places should be united in districts for the repair of the highways throughout England and Wales.' On that occasion I adverted to the evil of the unnecessary multiplication of new establishments as well as new officers, to their inevitable inefficiency and to the expense and obstruction to improvement which they created; and I submitted these, amongst other grounds, for proposing that the new duties should devolve on the boards of guardians of the new unions, as such duties had been in various instances combined under local Acts. The committee recommended the proposal for adoption. On the premises then placed before me, as to the expediency of establishing a new administrative body with new clerks and officers for the collection and management of the fund for repairs of the highways *alone*, and in small districts for which even the areas of unions were thought large, I should still adhere to the same conclusion.*

The present inquiry, however, has shown the general primary importance of the works of sewerage and drainage throughout the country. The execution of those works would properly devolve upon the commissioners of sewers already in existence in the towns, or in the marsh districts, or upon commissions of sewers which it will be found necessary to issue to places where there has been no need of surface drainage, but which stand in need of under-drainage. These being the primary works for making the ground clear and keeping it clear for all other works, would necessarily require the highest science and skill, and the strongest establishment; and it would be only carrying farther the principle of consolidation, as the only means of obtaining the most efficient service, the most conveniently and at the lowest cost, now to recommend that the care of the roads should, of all structural works, be made to devolve upon that body which has the best means of executing them, namely, the commissions of sewers, revised as to jurisdiction, and amended and strengthened as to power and responsibility.

* Except in endeavouring to give more emphatic recommendations as to the importance of making all the paid officers really responsible, I should not vary the representation I had then the honour to make in respect to the means of giving efficiency to local administration. 'With respect to the allusion of Mr Earle, as to the cry of centralisation, I conceive that it is a cry to which the few who use it can attach no definite ideas, and it has certainly had little influence except with the most ignorant. The phrase has been used abroad against the destruction of the authority of local administrative bodies, and the substitution of an inefficient and *irresponsible* agency by the general government. But even abroad, all those who call themselves the friends of popular liberty do not declaim against centralisation, but against *irresponsibility*. Here the phrase is used against a measure by which strong local administrative bodies of representatives have been created over the greater part of the country, where nothing deserving the name of systematised local administration has heretofore existed. The central board may be described as an agency necessary for consolidating and preserving the local administration, by communicating to each board the principles deducible from the experience of the whole; and, in cases such as those in which its intervention is now actually sought, acting so as to protect the administration being torn by disputes between members of the same local board; between a part or a minority of the inhabitants and the board, and between one local board and another, and in numerous other cases affording an appeal to a distant and locally disinterested, yet highly responsible authority, which may interpose to prevent the local administrative functions being torn or injured by local dissentions. I feel confident that the more the subject is examined, the more clearly it will be perceived that the great security for the purity and improvement of local administration must depend on a central agency.'

1.6 From the 'Second Report of the Commissioners for Inquiring into the State of Large Towns and Populous Districts of England and Wales, 3 February 1845', *HCP* (1845), Vol. XVIII, p. 13.

This enquiry largely endorsed the views of Chadwick about the kind of reforms necessary to achieve efficient machinery for safeguarding the public health.

In all the local investigations carried on under this Commission, an increasing opinion of the very special nature of the works under consideration, and of the special provisions required for their execution, was manifested. In several towns where the present constituted authorities have fully and fairly entered into the consideration of the means of relief from the more pressing evils in question, they have concluded by avowing their conviction of the necessity of special and distinct administrative arrangements to provide for them.

These defects in the administration of the duties entrusted to the local authorities, appear to have suggested to many of the witnesses who have been examined before us, and to others from whom we have received much valuable information in the country, the necessity of a superior authority for supervising the execution of all local Acts relating to drainage, paving, cleansing, and other sanatory objects.

The importance of such a superior authority is also established by the concurrent testimony of all the visiting commissioners, proving how inefficiently the provisions of these Acts are carried into execution by the local authorities even where they exercise the powers entrusted to them. These defects are attributed generally to their imperfect knowledge of science, with reference to structural improvements, to the absence of the means of comparing, in point of execution and economy, works executed in their own vicinity with those in other parts of the kingdom, and to the opposition of party, and the supposed interests and prejudices of individuals with which they have to contend.

We therefore recommend, that in all cases the local administrative body appointed for the purpose have the special charge and direction of all the works required for sanatory purposes, but that the Crown possess a general power of supervision.

1.7 From *Hansard*, 3rd Series, Vol. XCI (30 March 1847). Cols 625-6.

Viscount Morpeth gave great support in Parliament to the public health movement. The beginning of the concept of multi-purpose authorities can be detected in his comments about the type of authority needed to deal with the health of towns.

As almost the cardinal point upon which almost all the inquiries, reports and recommendations have turned, is that the various functions of sewerage, drainage, the paving and cleansing of streets, should be put under the same control, we have thought it the most expedient, if not the absolutely necessary, course, to place these powers of sewerage, drainage, paving, cleansing and supplying water under the same jurisdiction and control . . . we propose to combine all these different powers in a local administrative body.

1.8 From *The Economist* (20 May 1848), pp. 565-6.
The extensive provisions of the Public Health Bill of 1848 were an easy target for those who opposed 'state interference'. This extract gives the views of *The Economist*, then a very young journal.

We might go at much greater length into the bill, for there are not many clauses not liable to the objections of being much too minute, of relating to subjects that legislation ought not to meddle with, and being mischievous by commanding and enforcing a line of conduct by penalties which there are powerful motives for following, independent of all law. We have, however, said enough to indicate the principles and objects of this extensive measure. To promote the health of towns may be made the pretext for interfering with all the pursuits and occupations of the inhabitants; but certainly we were not prepared to find a bill under this title embracing so much of the business of the most industrious and intelligent portions of the community. If this bill become a law, we are not aware of a single business or amusement which may not be drawn into the vortex of legislation – not a single old or new art which the general board may not control and regulate. Cutlers, grinders, painters, and a variety of other labourers, are notoriously short lived; the general board and the local boards, to be consistent, must take one and all of them under protection. Gaming-houses, with the bad passions they engender, affect health and destroy life as well as factories; close theatres and cold churches as well as soap boiling and the smoke from steam-furnaces: and the same principle which justifies an interference with much of the business of life will warrant an inspection of all its amusements – of private parties and balls, as well as soap-boilers' premises and knackers' yards. Nay, we are disposed to think that, as many of the amusements may be dispensed with, while the businesses are the means of living for all, there is a far stronger justification for regulating those than these. We understand, on the principle that the government is to provide for the health of the people, if that be possible, why blood-boiling and soap-making are brought within this bill; but we do not understand why a single business or a single amusement in towns, in any way noxious to health and life, is left out.

From what is inserted and what is omitted, it looks as if this bill were generated by the narrowest and most superficial antipathies; and that it is based on bad smells and disgusting associations with peculiar manufactures. It is dictated rather by the fastidious taste of idle gentlemen than by the deliberate conviction of what legislation can effect to promote health. Either it should interfere with, and regulate, every part of every building, and every part of every business, and every amusement, or it should leave all uninterfered with. The former is clearly impracticable, and, therefore, the latter is the only policy.

The bill is but the beginning of an attempt, under the pretence of providing for the public health, to regulate by legislation, by boards and commissioners, every business in every town of the empire, just as working in factories and mines has been lately taken in hand by legislation, to the punishment of the men and the dismay of the masters. If there was any pretext for thus meddling in the growing negligence of the inhabitants of towns to their own improvement, we might be silent; but whatever may be said on the score of unhealthiness against Liverpool, London, Manchester, Birmingham, and Sheffield, the spirit of improvement is alive in them, and in every town of the empire; it has altered the whole face of them within the memory of man, and requires only to be enlightened by science, not impeded by quackish legislation, to make them in a short time abodes worthy of our intelligent people. In all of them the great source of evil is poverty, and therefore the helplessness of numerous classes. That is more likely to be aggravated by the restrictions on employment and the cost of the law than relieved. While it will increase poverty it will put an end to neighbourly assistance; it will check enterprise and self-exertion; it will beget reliance on boards instead of reliance on self; and by weakening the intellect and increasing the dependence of the people on government, will in the end more retard than promote the improvement of health.

1.9 From J. Toulmin Smith, *Local Self-Government and Centralization* (London, 1851), Chap. III, pp. 54-8 and 67-9.

Toulmin Smith was one of the most prolific of mid-century writers in defence of local institutions. This extract is essentially a blast against Chadwick, and was the beginning of the movement to unseat Chadwick from the General Board of Health.

The fundamental idea of Centralisation is, *distrust*. It puts no Faith in Man; believes not in Hope, nor in the everlastingness of Truth; and treats Charity as an idle word.

Its synonymes are, irresponsible control; meddling interference; and arbitrary taxation.

The system, and the results, of Local Self-Government have been so fully explained that it will be unnecessary to dwell at much length on that which is, on every point, its converse. And, as several forms which Centralisation has assumed in England will have to be hereafter noticed, it will be enough, now, to glance at what will always be some of the practical results of the system, in the same order as was done in treating of Local Self-Government.

And first: of the practical results, *Politically*.

How Local Self-Government leads necessarily on, by its own inherent force, to steady Progress, has been shown. Under Centralisation the forces always acting to this end are crushed out. Should it ever happen that the assumers of authority seek the good of others, instead of self-interest, it is a logical and physical impossibility that the true steps of progress can be taken. Whatever is done will be by fits and starts. The ground which alone can be fruitfully worked is kept untilled and barren. At length, some great and accumulated wrong, suddenly seen in its enormity, arouses a spirit of uncontrollable indignation, – the stronger because ignorant, – and a Revolution follows. And revolution may follow revolution; but, until Local Self-Government – the only system which gives free men a place, and implants the consciousness of duties and responsibilities – has rooted out Centralisation – the prop and means of despotism and tyranny – there can be no hope of lasting peace, a sound condition of society, or a steady progress.

The minds and energies of those whose welfare is in question, instead of having been habitually roused, themselves to grapple with each want that rises, have been systematically dwarfed and deadened. Though the might of the people has been spasmodically asserted, the paroxysm soon subsides, and others step in, instead, either to order or to control the ordering.

To tie up all to the tether of the leading strings which its various irresponsible functionaries shall hold, and to guide all according to the crude pedantries of individuals, is the object, and the result, of Centralisation. What the end is when, those leading strings once burst, unbridled fury and just indignation are poured upon the upholders of the system, the history of France supplies sad illustrations. The same history has been for some time assiduously weaving for England.

The earnest man, unshackled by the blighting influence of Centralisation, will always know that steady perseverance and unswerving confidence in truth will be crowned with sure success. It is the man who is unearnest that seeks to gain his ends by means of Acts of Parliament, which shall enforce and control free thought and action.

Nominated by the usurped power of what should be a merely ministerial executive, and dependent on its pleasure, the functionaries who thus get themselves appointed, neither acknowledge nor have any responsibility to the nation, or to any part of it. The 'reports' which they may, with officious parade, sometimes make public, instead of helping progress and truth forward, and putting their authors in a more responsible position, are merely a convenient means to disseminate manufactured evidence, the distorters of the truth, and always utterly untrustworthy. They but serve the further to blind and mislead those who have already ignobly submitted to a degrading system. They are but some of the crafty devices by which the shackles are being continually the tighter fitted on.*

Centralisation is only Communism in another form. Its object is, to take away the free action of every man over his own property; to stay the free use, by every man, of his own resources, his own ingenuity, and his own free action and enterprise. Universal obedience to the pedantic schemes of a few closet theorists, is proclaimed to be more conducive to human progress than the spreading of the truths wrought out by the ceaseless and multi-

* See *Government by Commissions* (1849), p. 173-8, 232, etc.

tudinous energy and enterprise of millions of active, thoughtful, and practical men, daily meeting, face to face, the difficulties to be overcome, and conscious of the responsibility that lies on them to grapple with and overcome them; and directly interested in attaining the best results. This is what Centralisation really is, stripped of the disguises under which its advocates always seek to cover its natural repulsiveness. The empirical and undiscussed projects of interested individuals are enforced as law over the whole land, instead of that law which the folk and people shall have chosen by their own counsel and consent. Every man is permitted to do that only with his own property and powers of body and of mind which irresponsible officials may be pleased to let him.

By those who have usurped, or who are seeking to usurp, powers inconsistent with the rights and responsibilities of a free people, the machinery of Centralisation will always be delighted in. To make stronger their hold on power, they thus spread, through all the ramifications of society, a system of bribery and corruption the most insidious and powerful; namely, the temptations of offices and appointments on which to live in ease at the expense of the public; and by means of which there shall exist, throughout all ranks, an army self-interested to uphold a corrupt and blighting system. Under such a system the functionaries, as it has been well said, 'are not there for the benefit of the people, but the people for the benefit of the functionaries'.* 'A numerous body of civil functionaries,' is created, 'living upon the people for the performance of duties, partly useless, partly such as a people imbued with public spirit would discharge for themselves; and extending over them, in their private affairs and movements, a superintendence and interference which a people with any sense of liberty and personal rights would not tolerate.'†

The consequences of Centralisation are, then, the 'crushing and brutalising of every human soul'. It goes about 'prying, with suspicious inquisitive eyes and ears, into the most secret words, actions, and even thoughts; and repressing, with irresistible force and promptitude, any attempt of the human intellect and will to shoot forth as God and Nature intended them to do'. The specious pretences put forth for its intermeddling are, in truth, but 'dictated

---

* Laing's *Observations on the Social and Political State of Europe, in 1848 and 1849* [1850], p. 184; a volume well deserving, throughout, of the most attentive perusal.

† *Ibid.*, p. 182.

by vanity, fraud, and avarice'; and all the results achieved are 'mere palliatives and works of ostentation, without striking at the root of any evil,'–the 'wild schemes of projectors and adventurers, most of which, upon trial, have been found to be either pernicious or impracticable.'*

This system may be carried out under any of the forms which are pedantically reckoned as modes of government. Equally under the form of autocracy, aristocracy, or democracy, may centralisation flourish; for neither of these names is in itself any other than a form and a disguise. Under each name the freedom of the nation may be trampled down, and functionarism ride rampant over it. Examples have not been wanting of Centralisation under each form, in Europe, in the first half of the 19th century. When Democracy, in the shape of universal suffrage, erects an oligarchy, the nation is, as has been seen in France, as much subjected to an irresponsible and burthensome yoke as if a Dictator ruled or an hereditary aristocracy governed.

Let the spirit of Centralisation be once admitted, under which-ever of these forms and names, and the true functions of government are departed from; meddling interference is carried into local and domestic details; the course of Law is disregarded and violated; and the interests of one class are sacrificed to those of another. Any misdeeds, neglects, or outrages are covered by the shield of government authority.† No responsibility anywhere exists, and no redress can be had; for at the same time that the right and responsibility of a free people to make the law, and assent to it, are taken away, the always co-extensive and equally essential right and responsibility to administer the Law are taken away too.

Compare the results of Local Self-Government with those of Centralisation. The difference is, between a healthy and an unhealthy state of the social and national union; between that which ensures confidence to individuals, security to person and property, reliance upon self dependence, and encouragement to enterprise and energy, – and that which takes away all these, and leaves each

---

* See the valuable and highly interesting collection of *Memoirs and Papers of Sir Andrew Mitchell, K.B.*, Minister Plenipotentiary at the Court of Berlin; published under the able and judicious editorship of Mr Bisset (Chapman and Hall, 1850). The above is the language in which the centralising policy and conduct of Frederic (called 'the great!') is characterised by one of the shrewdest of statesmen. See Preface, p. ix; Vol. i, p. 133; Vol. ii, pp. 343, 345, 367; as well as many other places remarkably illustrative of this subject.

† See 'Government by Commissions', p. 255, 315, etc.

prostrate at the feet of irresponsible authority. Centralisation, however small its inroads, will, just so far as it has gone, give rise to a sense of insecurity and uncertainty among all thinking men; to vexatious interference with personal and private rights; and to capricious restraints on enterprise and energy. Its constant tendency must always be to breed discontent and irritation, and to beget and foster dangerous, however for a time silent, tendencies to the disorganisation of society. . . .

The system of Centralisation, then, is one by which the energies and activity and enterprise of men in their political, social, moral, and intellectual relations are fettered and tied down, and subjected to the caprice and made liable to the arbitrary interference of a few irresponsible functionaries. It is demoralising, degrading, and inconsistent with a spirit of freedom and with the existence of free institutions. It is a system of which the necessary effects and entire tendency are the smothering of truth; the obstructing of investigation and true enquiry; the promulgating and enforcing of individual and interested schemes and crotchets, instead of the encouragement of careful, reasoned, elaborated truth. It is a system whose necessary result will always be, in a greater or a less degree according as it gains ground, to dwarf and stunt the development of the human faculties, and to check the putting forth of those energies which can never have free play but under that system with which centralisation is in direct and perpetual antagonism – the system of individual, local, and general self-dependence, as carried out by Institutions of true Local Self-Government.

It is well remarked by Adam Smith, in order to illustrate the folly of speculation in money lotteries, that, if you 'adventure upon all the tickets in the lottery you lose for certain: and the greater the number of your tickets, the nearer you approach to this certainty. There is not a more certain proposition in mathematics, than that the more tickets you adventure upon, the more likely you are to be a loser.'* With profound truth the observation applies to Centralisation. It is always the crafty course of the bringers in of this system, to attempt to soften down the repulsiveness of its first steps, as being only applied on a single or a trifling matter. So, by little and little, it creeps on, each step making the next easier. But, – if it is certain that no honest and freeborn man would accept, on any terms, nor on any assurance of increased material

* *Wealth of Nations*, Vol. i, p. 165 (ed. 1791).

well-being and convenience, the abjectness of a state of entire and unmixed moral and intellectual servitude, in exchange for the manly self-respect of freedom and independence, – let every honest man lay it well to heart that the principle is the same, and the mathematical certainty of mischief the same, at each step he allows to be taken in the course of Centralisation; from each new ticket that he suffers to be bought, by the nation, in that lottery the entire ticket of which is the unlightened abjectness of unbroken servitude. Today Poor Law may be made the specious pretext; tomorrow Public Health; next day Police: till, one by one, – each step rivetting the bondage firmer, and making surer the next step, – every attribute of a free people and of free Institutions has faded away, to exist no more except in History.

'Centralisation is the grasp of Despotism: Municipalities are the commons and promenades of a Free People. By the contraction of the one and the enclosure of the other we are losing our strength and freshness every day.'*

But let it never be forgotten that, while every step towards Centralisation must meet with the determined and unflinching resistance of every honest man, the alternative is not, and must never be allowed to be represented as, the old doctrine of simply 'let us alone'. The true sentiment of free men will always be, to assert the principles of self-government as their inherent right, their dearest inheritance and highest dignity; but to remember that such Right only exists as coextensive with Duty and Responsibility. It is not only that free men will not let others interfere to manage and control, for them, their affairs; but it is, that free men have the consciousness of the duty and responsibility not, themselves, to leave undone that by which the welfare of the community may be best advanced. It is because such sentiments are the natural and necessary growth of true Institutions of Local Self-Government, that, while 'to centralise is the art and trick of despots, to decentralise is the necessary wisdom of those who love good government.'†

* Walter Savage Landor; from a private letter, dated 20 October 1849, quoted here with the writer's permission.

† F. W. Newman; Letter dated 13 October 1849, published in the *Daily News* Journal.

1.10 From the 'Second Report of the Royal Sanitary Commission, 1871', *HCP* (1871), Vol. XXXV.

The work of this Commission led to the second round of reforms relating to public health in the nineteenth century. The following recommendations were the basis of the Public Health Act, 1872.

One local authority for all public health purposes in every place, so that no area should be without such an authority or have more than one.

That the laws concerning public health and the relief of the poor should be presided over by one Minister as the central authority.

1.11 From *Hansard*, 3rd Series, Vol. CCV (3 April 1871).

Mr Goschen, introducing bills to set up the Local Government Board and to reform the structure of local government and the rating system, summed up the complexities of the existing mass of authorities with a phrase which was destined to become one of the classic sayings of the nineteenth century.

The truth, Sir, is that we have a chaos as regards authorities, a chaos as regards rates, and a worse chaos than all as regards areas.

1.12 From *Hansard*, 3rd Series, Vol. CCIX, Cols 596-8 (16 February 1872).

Mr Stansfield, President of the Poor Law Board, speaking in support of the Public Health Bill which was designed to create a country-wide system of sanitary authorities, explained the chaotic state of affairs which then existed.

One object of the Bill was the reconstruction of the local sanitary authorities, and the other was the investing them with new sanitary powers. Of the two, he regarded the reconstruction of the sanitary authorities as the one of the greater importance. The Sanitary Acts might be divided into two classes – those which affected the sanitary authorities, whom they in future proposed to call urban, and those which applied to the country at large. The urban Acts were the Public Health Act of 1848, and the Local Government Acts of 1858, 1861 and 1863. The Nuisance Removal and the Sewage Utilisation Acts contained such very large and comprehensive powers that for whatever failure or laxity of sanitary administration there had been, they must look to something more than

C

the absence of power for an explanation. The first important Nuisance Removal Act to which he need refer was the Act of 1855, which defined a nuisance, among other things, to be any premises so kept as to be a nuisance or injurious to health. Power was given, too, among other things, for the appointment of sanitary inspectors, to seize unwholesome food, and to prevent overcrowding. The Nuisances Removal Act of 1855 was followed by similar Acts in 1860, 1863, and 1866, and under these Acts the definitions of nuisances were enlarged, powers were given for cleansing houses, for providing ambulances, for the removal of the infected to hospitals, for the disinfection of clothing, and for the establishment of mortuaries for the reception of the dead. On the other hand, the Sewage Utilisation Acts of 1865, 1866, 1867, and 1868 gave powers for the construction of sewers, to provide a supply of water for the inhabitants of different localities, to invest the local authority with the power of taking legal proceedings to prevent the pollution of streams, to provide hospitals for the reception of the sick, and, among other things, in cases of emergency, to furnish medicine and medical attendance for the benefit of the poorer classes of the population. The authorities on whom these powers were conferred were the vestries, and the House would not, perhaps, be surprised that these bodies had not universally availed themselves of the powers so bestowed. The nuisance authorities had changed from time to time. Before 1855 they were the Boards of Guardians; between 1855 and 1860 various bodies exercised the powers conferred by the Acts; between 1860 and 1868 they were again lodged in the Boards of Guardians, but in 1868 the most important of their functions – that was as regarded the nuisances connected with sewage and drainage – was taken from them and vested in the sewer authorities; in other words, in the hands of the inhabitants themselves, instead of in Boards of Guardians. While, therefore, the vestries had not sufficiently availed themselves of the powers placed in their hands, he was, he thought, entitled to say that the Boards of Guardians had not had sufficiently fair or continuous opportunities of performing the duties of nuisance authorities. He could not help thinking that the House would come to the conclusion expressed the other day at Liverpool by Lord Derby, that the first object of sanitary reforms was the construction of proper machinery for carrying them into effect. They required three things. The first, some central and governmental supervision and inspection, was, he thought, practically provided last year.

Then came the institution of defined authorities with defined responsibility. By defined authorities, he meant, in the words of the Sanitary Commission, authorities so constituted that there should be one sanitary authority for all sanitary purposes in one place; and by defined responsibility he implied that our legislation should cease to be so much as it had been permissive, and that distinct duties and responsibilities should be placed upon these bodies. With regard to the constitution of authorities they had followed the recommendations of the Sanitary Commission. They proposed to divide the sanitary authorities into urban and rural. Urban authorities were the Town Councillors in boroughs, Improvement Commissioners in Improvement Act districts, and Local Boards in Local Board districts. The rural authorities would be the Board of Guardians, with the exception of those that might be said to represent urban districts. Upon these bodies they proposed to bestow all the powers both of the Sewage Utilisation and the Nuisance Removal Acts. With regard to the urban authorities, they would have allocated to them the same powers they already possessed, with an extension. Then powers were taken to combine these authorities for certain purposes, such as the constitution of port authorities, dealing with rivers and vessels thereon, which was eminently necessary in cases of epidemic invasion. Next, by Provisional Order, it would be sought to combine districts for any sanitary purposes which might seem to call for a wider area, such as the conservancy of rivers, the enlargement of sewer works, etc., and by such arrangements, at once simple, elastic, and comprehensive, it was hoped that the recommendations of the Commissioners would be effectually carried out.

1.13 From the 'Report of the Select Committee on Boundaries of Parishes, Unions and Counties' (17 July 1873), *HCP* No. 308. Appendix, No. 4, pp. 197-8.

The chaotic welter of districts and boundaries is illustrated in this letter from the Registrar-General, which was one of the pieces of evidence brought before the Select Committee.

REGISTRAR GENERAL'S LETTER TO MR BRUCE

Administrative Districts
The absence of symmetry and system which is a peculiar feature in

our national organisation may be easily explained by a reference to the course of English history. At no period has there been attempted in this country a deliberate and scientific mapping out of the whole field of national activity, harmonising and co-ordinating the various parts under a comprehensive and well-balanced general scheme. We do not, indeed, suppose that many Englishmen desire the symmetrical simplicity of a political organisation like that of France, where all the old names and memories, divisions and jurisdictions, thrown down and trodden level by the great convulsion of the last century, have been supplanted by a local sub-division and political nomenclature absolutely severed from the history of the country. The names of Picardy, Normandy, Brittany, Provence, Burgundy, no longer appear on the authorised maps or in official documents, though they have not yet slipped out of popular language and recollection. The departments named after rivers and mountains are subdivided according to a systematic principle, and on the framework of these divisions and sub-divisions the whole administrative organisation of France rests. There is no overlapping of jurisdictions, no confusion of boundaries, no entanglement of masses of population grouped for different purposes in different sections and proportions. Such are the advantages, not inconsiderable it must be admitted, of the complete reconstruction for which the sweeping scythe of the Revolution cleared the ground. But, in our insular judgment, this gain is more than balanced by many moral and political losses. We do not desire to obliterate our provincial distinctions, to erase the names of our counties, hundreds, and parishes from the map, or to break with the history of the kingdom; and, in the main, it is a wise and wholesome conservative instinct that makes us hesitate in this way to pour the old wine of an independent national life into the new bottles of a centralised administrative organisation with strange names and a scientific system of arrangement to mark the change.

Yet there is reason to believe that our national dislike of innovation and distrust of symmetrical schemes might be relaxed with some practical benefit. A letter addressed to the Home Secretary by the Registrar General and the officers who co-operate with him in the vast work of the Decennial Census brings conspicuously into relief the difficulties and the waste of time and toil occasioned by the want of harmony among our administrative sub-divisions. The Registrar General and his fellow-workers complain that this defect has more than doubled the length as well as the severity of their task, and when we review the figures which have been laid before Mr Bruce, we feel no hesitation in accepting the statement. In the first place, the impossibility of properly co-ordinating the existing divisions of the country has necessitated a distinct system of sub-division for registration purposes, of which the Decennial Census may be considered an occasional development. The Poor Law union has been as far as possible taken as the unit, and has been constituted a 'registration district', divided into sub-districts. The districts are massed into 'registration counties'; and the counties, again, are arrayed in 'eleven great regional divisions'. The characteristic feature of this system is that there is no over-lapping or splitting up of either the unit of organisation or of its subdivisions or agglomerations. Thus every registration district consists of entire subdistricts; every registration county of entire districts. This is so plainly requisite for smooth and effective administration that the inexperienced may wonder why it should be looked on as a reform. But, in fact, the Poor Law union, which is taken roughly as the unit of organisation, has been defined on quite different principles from the county, which is constituted the next higher division; and the aggregation of Poor Law unions included either wholly or partially within the boundaries of a county in many instances considerably exceeds the county itself in area and population. Hence the necessity for mapping out the country into registration districts and counties not corresponding to the ordinary divisions. But this was only a trifling element in the confusion, the origin of which is succinctly pointed out in the Registrar General's letter. 'It is a peculiarity', we are told, 'of the administration of this country, that nearly every public authority divides the county differently, and with little or no reference to other divisions; each authority appears to be unacquainted with the existence, or at least the work, of the others.' Counties and their sub-divisions, however, of whatever kind, or discriminated on whatever principle, have to be enumerated, described, and defined in the statistical tables of the Census. Is it surprising that the Registrar General's Office protests against the multiplication of distinctions which, if not wholly without meaning, have long ceased to have a practical meaning? The Government and the country is now asked, through the medium of this appeal to Mr Bruce, whether nothing can be done to simplify by re-arrangement, a game of cross purposes that perplexes not merely the work of the

Census, which comes on us only once in 10 years, but ordinary every-day administrative business.

The English counties have been divided ever since the Saxon period into hundreds or wapentakes; but besides this historical sub-division have grown up the Parliamentary divisions, the lieutenancy districts, the petty sessional districts, the municipal, local board, police, and ecclesiastical divisions, and the Poor Law unions. Hardly any of these, though frequently called by the same names, have the same boundaries; and the result is that England exhibits a curiously confusing reticulation of mutually intrusive and intersecting jurisdictions. A map of the country which attempted to show in coloured outline the complexity of these concurrent systems would probably convey a better general notion of the existing difficulty than any verbal comment. It is remarkable that even where within our own remembrance a completely novel partition of the country was determined on for the purposes of the County Courts Act, no attempt was apparently made to bring the new divisions into any harmonious relation with the division adopted for the work of the superior courts. 'The circuits of the judges', the Registrar General remarks, 'do not consist of any definite number of county court circuits, nor are the county court circuits aggregates of the petty sessional divisions.' But perhaps the most striking example of the multiplied jurisdictions is London itself. We have London 'within the Tables of Mortality' differing from London as defined by the Metropolis Local Management Act, from London as subject to the authority of the Central Criminal Court, from London as protected by the Metropolitan Police, from London as represented in the Legislature by the members for its Parliamentary constituencies, from London as marked out by the regulations of the Post Office, from the City of London and the Diocese of London. It is needless to say that the Capital, the boundaries of which are thus variously defined, is cut up with an infinity of sub-divisions, which not one Londoner out of 10,000 professes to understand. Poor Law unions and parishes, vestries and local board districts, ecclesiastical parishes, police divisions, postal districts, Parliamentary cities and boroughs, and a dozen other sub-divisions make the Directory a puzzle, and contribute to frighten away numbers of excellent and intelligent persons from that singular problem, 'How is London governed?' But though the metropolis is perhaps the worst case of all, as we might expect from the greater complication of interests in the centre of national life, it is typical of a mass of similar cases. The commonest case of all is the small town with its Parliamentary representation, its municipal organisation, its Poor Law organisation, in which we find Parliamentary, municipal, and Poor Law boundaries all different. No wonder that the task of the officers who have been intrusted with the work of taking the Census has fallen a little behind the anticipations of the public. The difficulty of unravelling so many tangled webs can hardly be estimated by unskilled persons. The Registrar General and his subordinates have brought two facts to light which will receive, we may hope, the attention of Parliament as soon as local taxation comes on for discussion. The one is the cumbrous and inconvenient interlacing of administrative boundaries and jurisdictions; the other is the simplicity and symmetry of the system of division adopted for the purposes of registration. The latter, which retains the Poor Law union as the unit, and which accepts the county with a slight correction of limits as the next grade, has the merit of leaving names and associations untouched. We do not want to make a clean sweep of old memories, or to parcel out England into departments, but if we find a workable plan of administrative subdivision already approved by experience, we do not see why we should cling persistently to complications which have nothing venerable about them but age, and often not even that.

1.14 From *Hansard*, 3rd Series, Vol. 326 (8 June 1888), Cols 1554-8.

This extract from *Hansard* records the debate on the Committee Stage of the Local Government Bill, and shows how the Government's original intentions in relation to the grant of county borough status were frustrated by stages. Had these changes not occurred, the problems of local government reform in the mid-twentieth century would not have been so acute.

Amendment proposed,

> In page 1, at end, add – 'Provided, that every borough containing at the time of the passing of this Act fifty thousand inhabitants (which are the boroughs named in the Fourth Schedule to this Act) shall, for the purposes of this Act, and subject to its provisions, be a county of itself.' – (*Sir Henry James*)

Question proposed, 'That those words be there inserted.'

Mr Ritchie said, that as the Bill was originally introduced, the Committee would be aware that the limit which the Government thought proper to treat as a county in itself was a borough with a population of 150,000. He did not wish to disguise from the Committee that his own feeling was that it would, on the whole, have been better that the towns which were to be taken out of the counties, and to be created practically into counties themselves, should be only the largest and most important boroughs in the Kingdom. But, notwithstanding the belief on his part that the Bill, if it had been allowed to remain as it stood, would have been in many ways better than any other provision that could have been made, the Government had felt themselves unable to adhere to the limit originally fixed. Of course, there had been a very natural and, in many respects, a most laudable desire on the part of boroughs below 150,000 inhabitants to participate in the advantages proposed to be given to boroughs with over 150,000 inhabitants, and, therefore, the original figure had been reduced to 100,000. Still further pressure had been brought to bear on the Government to include boroughs even below 100,000 inhabitants, with the result that they had come to the conclusion to assent to the principle of this Amendment. The arguments which had been made use of were arguments which they had felt to be very strong indeed, and the announcement he had to make today was that, although the right hon. and learned Member for Bury (Sir Henry James) would probably, after the explanation he had given, not think it right to press his Amendment, because this would not be the place for any Amendment of the kind, the right hon. and learned Gentleman would undoubtedly expect from the Government some expression of opinion in regard to the decision they had arrived at, and what arrangements they proposed to make in the Bill, and what the boroughs were which would be included in the fourth schedule. As he had said, the Government had come to the conclusion upon the whole to accept the proposition of the right hon. and learned Gentleman. They proposed, therefore, that when they came to that part of the Bill which dealt with this question, to make provision that all boroughs which had 50,000 inhabitants in 1881, and which desired to come into the schedule, should be admitted into that schedule. With regard to the boroughs which could give satisfactory proof that they had now 50,000 inhabitants the Government had decided that they also should be included in the schedule. As to this latter class, however, they had not, at this moment, any reliable information. The only statistical information they had on the subject of population were the Registrar General's Returns, and they had been made up by taking as the increase since 1881, the same rate of increase as occurred between the Census of 1871 and 1881. Of course, this had been simply a work of calculation, and in many respects the figures might be fallacious. There might be boroughs which had had their area increased since 1881, and others which had not. The result of the decision of the Government was that all boroughs which desired to be admitted into the schedule which had a population of 50,000 in 1881 should be admitted, and all such boroughs as could satisfy the Government that their population had increased to that figure since 1881. As the right hon. and learned Gentleman was aware, there existed a means of finding that out by ascertaining how many additional houses had been built since the last Census, and that the Government would be prepared to accept as sufficient proof. Now that they had gone down so far in population as 50,000, there arose certain considerations with reference to the admission of other boroughs which had not so large a population as 50,000, and yet had their peculiar claims for consideration. He was speaking now of certain counties of cities. When the Bill was originally drafted, it was found impossible to take the claims of these cities into consideration, however great and substantial they were, and, therefore, boroughs and cities which formed counties – some of which had a population as low as 30,000 – were not included. But now that it was proposed to come down as low as 50,000 inhabitants, the Committee would see that the condition of things had altered, and while the Government would have been justified in refusing to recognise the position taken up in regard to these cities of counties, they were no longer prepared to insist on their exclusion. Therefore they were prepared, in addition to the boroughs he had spoken of, to admit these cities of counties, which from their antiquity, their associations, and ancient usage gave them a very strong claim to be included in the schedule. That claim was more accentuated by the fact that these boroughs had never been within the jurisdiction of the county at all. The population of three or four of these cities was exceedingly small, and he did not propose to deal with them in this way. But in reference to the cities whose names he would read, it was proposed to include them in the fourth schedule – namely, Warwick – which, of course, had a population of more than 50,000, and might be left out of the question – Exeter, Lincoln,

Chester, Gloucester, Worcester, and Canterbury. The population of Canterbury was considerably below that of Worcester, but they felt that if Canterbury did desire to come in, the historical claims of that City, notwithstanding the smallness of its population, would probably be recognised by the Committee. Therefore, if Canterbury desired to come in, it would be admitted. He hoped the Committee would understand that they did not propose to force any of these boroughs or cities to go out of the counties. It was quite optional with them, and perhaps they would take some other means of letting the Government know whether they desired to be included in the schedule or not, because, as they did not propose to force any of these boroughs or cities to take up this particular position, so also they were prepared to provide means in the Bill by which at any time in all these boroughs or cities, if they thought it more advantageous to their own interests, they could become part of the county to which they belonged. There was another consideration which they were bound to regard now that the number of boroughs included in Schedule 4 had been so greatly increased. A large and very influential deputation from Lancashire waited upon him at the Office of the Local Government Board a few days ago, to represent to the Government that the counties in which these boroughs were situated might be placed at a very great financial disadvantage if the boroughs were taken out of the counties and placed in an independent position by being put in the fourth schedule. He was bound to say that the representations made to him at that time seemed to him to have great force and weight, and that it was impossible for the Government to ignore them. He did not believe that any of these boroughs desired that the counties from which they were taken should suffer financially from the severance. He had always, when representations were made to him on behalf of the boroughs, said to the deputations who placed the cases before him, that in any event they would take special care that the county finances were not adversely affected, as far as the existing contributions were concerned, by such boroughs being taken out of the counties. In no single case had there been the smallest objection on behalf of these towns to an arrangement whereby these contributions should be maintained as at present. But the circumstances of the various boroughs were so different, that it was absolutely impossible for the Government to lay down a hard and fast rule by which each case should be settled. They, therefore, resolved to prepare a large clause of an equitable character providing for the establishment of a Commission, to which all these cases might be referred in the absence of agreement between the boroughs and counties affected; and such a Commission should have power to decide each case upon equitable grounds. Of course, the Commission was said to consist of a system of arbitration. The Government had felt it of extreme importance that whatever machinery they established, it should be as little costly as possible, and hon. Gentlemen would be aware that in resorting to arbitration heavy costs were sometimes incurred. It was, therefore, thought better to set up a small Commission, whose names would inspire confidence all over the country. By that means a tribunal would be provided which would settle all these matters in a fair and satisfactory manner, with the least possible amount of expense. These were the proposals the Government had to make. He hoped in a few days to be able to lay on the Table of the House the clause or clauses by which this object was to be effected, so that Members who were interested should have the fullest opportunity of studying the provision proposed to be made, and of seeing whether it met with the justice and the necessities of the case. Under these circumstances, and as the Government undertook at the proper time, and in the proper place, to insert the names of the boroughs that were to be included in the fourth schedule, he hoped the right hon. and learned Gentleman would consent to withdraw the Amendment.

1.15 From *The Times* (18 September, 1888).
This extract is from the first of a series of articles which appeared in *The Times* after the Local Government Act, 1888, had been passed. This comment is about the contemplated transfer of supervisory powers over the local boards from the Ministers to the County Councils.

When the contemplated further powers are transferred from the Local Government Board and the Board of Trade to the county councils, then these bodies will become of still more importance and will be far more powerful than they are as immediately created by the Act. They are, in fact, huge machines capable not only of doing their own work, but of furnishing the motive power for the vast and complicated mechanism that must exist throughout all the country districts of England and Wales. By the Bill it was proposed at once to transfer certain important powers to the county councils.

But in Committee these powers were struck out, and it was left to the Local Government Board to transfer these and other powers by provisional order. Indeed, the county councils may have transferred to them all such powers, duties, and liabilities of the Privy Council, of the Board of Trade, Local Government Board, Education Department, Secretary of State or Government Department as are 'conferred by statute and appear to relate to matters arising within the county and to be of an administrative character'. Thus the county councils may, without further legislative action, become really county parliaments.

1.16 From *The Times* (23 October 1888).

This extract is the concluding remarks of the leading article in *The Times* about the prospects for the new County Councils.

Before we see the County Councils actually at work it is difficult to anticipate with any approach to accuracy the direction in which the transfer of power from the hands of the magistracy to that of a representative body will first manifest itself in any decided change of policy or result. There is, undoubtedly, room for improvement in the management of pauper lunatic asylums, and the County Councils will certainly be expected to ascertain for themselves whether the ribs and breastbones of lunatics – especially pauper lunatics – are quite so brittle as they are sometimes represented to be, and why it is that lunatics – especially pauper lunatics – are so very apt to tumble into over-heated baths. In the administration and enforcement of the Rivers Pollution Acts, again, the County Councils are likely to prove stronger and more exacting than local sanitary authorities have been, though here it must be recollected that manufacturers who find it convenient to pour their refuse into the nearest rivers will be very apt to seek a place on the County Councils and to endeavour to persuade their colleagues that their particular refuse is the most harmless substance in the world. In sanitary matters it is to be expected that the County Councils will be neither much more nor much less enlightened than the constituencies to which they will owe their existence. Probably more attention is now paid to sanitary science in England than in any other country in the world, but there is still plenty of room for improvement even in England; and we suspect that, if the whole truth were known, there is quite as much room for improvement in rural England as there is in urban England. In towns self-interest almost compels us to be sanitary, the penalty for indulgence in insanitary conditions is so heavy and so certain to be exacted sooner or later. In rural districts, on the other hand, the mischief is more insidious and less palpable, though not less destructive in proportion to the sparser population. There is plenty of room, therefore, for the energies of a County Council in the development of rural sanitation. On the whole, the duties of a County Councillor,though not exciting in themselves, and not attractive to every one, should be of sufficient importance to induce good men and good citizens to undertake their discharge. If the Local Government Act failed to quicken the civic life of our rural districts and to raise it to higher levels of virtue, capacity, integrity, and intelligence, then, indeed, we should have to admit that representative institutions themselves are on their trial.

1.17 From the *First Report of the Royal Commission on Local Government* (7 August 1925), Cmd. 2506, pp. 452-3 and 469-71.
These extracts give the views of the Royal Commission about the methods to be used for creating and extending County Boroughs, and the Commission's arguments for recommending that the qualifying population for county borough status should be raised to 75,000.

1194. Proposals for the constitution of County Boroughs require separate consideration from proposals for the extension of County Boroughs, owing to the degree of opposition which they generally attract.

The application of the Provisional Order procedure to these proposals is open not only to the objections which we have already indicated, but also to the objection that it involves the expense of a Local Inquiry which does not have the result of removing opposition in Parliament, and therefore leaves the expense of Parliamentary proceedings where it would be if the proposal had been made in the first instance by Private Bill.

1195. We are of opinion that in these circumstances it is not necessary to leave Town Councils with their existing option of making a proposal for the constitution of a County Borough either by application for a Provisional Order or by promoting a Private Bill; and we recommend that the existing law should be altered so as to provide that all proposals for the constitution of County Boroughs should be made by Private Bill.

1196. The facts in regard to past proposals for the extension of County Boroughs differ from those in regard to proposals for the constitution of County Boroughs. Some proposals for the extension of County Boroughs have not been opposed by other Local Authorities at any stage, and opposition to a number of other proposals has not persisted beyond the stage at which a Local Inquiry was held.

In so far as opposition to these proposals does not arise, or is removed before the Parliamentary stage, there are, in our opinion, substantial reasons for preserving the existing option of County Borough Councils to make proposals for extension under the Provisional Order procedure.

1197. At the same time, the lack of confidence in this procedure is felt as much in regard to its application to proposals for the extension, as in regard to its application to proposals for the constitution, of County Boroughs. We think that it must be recognised as being more important that a procedure should command the confidence of those who are affected by it than that it should in certain cases be cheap and convenient. We have, therefore, sought for a solution of the present difficulties in a procedure under which it should be the rule that proposals for the extension of County Boroughs would be made by Private Bill, while in any case in which the Local Authorities concerned, other than the County Borough Council, do not object to the employment of Provisional Order procedure, it should be open to the County Borough Council, if they so desire to resort to that procedure instead of promoting a Private Bill.

THE FIGURE OF POPULATION WHICH SHOULD ENTITLE A TOWN COUNCIL TO PROPOSE THE CONSTITUTION OF A COUNTY BOROUGH

1259. We heard very full statements from witnesses of the arguments by which they supported their widely different views on this question. The witnesses on behalf of County Councils took their stand, first, on the fact that in 1888 the Government, when they submitted to Parliament a figure of the population which towns should be required to have as a condition of being constituted into County Boroughs, submitted the figure 150,000; secondly, on the growth of the population of England and Wales since that date; and thirdly, on the growing scope and complexity of the administration of local government since 1888, which had, in their view, rendered it impossible for a Town Council to administer services for the inhabitants of the town as efficiently and economically as may have been possible in 1888, if the population of the town were not more than 50,000.

1260. The witnesses on behalf of Town Councils, on the other hand, based their arguments for the retention of the existing figure of 50,000, first, on the fact that Parliament had decided that this figure was a proper one, and had not thought fit to change it in the light of the circumstances which had been common knowledge since 1888; secondly, on the evidence which they adduced that Councils of towns of this size were administering services for their inhabitants with proper efficiency and economy, and that other towns of the same size could be equally well administered if they were constituted into County Boroughs; and thirdly, on the ground that it would be undesirable for Parliament to require the population of a town to reach such a size before the town could be constituted into a County Borough that reasonable expectations, and valuable incentives to good government, would receive a check.

1261. This question is one of the most difficult which we have had to consider, but we have taken the view that the proper manner in which to deal with it was first to secure that when a proposal for the constitution of a County Borough is made by a Town Council under the law existing for the time being, the procedure by which the proposal is considered should be such as to satisfy both the Town Council and the County Council concerned that they are being fairly dealt with. The recommendations set out in the preceding Chapter of this Report are directed to this end.

1262. We regard the present statutory figure of population as a figure intended to prevent unreasonable proposals from being made, but not as a figure which indicates that every proposal which can be made ought to be put into effect. It has been well said to us that the quality of the administration of the Local Authority is of more importance than the quantity of the population in the town.

At the same time, we have come to the conclusion that the arguments based upon the growth of the population of the country as a whole since 1888, and the tendency of Parliament to entrust local government services to Authorities having jurisdiction over considerable aggregations of population, are entitled to a certain weight. We are no less impressed by the desirability of encouraging Town Councils, who attach great value to winning for the towns the status of County Boroughs, to do everything which will enable them to show, when their population reaches the necessary size, that they have by the efficiency of their government satisfied the other, and the main, conditions which justify the grant of County Borough status.

1263. We accordingly recommend that in future the number of the population of a Borough which should entitle the Town Council to promote a Private Bill for the purpose of constituting the Borough into a County Borough should be 75,000.

1.18 From the *Second Report of the Royal Commission on Local Government* 1923-9 (October 1928), Cmd. 3213. And from the *Local Government Act* (1929).

These extracts show the recommendations of the Royal Commission in relation to the review of the areas of county district councils, and the actual provisions of the Act which gave effect to these recommendations. This is one of the few instances in which the recommendations made by a Commission are enacted without much alteration.

18. On the 1st April, 1927, there were 1,698 County Districts in England and Wales, made up as follows:

Rural Districts	658
Urban Districts	785
Non-County Boroughs	255

CHAPTER I – REORGANISATION OF AREAS

Section I – Evidence on behalf of the Minister of Health
... As the result of the circumstances in which Non-County Boroughs, Urban Districts and Rural Districts have been constituted during the last 60 years, there are wide variations in the size and financial resources of the Authorities within the three groups.

19. The following table, derived from the figures given in the memorandum of the Minister of Health, show the distribution of population according to the Census of 1921 between the 1,698 County Districts as constituted on the 1 April 1927:

20. The number of Authorities with very small populations is considerable. In the case of Urban Authorities this may be traced partly to the fact that in the years 1862 and 1863 the inhabitants of a large number of quite small places (some with a population of

	Non-County Boroughs	Urban Districts	Rural Districts
TOTAL NUMBER OF COUNTY DISTRICTS	255	785	658
DISTRICTS WITH POPULATIONS OF			
Under 1,000	1	16	10
Between 1,000 and 2,000 ..	13	63	17
,, 2,000 and 3,000 ..	19	72	29
,, 3,000 and 4,000 ..	20	74	28
,, 4 000 and 5,000 ..	13	77	42
5,000 or less	66	302	126
Between 5,000 and 10,000 ..	40	222	216
,, 10,000 and 20,000 ..	53	178	229
20,000 or less	159	702	571
Between 20,000 and 30,000	33	45	67
,, 30,000 and 50,000	50	28	15
,, 50,000 and 100,000	12	6	5
Over 100,000	1	4	—
Over 20,000	96	83	87

less than 100 persons) adopted the urban form of local government under the provisions of the Local Government Act, 1858, in order to avoid the inclusion of their parishes in Highway Districts formed under the Highway Act of 1862. Figures have been put before us to show how far in one large County, the West Riding of Yorkshire, local administration has still to be conducted within urban areas originally delimited in 1862-3, from which it appears that of the 22 Urban Districts in the County originally formed in those two years, 14 had populations in 1921 of less than 5,000, and, further, that of these 14, three had populations of less than 1,000, and six had populations of between 1,000 and 2,000.

21. Between the passing of the Local Government Act, 1888, and the 1st April, 1927, 270 Urban Districts have been formed, in 183 of which the populations according to the last Census before formation were under 5,000. Between the same dates, 118 Rural Districts have been formed, of which 71 had less than 5,000 population. It is, however, to be noted that in some of these cases the creation of a small Rural District resulted from the subdivision

of an existing District in compliance with the requirements of the Local Government Act, 1894, which were designed to ensure that the whole of each Rural District should be within one Administrative County.

We should perhaps observe that in our opinion the bearing of population on the problem of local government in Rural Districts necessarily differs from that in Urban Districts.

22. It will be seen from the figures presented on behalf of the Minister of Health that the financial capacity of many small areas is restricted. There were, on the 1st April, 1927, 494 County Districts (66 Boroughs, 302 Urban Districts, and 126 Rural Districts) with 5,000 or less population. Of these 494 Districts there were 430 (65 Boroughs, 264 Urban Districts, and 101 Rural Districts) where a 1d. rate produced less than £100. . . .

26. The Minister of Health represented to us that the existing numbers of Councils of County Districts might advantageously be reviewed, and suggested for our consideration the principles on which any reorganisation of the structure of local government should proceed. These may be summarised as follows:

(i) That any proposal for change should be directed to encouraging the confidence of the inhabitants of any area in their representatives, and the extent of their active and effective interest, both in the election of representatives and the provision of local government services in their area;

(ii) That due regard should be paid to the history and prestige of the form of local government at present applied to the areas affected, and to the sentiment with which it is looked upon by the inhabitants of those areas; and

(iii) That, so far as the reasonable observance of the preceding principles allows, the areas of Local Authorities should be so delimited as to provide a form of local government under which all Local Authorities are not only willing to discharge, but capable of discharging, the functions assigned to them in such a manner as to secure the fullest possible return for the time and money spent on their work. . . .

SECTION III – CONCLUSIONS AND RECOMMENDATIONS

39. We are of opinion that the need for a general review of areas of County Districts and Parishes has been established. The representatives of the Local Authorities have not dissented from the view that there are at present Authorities who cannot efficiently

discharge the functions entrusted to them, and that a review of areas should be undertaken in order to see how far ineffective units can be eliminated by reorganisation.

40. Under the present law a Rural District Council can, and in many cases do, appoint Parochial Committees under section 202 of the Public Health Act, 1875, for the more urban parts of their District. If the suggested reorganisation of areas results in the elimination of any small Urban District, some similar provision to give additional local powers deserves consideration.

41. In our First Report (paragraph 1189), when dealing with the subject of the constitution and extension of County Boroughs, we expressed the opinion that the governing consideration should be to secure the welfare of the populations affected and the best and most efficient method of providing for their local government. The same principle should be applied in the reorganisation of County Districts; and it should also be borne in mind that efficient administration depends not only on area but also on there being assigned to each unit functions of such variety and importance as will ensure local interest, and secure as members of Local Authorities persons best fitted to render service.

42. There is a considerable measure of agreement as to the procedure by which the reorganisation should be effected, subject to adequate safeguards, particularly with regard to effective consultation between the various Authorities concerned.

It appears to us that the proposals submitted on behalf of the Minister of Health provide the basis of a satisfactory scheme for effecting a reorganisation of areas; and, with certain modifications and additions, we have decided to recommend its adoption.

Our conclusions and recommendations in regard to the reorganisation of areas are as follows:

43. With a view to securing efficient units of administration the existing law and procedure, under which a reorganisation of areas may be effected, should be modified:

(i) By making provision for a general review of the existing County Districts and Parishes within a specified period after the date when Parliament passes the necessary legislation.

(ii) By making provision to facilitate further general reviews from time to time as they become necessary.

(iii) By amending the existing law as to alteration of particular County Districts and Parishes which may become desirable in the intervals between the reviews.

REARRANGEMENT OF COUNTY DISTRICTS

46. (1) The council of every county shall as soon as may be after the commencement of this Act, after conferences with representatives of the councils of the several districts wholly or partly within the county, review the circumstances of all such districts and consider whether it is desirable to effect any of the following changes:

(a) any alteration or definition of the boundaries of any such district or of any parish;

(b) the union of any such district or parish with another such district or parish;

(c) the transfer of any part of such district or parish to another district or parish;

(d) the conversion of any such district or any part thereof, if it is a rural district, into an urban district, or if it is an urban district, into or so as to form part of a rural district;

(e) the formation of any new district or parish;

and shall forthwith after the review is completed as respects the whole or any part of the county, and before the first day of April, nineteen hundred and thirty-two, or such later date as the Minister may in any case allow, send to the Minister a report of the review, together with proposals as to the changes, if any, which they consider desirable. . . .

47. (1) A county council may subsequently whenever they think it desirable, and shall if so required by the Minister, review generally the circumstances of the districts within the county, so, however, that the interval between the original review and the first review under this section, or between any two reviews under this section, shall in no case be less than ten years.

1.19 From the *Reform of Local Government* by the Nalgo Reconstruction Committee, pp. 25-8, and *The Future of Local Government* by the Labour Party, pp. 7-8.

These two pamphlets from which the following extracts have been taken are examples of the suggestions for local government reform which were being circulated towards the end of the 1939-45 war.

III. THE ALL-PURPOSE AUTHORITY

. . . We recommend that the ultimate objective of local government reform should be the division of the whole of England and Wales into a number of directly elected local authorities, each adequate in area, population, and financial resources, and possessed of the necessary powers, to administer efficiently all local government services within its area; and with the right of direct access to all government departments. This proposal is, however, as has already been stated, subject to the reservation discussed more fully in Section VI below, that some local government services may require to be planned and co-ordinated (though not directly administered) over wider areas than most of the all-purpose authorities will be able to provide, and that it will, therefore, be necessary to introduce the machinery for co-ordination and planning outlined in that section.

IV. SIZE OF THE ALL-PURPOSE AUTHORITY

54. We consider it undesirable, in view of the differing circumstances of each area, to lay down any precise standards of population and financial resources for the proposed all-purpose authorities. Since, however, it is necessary to indicate some standard, we suggest that, for efficient and economical government, the authority should, where practicable ... have a population in the neighbourhood of 250,000.

VI. PROVINCIAL COUNCILS

59. The division of the whole country among a number of all-purpose local authorities of the type suggested would solve many of the problems indicated above. Without further provision, however, it would fail adequately to meet the needs of those specialised or large-scale services which call for planning and co-ordination over a wider area than any single all-purpose authority of the size suggested could cover.

60. To ensure this co-ordination, we therefore further recommend that there should be established by law a number of Provincial Councils.

61. These Provincial Councils should be composed of representatives appointed by the all-purpose authorities within the province, in proportion to the population of each. Their function should be solely to secure efficient planning and co-ordination of the services remitted to their consideration. They would thus possess no executive or administrative powers – but their recommendations, subject to the approval of the government departments concerned, should be mandatory upon all the local authorities within the province.

62. The services over which the Provincial Councils would exercise their planning and co-ordinating function would include:

Town and Country Planning;

General Hospitals, Specialist Hospitals, Mental Hospitals, and certain Public Assistance Institutions;

Major Highways Developments;

Provision for Specialist and Technical Education;

Main Drainage and Sewage Disposal;

Provincial Library Provision;

The Development and Co-ordination of Public Utility Services; and

Any other services whose adequate provision requires a larger population than the local authorities in the area can provide individually, or which would benefit from broad planning and co-ordination over wide areas.

63. The area covered by each Provincial Council should be that within which co-ordination of the services remitted to it is desirable. It is probable that this would, in respect of most services, coincide with the Provincial Planning area. There may, however, be some services which would require different areas and for which it would be necessary to have different Provincial Councils. In general, however, it should be the aim to concentrate as many services as possible under one Provincial Council.

64. As has already been explained, the Provincial Council would possess no executive powers. Its function, as we visualise it, would be to consider the needs of its area in regard to each of the services enumerated above, to determine the nature of the provision to be made, and to select the appropriate all-purpose authority or authorities which should make that provision. The cost both of provision and maintenance would be apportioned among the areas served on an agreed basis. Institutions which already serve, or would serve, an area more extensive than that of a single all-purpose authority would be administered by the authority in whose area they are situated, the costs being similarly apportioned on an agreed basis among the authorities making use of the institutions. In some instances, one all-purpose authority might provide the institution and make charges for user by others, on lines already familiar in some services.

PROPOSALS FOR REORGANISATION

Regionalism

There is now a widespread recognition of the need for a change in Local Government, but there is by no means agreement as to the form of change desirable. Discussion of the subject tends to become confused with the war-time expedient of dividing the country into twelve Civil Defence Regions, and the appointment of Regional Commissioners. This development, however, cannot be regarded as a regionalisation of Local Government. It is rather a devolution of the responsibilities of the central Government, so that the functions of government can be carried on in a war emergency. This form of regionalism is more than a war-time measure, however; it is a tendency that has grown throughout the present century. Before the war there were regional organisations for electricity, the Ministry of Labour, the Ministry of Health, the Advisory Services of the Ministry of Agriculture, Milk Marketing Boards, Assistance Boards, etc., while during the war a number of Ministries have adopted the Civil Defence Regions for special administrative purposes. This is not the place to discuss the future administrative set-up of the central Government. It must be emphatically stated that this type of organisation cannot be permitted to supplant a system of democratically elected Local Authorities. Nor must these Regions condition the area of the new, bigger Local Government Authority, since they are much too large and unwieldy and therefore too remote to maintain a common interest.

The Single All-Purposes Authority

Among the proposals for reform is one which suggests the reorganisation of Local Government on the basis of a single all-purposes Authority, similar to the existing County Borough Council. This view is unacceptable because:

(1) In rural areas the resources available would be so limited that the area required would be too large for all purposes, with a danger of the structure becoming remote, particularly in relation to purely local services, and would necessitate the delegation of some of the responsibilities upon co-opted Committees. Purely local services, with other responsibilities delegated from the major Authority, should be administered by a democratically elected Local Authority.

(2) In the large conurbations, there is a two-tier system in being which will continue to be necessary in all centres of large population if local interest is to be preserved.

It is imperative that any change in Local Government should seek to fuse the interests of town and country, and to have within each major unit a well-balanced grouping, actual or potential, of diversified industry, agriculture, commerce, and residence. This cannot be done by merely adding tracts of rural land to an existing town, because this would merely accelerate urban sprawl, often over good agricultural land. In this connection, it is significant that the Land Utilisation Survey revealed that of the 30,000,000 acres of farm land, not more than 2,500,000 acres were of the highest quality capable of intensive cultivation. Some of this land had been built on during the housing boom, while a considerable proportion of the remainder was on the fringe of great cities, and was in the market as building land. If the exercise of planning powers is to ensure the best use of land, the planning Authority must operate in an administrative area wider than would be possible by the proposed extension of town government.

Planning the New Structure

Any change in Local Government structure must vest full authority in the elected representatives of the people. The democratic tradition in Local Government is very powerful, and nowhere more so than in the ranks of the Labour Movement. It is not enough merely to affirm this principle. Efforts must be made to translate Labour's ideas and ideals into a constructive system of government that will conform to the necessities of historical development. Due regard must therefore be paid to the organisations which now exist, all of which have played a vital part in developing the social services and in training large numbers of people in the art of public administration. Nevertheless, the immensity of the task of post-war reconstruction must be recognised. It will require a smaller number of Authorities than now exist, since no change adequate for modern needs could avoid their supersession. Suitable machinery should be established by the Central Government to survey the country as a whole to determine the areas suitable for a Regional or Major Authority, adequate for the efficient performance of large-scale services, particularly those which need for their efficient and economical development considerable area, population, and sufficient financial resources. It should be emphasised that the use of the word 'Region' in this connection is in no way related to the organisation or area of the Regional Commissioners, but is used merely to indicate a suitable geographical area. The new Regions must not be so large that the sense of a common interest in their government would be lost, or cause various areas on their outskirts to feel that they had too little in common, but must be large enough to permit an adequate area for development. Their resources must be such that they can with little difficulty command administrative and technical staffs of the highest efficiency. They may well be adaptations of the existing administrative County areas, provided that present boundaries, many of which were determined by historical conditions which bear no relation to modern needs, are not regarded as sacrosanct or unalterable. Where necessary, amalgamations and absorptions of existing Authorities should take place to achieve a satisfactory unit.

Area Authorities
Within each Region there should be a suitable number of Area Authorities to administer the purely local services, and others delegated to it by the Major Authority. The size and number of the areas could be determined by population, rateable value (actual and potential), administrative convenience, and the balance of town and country. They should be as few as will make efficient democratic Local Government reasonably possible. This would require amalgamations of many Urban and Rural Authorities, and where possible these would be based upon existing County Boroughs.

Division of Functions – Standard of Service
In addition to revising the structure of Local Government, steps should be taken to extend its powers to enable it to play a full part in the democratic government of the people. Thus, in addition to ensuring a minimum standard of performance by the exercise in suitable cases of the powers of default by the Region in the case of default by the Area Authority, and by the Minister in the case of the Regional Authority, a general Enabling Bill should extend the opportunities of development by Local Authorities. In the allocation of powers to the respective Authorities two principal considerations will have to be borne in mind. These are:

(1) The control and administration of such services as are best provided and administered by, and the cost borne equitably

73

over the Region, must go to the Regional Authorities.

(2) The powers and duties of the Area Authorities must be such as will give them a status and their powers such an importance as will attract the right type of person as members.

1.20 From the Ministry of Health White Paper, *Local Government in England and Wales during the Period of Reconstruction* (January 1945), Cmd. 6579. Part I, The Future of Local Government, p. 4.

The reasons which have led the Government to the view that the time is not opportune for a general recasting of the local government structure have been stated in Parliament and were elaborated in a letter addressed in September 1943, by Sir William Jowitt, then Minister without Portfolio, to the Association of Municipal Corporations and the County Councils Association. Broadly, they may be stated in two propositions – first, that there is no general desire in local government circles for a disruption of the present system, or any consensus of opinion as to what should replace it; and secondly, the making of a change of this magnitude, which would by common consent have to be preceded by a full-dress inquiry, would be a process occupying some years and would seriously delay the establishment of the new or extended housing, educational, health and other services which form part of the Government's programme.

As against this it may be – and, indeed, has been – said that the present local government structure was not designed to bear the weight of these new and extended services and will prove inadequate; and that to establish the services in advance of a reconstruction of the system is to pour new wine into old bottles. This argument is usually based on two main contentions, both of which call for examination:

(1) that certain of the services, such as town and country planning and hospital services, need to be planned, and in some cases administered, over a wider area than a county or county borough; and

(2) that the reconstruction programme will place an impossible burden on local government finance.

1.21 From the *Local Government (Boundary Commission) Act* (1945), sections 1 and 2, and from the 'Local Government Boundary Commission's Annual Report for 1947', *HCP* 86 (1947–8), pp. 10-13 and 19-21.

The powers of the Local Government Boundary Commission, as set out in the Act, were to reorganise the areas of local authorities within the existing system. There were two limitations: though it could demote a county borough to a non-county borough, it could not get rid of borough status; and the Commission was given no power to redistribute local authority functions. The three extracts which are taken from the 1947 Annual Report show how seriously the Commission regarded these limitations.

1. (1) There shall be established a Local Government Boundary Commission (in this Act referred to as 'the Commision') which shall be charged with the duty of reviewing the circumstances of the areas into which England and Wales (exclusive of the administrative county of London) are divided for the purposes of local government, and exercising, where it appears to the Commission expedient so to do, the powers of altering those areas conferred by the following provisions of this Act. . . .

2. (1) The Commission shall have power:

(*a*) to alter or define the boundaries of a county, county borough or county district;

(*b*) to unite a county with another county, or a county borough with another county borough, or to unite a non-county borough with another non-county borough, or an urban or rural district with another district, whether urban or rural, or to include an urban or rural district in a non-county borough or any county district in a county borough;

(*c*) to divide a county into, between or among two or more counties or an urban or rural district into two or more districts, whether urban or rural, or between or among two or more areas, whether county boroughs or county districts;

(*d*) to constitute a borough (either by itself or together with the whole or any part of another county district) a county borough;

(*e*) to direct that a county borough shall become a non-county borough and specify the county in which it is to be included;

(*f*) to constitute a new urban or rural district, or to convert a rural district into an urban district or an urban district into a rural district;

(*g*) so far as appears to the Commission to be requisite in connection with any exercise of their powers under the foregoing paragraphs, to alter the boundary between a

75

parish and another parish, to unite a parish with another parish, to divide a parish into, between or among two or more parishes, or to constitute a new parish:

Provided that no part of the administrative county of Middlesex shall be constituted a county borough.

SIZE OF LOCAL GOVERNMENT UNITS

17. It is not possible by any process of arithmetic or logic to arrive at exact figures for an optimum size of a local government unit either in relation to local government as a whole or to any one function or group of functions. At best one can – to use an engineering term – arrive at a reasonable tolerance, and it is fairly certain that even in regard to that there will be special cases demanding exceptional treatment. Moreover, the process is largely one of weighing conflicting aims and deciding where on balance the advantage lies. Opinions on these matters differ and will continue to differ.

If we were dealing with a new country having an evenly distributed population and without marked physical features, it would be fairly simple, though not necessarily desirable, to design a single uniform system of local government – whether one-tier, two-tier or many-tier – and to carve up the country into units of suitable size and shape. The actual problem is a very different one. We have to take England and Wales as we find them. Their main features – massive concentrations of populations in London and in the industrial North and Midlands, mining areas, agricultural areas, ports and centres of commerce, cathedral and university cities and towns, seaside resorts – all of these are there. Local government administration must be made to fit them as best it can, and it would be surprising if all units could be cast in the same mould. Moreover, the physical structure of the two countries with their rivers and estuaries, their indented coast lines, their ranges of mountains and hills, their forests and moorlands would, apart from anything else, forbid any division into neat and tidy shapes and sizes. Incidentally, such a division would involve alterations far more drastic than anything we shall propose. The real problem is to decide how far existing local government areas based, as for the most part they are, on long-standing tradition and sentiment and broadly corresponding with the physical characteristics of the country are suited to modern requirements, and how far growth and re-groupings of population, changes in methods of communication and transport, and generally new ways of life, have made obsolete some units which in their day were natural and appropriate.

18. The task is complicated because different local government services need different-sized units of administration. This may even be true of different parts of the same service; for example, the maintenance of county and district roads in urban areas has long been assigned to different authorities. Again, physical features are the important factor in some services, for instance, land drainage, sewerage, or water supply. . . .

20. Another factor is what may be called the population catchment area of a service. An important part of the work of local authorities relates to special classes of the population and, in particular, to children and others who in various ways and degrees are handicapped, whether physically or mentally or by their environment. The work is difficult, but happily the beneficiaries form a relatively small portion of the total population. If the service is to be carried on with reasonable economy in terms of money and of the highly specialised officers and equipment necessary, the unit of administration should be a wide one. On the other hand, much of this work is of a kind in which personal oversight by members of the responsible authority and a personal knowledge of and interest in the beneficiaries of the service are invaluable. Here, as so frequently happens, there are conflicting advantages and a balance has to be struck.

21. The need for different units of administration for different services could in theory be met by having for each service a separate body operating over the appropriate area. We need not spend time on this suggestion. Last century the system was tried on a large scale, not as a matter of conscious design, but as a stage in the piecemeal development of local government services. There are, so far as we know, no present-day advocates of a series of unrelated school boards, highway boards, poor law boards and the like. . . .

23. The main disadvantage of a large unit is remoteness of administration, leading to loss of interest on the part of the electorate and to lack of intimate knowledge of the area on the part of members. Local government loses vitality in proportion to the remoteness of the individual member or officer of the council from the individual citizen. Long journeys to and from the council offices make it difficult, if not impossible, for persons whose time

for public work is limited, to undertake membership of a council, particularly under present-day conditions when, apart from meetings of the council itself, the almost continuous committee work imposes a heavy strain. This disadvantage does not exist to the same degree in services in which detailed control by members is not necessary, but, even in these cases, long distance travelling by officers in the course of their work adds to the administrative cost of the service.

The size, too, of the council in relation to the electorate is an important consideration, as is also the number of electors proper for one electoral division, and there is plainly a point at which an executive body becomes unwieldy and a constituency unmanageable. Where the population is scattered there is no doubt a case for a lower proportion of electors to representatives.

24. The following are some of the main points in favour of large units:

(a) In their ability to attract officers of high capacity, large units with their greater financial resources have obvious advantages, as they have also in services which call for elaborate and expensive equipment.

(b) A single large unit should be able to achieve economies in terms of man-power and money more easily than several smaller ones. We need not stress the importance in present conditions of economising in the use of highly trained technical officers – educational advisers, town planners, doctors, engineers – and of the higher grades of administrative officers. The engagement of specialists by a small authority may, besides imposing an undue burden on the ratepayers, involve a waste of valuable skill and experience.

(c) A reduction in the number of administrative boundaries is in itself valuable. The cost of handling 'fringe' questions, of deciding whether a person taking advantage of a service in an area is, in fact, resident in the area, of book-keeping connected with the financial transactions between authorities for services rendered to each other's residents, is by no means negligible; nor is the risk of overlapping provision, or of such extravagances as unnecessarily long distance conveyance of children to school merely because of boundaries.

(d) In some services the size of the group of persons employed – policemen, teachers, nurses, midwives – is an important factor in favour of larger rather than smaller units. If the force is a small one, promotion prospects may become a matter more of chance than of merit.

(*e*) Uniformity of administration, to the importance of which we have already drawn attention, in supervisory and enforcement services is more easily secured in large units.

25. There will frequently be a conflict between 'effectiveness' and 'convenience' and the proper balance must be struck. And while there is undoubtedly a minimum below which an authority cannot be effective, there is equally a maximum above which effectiveness falls off. . . .

MAIN RECOMMENDATIONS

39. In the light of the survey contained in Parts III-VII of this Report we have had to consider what action we ought to take.

One course would be to accept the undoubted fact that we have no mandate to deal with the functions of local authorities and, upon the assumption that the distribution of functions between the various types of local authorities remains unaltered, to proceed to make Orders in accordance with our present instructions in the Act and in the General Principles creating fresh county boroughs or reducing the status of existing ones, uniting or dividing counties, and altering the boundaries of counties and county boroughs. We should then, after settling each case on its merits, submit each Order for review by Parliament. This is the course which one of our members (Mr Holmes) would prefer to adopt, and accordingly he does not wish to identify himself with those portions of the Report which are not consistent with the adoption of this course. Those portions are, therefore, the responsibility of the four other members of the Commission only.

An alternative course, and one which the Commission have decided to adopt, is to set out in this Report an analysis of the present position, to make recommendations for alterations, whether or not these alterations are within the jurisdiction of the Commission, and to ask either that fresh legislation should be enacted and fresh principles laid down, or that the Commission should be instructed to proceed on the present footing. We think it right to explain why this is in our view the proper course.

We are reluctant to proceed on our present instructions for two reasons. First, we have come to the definite conclusion that 'effective and convenient units of local government administration' cannot everywhere be procured (and that is our primary task) without a fresh allocation of functions among the various types of local authorities, particularly where the larger towns are concerned. Since the Act of 1888 the structure of local government has been based on the principle that local government functions can be divided broadly into two classes – major and minor. In county administration major functions are allotted to the county and only the minor functions are entrusted to those towns which are non-county boroughs. In towns of a certain size a single administration (the county borough) is responsible for both major and minor functions or, in other words, is an 'all-purpose' authority. The vast increase in variety, complexity and scope of local government services since 1888 and the radical changes made in the last four years have, in our view, made obsolete this division of boroughs into two classes only – 'all-purpose' authorities and 'minor-purpose' authorities. We think that the existence of a third and intermediate class of middle-size towns ('most-purpose' authorities) should now be recognised in the field of local government. Secondly, none of us is anxious to be forced to make Orders which would weight the scales so heavily in favour either of county (including county district) government or, alternatively, of county borough government as virtually to destroy one or other type in many areas. If the Commission continue to be limited, as now, to a choice between continuing the county borough system, unimpaired and expanded, or reducing many existing county boroughs to the staus of non-county boroughs and declining to create new ones, we cannot avoid this result. If we are faced with this choice, four of our members would regard, as the lesser of two evils, the reduction to non-county borough status of almost three-quarters of the existing county boroughs. Mr Holmes, on the other hand, would give his vote for the retention and some expansion of the county borough system.

It may be asked whether an escape from this dilemma is to be found in the first of the three courses to which we referred in our 1946 Report, a policy of moderate extension of county boroughs in accordance with past practice. Our answer is that this course would not solve the problem of many of the county boroughs. These towns are nearly all overcrowded and in need of redevelopment, and extensions on a larger scale than heretofore would be essential if they are to be effective as autonomous all-purpose authorities.

We have come to the conclusion that the creation of a new type of authority whose area would form part of the county, but the scope of whose functions would be intermediate between those of an 'all-purpose' authority and those of a 'minor-purpose' authority, may provide a solution which would enable the legitimate demands for county borough extensions to be met without crippling the county and at the same time secure an allocation of functions in accordance with modern requirements. We confess that in recommending this solution we have also been influenced by a keen desire to find a course which lies between the extreme views of the counties and county boroughs, but which is not a mere temporary patchwork, leaving the real problems outstanding for our successors. We believe that our solution includes such ground as is common between the views of counties and county boroughs and that it might form the basis of an agreed policy.

40. Before setting out our main recommendations we summarise them in the shortest possible form so as to give a bird's-eye view of what we have in mind. We then set them out in detail, and in the immediately following Parts of the Report we indicate what might be the effect on the pattern of local government in England if the policy we recommend were adopted (Parts IX and X), and suggest a number of possible re-arrangements in Wales (Part XI).

41. Our major recommendations may be summarised as follows:

(a) In future there should be three main types of local government units – counties, county boroughs and county districts. To distinguish the first two from existing units we refer to them in this Report as 'new counties' and 'new county boroughs'.

(b) The whole of England and Wales, *including* the areas of the existing county boroughs, would be divided into new counties. The bulk of these would be the existing counties, with some combined and some divided; and they would be administered, as now, on the two-tier system. The remainder of the new counties would be large cities and towns (with suitable alterations of boundaries where necessary) administered, as now, on the one-tier system. The general aim would be to secure a population in each new two-tier county of between 200,000 and 1,000,000, and in each one-tier county of between 200,000 and 500,000.

(c) The new county boroughs would consist broadly of the middle-size towns – boroughs with populations between 60,000 and 200,000. They would also include the Cities of Liverpool and Manchester which would form the centres

D

of two new counties. The new county boroughs would be part of the administrative county and would look to the county for certain services (including police and fire). But they would form a new and middle rank of authority with important autonomous functions – in particular, all education, health, and care of the old and disabled services, and parts of town and country planning and highways – in addition to all those of an ordinary second-tier authority.

(d) County districts would include all non-county boroughs (except those which would become new county boroughs), urban districts and rural districts. They would be responsible for all existing second-tier functions and, in suitable cases, for functions delegated by county councils. The distinction in title between Urban and Rural Districts would be abolished and all county districts would, after their boundaries had been reviewed, have similar autonomous functions.

(e) Delegation of functions by county councils would be effected by means of 'county schemes' prepared in accordance with General Principles approved by Parliament. The schemes would take into account the nature of the function to be delegated and the circumstances of the county and of each second-tier authority.

1.22 From the Ministry of Housing and Local Government White Paper, *Local Government Areas* (1956), Cmd. 9831, Appendix, pp. 13-15.

After the abolition of the Local Government Boundary Commission in 1949, the problem of local government reform was forgotten in the pressure of party in-fighting. The 1956 White Paper marks its re-emergence after a period of behind-the-scenes activity by the Ministry to get some measure of agreement between the local authority associations.

I. THE NATURE OF THE PROBLEM

1. The present system of local government is one-tier administration in the large cities and towns, and, in the administrative counties, two-tier in the smaller towns and three-tier in the rural districts. The approach in this paper is that this structure works well and that it should be maintained; but that it could be made to work better if certain matters were dealt with. . . .

II. POLICY PROPOSALS

Promotion to County Borough Status outside Conurbations

4. An application by a non-county borough or an urban district for promotion to county borough status should be considered in the light of:

  (a) its ability (having regard to population, resources and other factors) to discharge effectively and conveniently the functions of a county borough; and

  (b) the effect which the promotion if made would have on the county as a whole. (Among the relevant factors to be considered in this connection should be other applications for promotion and the possibility of adjustment in county boundaries or, in appropriate cases, of amalgamations of one county with another).

5. Two or more authorities should be entitled to make a joint application for amalgamation and simultaneous promotion to county borough status.

6. It should be permissible for an authority to apply for an extension of its boundaries and for promotion to county borough status, and for both questions to be considered at the same time.

7. In considering an application by a non-county borough or urban district for promotion to county borough status, there should be a presumption that an authority with a population of 100,000 or more (having regard to the provisions of paragraphs 5 and 6) is able to discharge effectively and conveniently the functions of a county borough (see paragraph 4 (a)).

8. An authority with a population of less than 100,000 which seeks promotion to county borough status should be required to show exceedingly good reason to justify promotion, having regard to both (a) and (b) of paragraph 4.

Extension of County Boroughs

9. An application by a county borough for an extension of its boundaries should be considered in the light of all relevant factors, including the effect on the administrative county.

Withdrawal of County Borough Status

10. The withdrawal of county borough status on the grounds of inability to discharge effectively and conveniently all the functions

of a county borough, having regard to population, resources and other factors, might be considered as part of any reorganisation.

Alteration of County Boundaries

11. The division, amalgamation, alteration and extension of counties might also be considered as part of any reorganisation.

Conurbations

12. By conurbations are meant large areas of more or less continuous urban development containing a substantial number of local authorities. (The definition of the areas to be regarded as conurbations for the purposes of local government reorganisation will need further consideration.) The pattern of local government in these areas should be looked at as a whole. The aim should be to ensure, throughout each conurbation, individually and collectively effective and convenient units of local government. Inside conurbations the case for the creation of a county borough or for the extension of the boundaries of a county borough should be looked at equally with the need for securing a proper organisation of local government on a two-tier basis in the parts of the conurbation outside county boroughs.

13. Subject to the previous paragraph, applications for promotion to county borough status inside conurbations (excluding Middlesex) should be treated on the same lines as applications from authorities elsewhere; but the minimum population for eligibility for promotion within a conurbation should be 125,000, subject to the provisions of paragraphs 5 and 6 above.

14. Middlesex should be preserved as a two-tier urban County, and its County Districts should be ineligible for promotion to county borough status. As part of any such arrangement, there should be some redistribution of powers between the County and the District Councils, including the conferment on the latter of some powers not at present exercised by the County District Councils. This would take place after any necessary boundary adjustments or amalgamations.

1.23 From the *Local Government Act* (1958), sections 17-20.

This Act set up the two Commissions, one for England and one for Wales, to review the structure of local government. It broke new ground in creating a separate Commission for Wales which had hitherto been considered along with England, and in creating separate processes and different objectives for the review of authorities in the conurbations.

REVIEWS OF LOCAL GOVERNMENT AREAS IN
ENGLAND AND WALES

Reviews by Local Government Commissions

17. (1) There shall be a Local Government Commission for England and a Local Government Commission for Wales, which shall be charged as respects England, exclusive of the metropolitan area, and Wales respectively with the duty of reviewing the organisation of local government:

(*a*) in the areas specified in the Third Schedule to this Act (hereinafter referred to as 'special review areas'),

(*b*) in the remainder of England (exclusive of the metropolitan area) or Wales, as the case may be,

and of making such proposals as are hereinafter authorised for effecting changes appearing to the Commissions desirable in the interests of effective and convenient local government. . . .

18. The changes which may be put forward in proposals of the Commission on the review of any area are changes to be produced by any of the following means or any combination of those means (including the application of any of the following paragraphs to an area constituted or altered under any of those paragraphs):

(*a*) the alteration of the area of an administrative county or county borough (including the abolition of any county district in the course of the extension of a county borough);

(*b*) the constitution of a new administrative county by the amalgamation of two or more areas, whether counties or county boroughs, or by the aggregation of parts of such areas or the separation of a part of such an area;

(*c*) the constitution of a new county borough by the amalgamation of two or more boroughs (whether county or non-county), the conversion of a non-county borough or urban district into a county borough, or the division of an existing county borough into parts and the constitution of all or any of the parts a county borough;

(*d*) the abolition of an administrative county or county borough and the distribution of its area among other areas, being counties or county boroughs;

85

(e) the conversion of a county borough into a non-county borough and its inclusion in an administrative county;

(f) the inclusion of the Isles of Scilly, as one or more county districts, in an administrative county.

19. In relation to proposals on the review of a special review area, the foregoing section shall have effect as if the following paragraphs were added thereto:

(a) the alteration of the area of a county district;

(b) the constitution of a new non-county borough by the amalgamation of a non-county borough with one or more other county districts;

(c) the constitution of a new urban or rural district by the amalgamation of areas being urban or rural districts or by the aggregation of parts of county districts or the separation of a part of a county district;

(d) the abolition of an urban district or rural district;

(e) the conversion of a rural district into an urban district or of an urban district into a rural district.

20. (1) Where it appears to the Commission, and it is so stated in their report, that the nature of a special review area or a part of it is such that the organisation of local government therein should take the form of a continuous county, but that there should be a redistribution of functions as between the county council and the councils of the county districts in the county, the Commission may put forward proposals for:

(a) the exercise of county functions by the councils of the said county districts or any of them,

(b) the exercise of district functions by the county council, either as respects the whole or as respects a part of the county.

(2) In this section 'continuous county' means a county within the extent of which there are no county boroughs, and in this Act:

'county functions' means functions which under the general law are exercisable by a county council, and includes the establishment, maintenance and administration of a police force and any other functions of the Standing Joint Committee,

'district functions' means functions which under the general law are exercisable by councils of county districts or of county districts of any description.

1.24 From the *Report of the Royal Commission on Local Government*

(1966–9), Vol. I, Cmnd. 4040, pp. 1-5 and from *The Memorandum of Dissent by Mr Senior*, Vol. II, Cmnd. 4040-I, pp. 2-6.

These are the basic principles for the reform of local government put forward by the main body of the Commission, and their confutation by Mr Senior. The memorandum of dissent makes history in that it is the first such memorandum to extend to greater length than the original statement. These two statements of principle are destined to be the cornerstones of arguments about local government reform for many years to come.

MAIN CONCLUSIONS AND HOW THEY WERE REACHED
Main Conclusions

1. The pattern and character of local government must be such as to enable it to do four things: to perform efficiently a wide range of profoundly important tasks concerned with the safety, health and well-being, both material and cultural, of people in different localities; to attract and hold the interest of its citizens; to develop enough inherent strength to deal with national authorities in a valid partnership; and to adapt itself without disruption to the present unprecedented process of change in the way people live, work, move, shop and enjoy themselves. These purposes have guided our assessment of the present and our proposals for the future.

2. We are unanimous in our conviction that local government in England needs a new structure and a new map. Ten of the 11 members of the Commission agree about the principles on which the new structure and map should be based.*

3. England (outside London which was not within our terms of reference) should be divided into 61 new local government areas, each covering town and country. In 58 of them a single authority should be responsible for all services. In the special circumstances of three metropolitan areas around Birmingham, Liverpool and Manchester, responsibility for services should be divided in each case between a metropolitan authority whose key functions would be planning, transportation† and major development, and a number of metropolitan district authorities whose key functions would be

---

* Mr Senior agrees with our diagnosis and with some of our principles but cannot accept many of the proposals we base on them. His alternative proposals are set out in his memorandum of dissent, printed as volume II of the report.

† 'Transportation' is used throughout this report to cover transport planning, the design, construction and maintenance of highways, traffic management, control of car parking and the provision of public transport.

education, the personal social services,* health and housing.

4. These 61 new local government areas should be grouped, together with Greater London, in eight provinces, each with its own provincial council. Provincial councils would be elected by the authorities for the unitary and metropolitan areas (including, in the south east, the Greater London authorities), but would also include co-opted members. The key function of these councils would be to settle the provincial strategy and planning framework within which the main authorities will operate. They would replace the present regional economic planning councils and collaborate with central government in the economic and social development of each province. They will therefore play an essential part in the future adaptation of local government to the changes in ways of life and movement that time and technical progress will bring.

5. Within the 58 unitary areas and, wherever they were wanted, within the three metropolitan areas, local councils should be elected to represent and communicate the wishes of cities, towns and villages in all matters of special concern to the inhabitants. The only *duty* of the local council would be to represent local opinion, but it would have the *right* to be consulted on matters of special interest to its inhabitants and it would have the *power* to do for the local community a number of things best done locally, including the opportunity to play a part in some of the main local government services on a scale appropriate to its resources and subject to the agreement of the main authority.

How main conclusions were reached

8. In considering what changes are needed to correct these structural and other defects there is one fundamental question. What size of authority, or range of size, in terms of population and of area, is needed for the democratic and efficient provision of particular services and for local self-government as a whole?

9. After examining each of the main services in turn, we decided that answers to that question must be found by seeking to apply to each part of the country the following general principles:

* 'The personal social services' are those studied by the Seebhom Committee: e.g. child care, various welfare services, care of the homeless, care of the handicapped, education welfare and child guidance, day nurseries, home help, mental health social work, adult training centres, social work services and welfare work undertaken by some housing authorities. (*Report of the Committee on Local Authority and Allied Personal Social Services*, Cmnd. 3703, HMSO 1968.)

(i) Local authority areas must be so defined that they enable citizens and their elected representatives to have a sense of common purpose.

(ii) The areas must be based upon the interdependence of town and country.

(iii) In each part of the country, all services concerned with the physical environment (planning, transportation and major development) must be in the hands of one authority. Areas must be large enough to enable these authorities to meet the pressing land needs of the growing population, and their inhabitants must share a common interest in their environment because it is where they live, work, shop, and find their recreation.

(iv) All personal services (education, personal social services, health and housing), being closely linked in operation and effect, must also be in the hands of one authority, as strongly recommended by the recent report of the Seebohm Committee.*

(v) If possible, both the 'environmental' and the 'personal' groups of services should be in the hands of the same authority, because the influence of one on the other is great and likely to increase. Further, concentrating responsibility for all main local government services in a single authority for each area, as in the present county borough, would help to make the idea of local self-government a reality. Through allocation of priorities and co-ordinated use of resources, a single authority can relate its programmes for all services to objectives for its area considered as a whole.

(vi) Authorities must, however, be bigger than most county boroughs (and all county districts) are at present, if they are to command the resources and skilled manpower which they need to provide services with maximum efficiency.

(vii) The size of authorities must vary over a wide range if areas are to match the pattern of population. But a minimum population is necessary. What this should be is a question of great difficulty and we received much evidence about it. We concluded that this pointed to a minimum of around 250,000. Though authoritative witnesses would prefer a higher minimum for education – perhaps as high as 500,000

* Cmnd. 3703, HMSO (1968).

– we did not accept that this was essential. Moreover, a minimum above 250,000 would be too high to provide coherent and reasonably compact areas in many parts of the country. It would also be unnecessarily large for the other personal services (the personal social services, health and housing), which must be kept together with education.

(viii) At the other end of the scale, authorities must not be so large in terms of population that organisation of their business becomes difficult and the elected representatives cannot keep in touch with the people affected by their policies. This is especially important in the personal services. There was little evidence to guide us but we concluded that a population of not much more than 1,000,000 should be the maximum for the personal services, though much would depend on the social and geographic characteristics of each area.

(ix) Where the area required for planning and the other environmental services contains too large a population for the personal services, a single authority for all services would not be appropriate; and in these parts of the country, responsibilities must be clearly divided between two levels, and related services kept together.

(x) The new local government pattern should so far as practicable stem from the existing one. Wherever the case for change is in doubt, the common interests, traditions and loyalties inherent in the present pattern, and the strength of existing services as going concerns, should be respected.

10. In considering what the new local government structure should be, we first concentrated on the 'city region' since this was the idea strongly advocated for the whole country by the Ministry of Housing and Local Government, the department with chief responsibility for English local government.* We examined various possible local government maps of England in turn, and the following points emerged:

(i) The city region idea has value because it takes account of the fact that people are now much more mobile than they were.

* According to the Ministry's evidence, a city region 'consists of a conurbation or one or more cities or big towns surrounded by a number of lesser towns and villages set in rural areas, the whole tied together by an intricate and closely meshed system of relationships and communications, and providing a wide range of employment and services'.

(ii) Witnesses put forward a variety of possible areas as city regions, ranging in number from 25 to 45 for the country as a whole. This suggested that the city region was not an idea which could be applied uniformly all over England, and in some parts of the country it did not seem to us to fit reality. In a number of areas it does provide the clue: around the great urban concentrations of Birmingham, Liverpool and Manchester, and also in areas where a big town is the natural centre for a wide area of surrounding countryside and smaller towns. But in others, such as the south west, insistence on the idea of the city region seemed to mean creating artificially constructed areas whose people have no sense of looking to a city centre or of sharing interests peculiar to themselves; and in the south east the idea leads to no clear local government pattern because the influence of London overshadows that of other centres.

(iii) Many suggested city regions would be so large as to need a second operational tier of authorities if local government is not to be too remote for effective contact between the elected representatives and the people. But many of these second-tier authorities would be too small to find the resources needed for the main local government services; and in any case the present splitting of personal services which ought to be concentrated in one authority would be reproduced over a large part of the country.

11. We therefore next considered various alternatives to applying the idea of the city region to the whole country. We examined a series of maps illustrating the other main proposals for a new structure put to us in evidence. These proposals were: a single tier; two tiers of various kinds and sizes; main authorities performing most functions but with a level above them, covering a 'province', to perform the rest. Other maps which our staff prepared for us showed that the country could be divided into 130 to 140 areas which had some measure of coherence because of internal social and economic ties, but many of these areas have populations far too small to enable them to employ the range of staff needed for the efficient provision of any of the main services.

12. Meanwhile we had become increasingly convinced by those who emphasised the need for an organ of community at grass-roots level. Our conclusion was that any new pattern of democratic government must include elected local councils, not to provide

main services, but to promote and watch over the particular interests of communities in city, town and village throughout England.

13. Our examination of England had also led us to the conclusion that local government, however organised, needs to include a new representative institution with authority over areas larger than any city region, not unlike the eight areas of the present regional economic planning councils. This provincial council would handle the broader planning issues, work out provincial economic strategy in collaboration with central government and be able to act on behalf of the whole province.

A DIFFERENCE IN APPROACH

4. My colleagues take as their starting-point the proposition that, in considering what changes are needed to remedy the ills we have diagnosed, there is one fundamental question – namely, what *size* of authority, or range of size, in terms of population and of area, is needed for the democratic and efficient provision of particular services and for local self-government as a whole. The answer they produce is expressed in terms of population only: it takes no account of the geographical requirements of democracy and efficiency.

5. They go on to lay down the principles by whose application to each part of the country the answer must be found, and one of these is that to concentrate responsibility for all main local government services in a single authority for each area (as in the present county borough) would help to make the idea of local self-government a reality. Thus stated the unitary principle is unexceptionable in itself; but the number of areas in which it is reconcilable with an equal regard for other stated principles and for the facts of social geography can be counted on the fingers of one hand. Elsewhere the only way to realise the theoretical advantages of unitariness would be to increase or reduce the populations of the areas which are coherent enough in terms of social geography to make functionally effective and democratically viable units of local government. Yet my colleagues all claim that coherent units conforming both with the unitary principle and with their specified range of population size can be identified in all but three areas – the three which can be divided into district units conforming with their minimum population size. . . .

9. In three extreme cases – the Merseyside, Selnec and West

Midlands areas – my colleagues recognise that unitariness is out of the question: the sacrifices entailed would be unconscionable. In four cases – the Cambridge, Peterborough, Lincoln and Leicester areas – I recognise that the advantages of unitariness can be realised without material sacrifice of other values. Elsewhere, however, it seems to me that my colleagues' pattern treats functional effectiveness, democratic vitality, responsiveness to changing local needs, economic viability and coherence in terms of human geography as aims to be pursued only in so far as they can be reconciled with the demands – as my colleagues see them – of the unitary principle.

10. What the unitary principle demands is, first, that each local authority's area should be populous enough to enable every service whose work-load is related to population to be fully and economically staffed. My colleagues express the view that on this ground an authority responsible for the personal services (among which they include education and house-building) ought to have a population of at least 'around 250,000'. Which functional requirements of which of these services, in what demographic circumstances, call for this figure rather than for one less than half or more than twice as large, I leave for later discussion; suffice it for the moment that this is the figure my colleagues have chosen.

11. By the same token, the unitary principle would seem to demand that each local authority's area should be of such a size and shape that the 'environmental' services (planning, transportation, etc.), whose problems are related to the regional scope of modern living, should also be able to operate properly. But such regions contain populations ranging up to well over 2,000,000 even if Merseyside, Selnec and the West Midlands are excluded, and all but one of my colleagues recognise that an all-purpose authority with a population in excess of 1,000,000 would be both undemocratic and unmanageable. What they conclude from this, however, is not, as one might expect, that these regions should be treated in the same way as Merseyside, Selnec and the West Midlands, so that their planning and transportation authorities can do their jobs properly. It is that they should be divided for all purposes into units each containing not much more than 1,000,000 people.

12. Thus the unitary principle is interpreted as demanding, over 'England as a whole', units with populations ranging from around 250,000 to around 1,000,000. In consequence, many of the geographical entities needing to be planned as wholes would have to

be fragmented and most of the coherent districts that could effectively deal with their own distinctive personal-service problems would have to be denied their democratic right to do so.

13. My colleagues seek to mitigate these consequences in two ways. On the one hand they would give indirectly elected provincial councils wide powers of control over the plan-making work of the unitary authorities, and on the other hand they would give 'local' councils for the areas of former county and non-county boroughs opportunities to 'play a part' in the running of statutory services with the consent of the unitary authorities.

14. But their provincial councils cannot be given development powers without destroying the unitary principle. Yet without development powers they would be impotent to get their own plans carried out, and ultimately unable, where development could not be indefinitely held up, to exercise even their powers of negative control. Their possession, as indirectly elected bodies, of an ineffectual power to interfere with the structural planning job that needs to be done on a regional scale would serve only to prevent them from exerting a positive influence, as the confidential advisers of central government, on the management of the provincial economy – a necessary job that only an appointed provincial council can do.

15. Similarly, the 'local' councils cannot be given decision-making powers over any part, however derisory, of local government's statutory services without destroying the unitary principle. They would therefore be unable to get the distinctive needs of their own people met. Their ineffectual 'participation', as passive agents, in statutory services that could be better organised on a district basis would serve only to distract them from their more important tasks of voicing local opinion and providing non-statutory amenities for the people living in their areas. In short, by calling in the provincial and 'local' councils to redress the deficiencies inherent in their unitary authorities, my colleagues would at best compromise what is most valuable in the concepts of the provincial and 'local' councils and at worst turn their one-tier system into a three-tier one with units inappropriate in scale and composition for most purposes at every level.

16. A minor premise which, as interpreted and applied by my colleagues, I also find unacceptable is that the new local government pattern must stem from that existing today. If (as we all agree) every existing administrative county, every county and non-

county borough and every urban and rural district must be abolished, and new units based on entirely different principles created, it seems to me that to distort the new pattern in order to resurrect as many as possible of the old boundaries can only prejudice both the acceptability of the new authorities and the prospect of their making a clean break with obsolete management practices.

17. Another of my colleagues' principles is that the areas of the new units must be based upon the interdependence of town and country – a proposition with which I am, of course, in complete agreement. My objection here is that the principle as stated does not go anything like far enough. It would be satisfied if we merely recommended, as some witnesses suggested we should, that the existing county boroughs be submerged in the existing counties. But this would not take us five per cent of the way towards creating a structure that would meet the functional requirements of the 'environmental' services. For nearly all the present county boundaries entirely fail to recognise the only kind of interdependence between town and country that is relevant to the organisation of local government – namely, the interdependence of a major urban centre with that particular tract of country (including lesser urban centres) whose inhabitants find that particular centre more accessible than any other offering a comparable range of opportunities. But to recognise this would be to introduce a socio-geographic parameter into the quest for the right answer to the 'fundamental question' of the appropriate size of unit for particular services. And that would make the unitary principle inapplicable to any of the more populous parts of the country.

18. This, I think, is the nub of the difference in approach between my colleagues and myself. They have adopted a principle of organisation – the unitary principle – and determined a range of *population* size for unitary authorities by analysing the theoretical requirements of functional efficiency and democratic viability in isolation from the geographical context in which local government must operate – though with a tender regard for the need to 'maintain the momentum' of the existing administrative pattern. Only when they come to examine possible boundaries for particular units within their predetermined range of population size do they take account of the realities of social geography – and then only as considerations to be weighed against others in striking a 'balance of advantage' and deciding whether exceptions to the unitary principle are unavoidable. I think the right approach is to start by

analysing the facts of social geography, the requirements of functional effectiveness and the conditions of democratic viability in relation to one another, to let the outcome of this analysis determine the appropriate scales of units for groups of related functions, and then to see what principle of organisation best fits the needs thus ascertained and the practicalities of the transition to a new structure.

19. Our motorised society organises itself in a series of more or less self-contained geographic entities (called city regions) ranging in continuous gradation from the simplicity of a single-centred rural region to the complexity of a hierarchical system of community relationships with a major conurbation centre as its unifying focus. In a few cases at each end of this range, both my colleagues' approach and my own lead to very similar proposals. But throughout the graduated continuum between these extremes my colleagues' approach entails sacrifices of community coherence, of functional effectiveness (especially in the 'environmental' field) and of democratic strength that become increasingly intolerable as the socio-geographic structure becomes more highly organised. If they had been content to acknowledge these sacrifices and argue that the benefits inherent in the unitary pattern justified them, it would have been sufficient for me to let the positive merits of my alternative structure speak for themselves. But since they profess to have identified a set (with variations) of unitary areas all of which are socially, economically and geographically coherent, satisfactory for planning purposes and democratically viable, I am obliged to controvert these claims by reference to specific areas.

1.25 From the *County Councils Gazette* (December 1969), Vol. 62, No. 12, pp. 362-4.

This is the text of a letter dated 14 November 1969, sent to the Permanent Secretary of the Ministry of Housing and Local Government setting out the views of the County Councils Association, the Rural District Councils Association and the Urban District Councils Association on the proposals of the Royal Commission on Local Government, 1966-9.

The three Associations are agreed that the local authorities of the future which have the responsibility for major planning, transportation and environmental functions and such services as education must be of sufficient size to carry out the duties without any doubt as to their viability or the sufficiency of their resources for doing so. They take the view that such authorities should have a minimum population of around 500,000 except where, due to sparsity, this could not be achieved within a reasonable area, and that in a number of instances (for example where there is fairly high density of population) authorities of a greater population – even in excess of 1 million – would be appropriate; the authorities contemplated would comply to a great extent with the principles of the Royal Commission.

At the same time, the three Associations broadly accept the Royal Commission's proposals for the system of local government in the area of the conurbations; nevertheless, they are firmly of the opinion that the boundaries of the so-called metropolitan areas which encompass the three conurbations concerned should be much more tightly drawn so as to exclude the rural and rural/urban fringes from the areas of those authorities.

The three Associations are also agreed that the system of two-tier government suggested for the conurbations – subject to some readjustment of the proposed allocation of functions, in particular of education which must be the responsibility of the larger area or first-tier authority – should also be applied to certain other parts of the country; this is so particularly where there are mixed areas of town and country with large high-density populations often with separate urban communities within a short distance of each other.

The Royal Commission's proposals for a unitary system have been criticised in varying degrees by each of the three Associations. The RDCA and UDCA consider that a major objection to the proposals is that they would involve an unacceptable reduction in the number of councillors involved in the administration of local government, in particular of the more local services, and they do not consider that the Commission's proposals for a sytem of local councils would meet this defect. In their view there should be in all the 'unitary areas', a second tier of district authorities each with a population of, say, 60,000–100,000 and in some areas with a higher population figure.

The County Councils Association have also expressed doubts about the democratic basis of the unitary authorities. Whilst acknowledging the advantages of this type of authority, they consider that in practice some positive arrangements are required to ensure the participation of more elected members in the administration of the services. For this purpose, the County

Councils Association have suggested that each unitary authority should decentralise administration of selected appropriate functions to district committees of elected members, these being, consitutionally, committees of the unitary authority. . . .

The Associations have given some preliminary consideration to the allocation of functions and already they have found scope for a considerable measure of agreement. Thus, it is accepted that the main authority (first tier) should be responsible for police, fire, transportation and principal highways (including traffic management), education, personal health services (including ambulance), social work services (Seebohm), water supply, consumer protection and refuse and sewage disposal.

With regard to the functions for the second tier, the Associations accept that house purchase and improvement, public health (including food and drugs and caravan licensing functions), sewerage, building controls, refuse collection, clean air, coast protection, arts, recreation (including picnic and caravan sites), parks and the provision of amenities generally (in parallel with any local or parish council) should be the direct responsibility of the second-tier authority.

The three Associations have also given some consideration to the selection of those services in which district committees could play a valuable part in the discharge of the functions of the main authority. They believe that the social work and personal health services may well be appropriate for this method of organisation; this will be particularly important in the larger of the main authorities, and they consider that these future authorities should be enabled to make appropriate arrangements for this purpose, possibly within a general statutory framework. . . .

The representatives of the three Associations believe that a reorganisation system on the lines they have indicated would meet the objections on democratic grounds to the Commission's proposal. They estimate that, under such a system, the number of elected members directly concerned in the administration of services might well be increased to between two and three times the number required by the Commission's present proposals – estimated by the RDCA as about 5,000.

1.26 From the Local Government Commission for Wales, *Report and Proposals for Wales* (10 December 1962), pp. 210-11.

This extract gives the Commission's own summary of its proposals for the reorganisation of local government in Wales. The Commission was eventually disbanded without any of its recommendations being achieved.

1036. The proposals which we have formulated and which we now submit to the Minister can be summarised as follows:

I. COUNTIES

The administrative counties of Wales should be reduced in number from thirteen to seven. These seven counties should be, in broad outline, as indicated below:

(1) Mid Wales, consisting of the existing counties of Montgomery, Radnor and Brecon (apart from the southern fringe), with southern Merioneth and northern Cardiganshire.

(2) Anglesey.

(3) Gwynedd, consisting of the existing county of Caernarvon with the northern part of Merioneth and the western part of Denbighshire.

(4) Flint and Denbigh, consisting of the existing county of Flint with the eastern part of Denbighshire, together with the Edeyrnion Rural District of Merioneth.

(5) West Wales, consisting of the existing counties of Pembroke and Carmarthen with the southern part of Cardiganshire.

(6) Glamorgan (including the existing county borough of Merthyr Tydfil), together with that part of Breconshire south of the watershed of the Brecon Beacons.

(7) Gwent, consisting of the present county of Monmouth together with (a) that part of Breconshire south of the watershed of the Black Mountains and (b) the western side of the Rhymney Valley (now in Glamorgan).

II. COUNTY BOROUGHS

(1) The county borough of Cardiff should be altered as described in paragraph 744.

(2) The county borough of Newport should be altered as described in paragraph 820.

(3) The county borough of Swansea should be altered as described in paragraph 841.

(4) The county borough of Merthyr Tydfil should be converted

to a non-county borough and absorbed in the administrative county of Glamorgan.

(5) We recommend that Rhondda Borough should not be granted the status of a county borough as proposed by its Council.

(6) We recommend that Wrexham Borough should not be granted the status of a county borough as proposed by its Council.

1.27 From *Local Government in Wales* (July 1967), Cmnd. 3340, pp. 1-2 and 23-6.

These are extracts from the White Paper giving the proposals of the Secretary of State for Wales for local government reform in Wales.

3. The Local Government Commission in its first report* produced in 1961 put forward draft proposals for creating, substantially by amalgamation, five administrative counties instead of the existing 13, the more densely populated areas of the north and south being associated with the more sparsely populated areas of Mid Wales. The 1961 report also proposed extensions to the county boroughs of Cardiff and Newport, a minor adjustment of the boundary of Swansea, the conversion of the county borough of Merthyr Tydfil into a non-county borough, and the rejection of suggestions that the non-county boroughs of Rhondda and Wrexham should be made county boroughs. These proposals met with opposition and, after conferences with local authorities and other interested bodies, the Commission, in their final report,† adhered in the main to their recommendations about the county boroughs but proposed that there should be seven rather than five new counties. At the heart of their final proposals for the counties was the concept of a Mid Wales county created by the amalgamation of Montgomeryshire, Radnorshire, most of Breconshire and parts of Merioneth and Cardiganshire. Pembrokeshire and Carmarthenshire were to be joined with the rest of Cardiganshire, and Flintshire was to be joined with most of Denbighshire and with part of Merioneth. Glamorgan and Monmouthshire were each to take in a part of Breconshire, and the whole of the Rhymney

* Local Government Commission for Wales, *Draft proposals* (published by the Commission, 1961).

† Local Government Commission for Wales, *Report and Proposals for Wales* (HMSO, 1963).

Valley was to be transferred from Glamorgan to Monmouthshire. Caernarvonshire was to be combined with part of western Denbighshire and the remainder of Merioneth. Only Anglesey was to remain untouched. This final report also had a mixed reception on publication and the Commission's proposals were again opposed by many local authorities. Further, it was generally accepted that the Commission had, as they themselves emphasised, been limited by the exclusion of functions and finance from their terms of reference. The Government of the day did not feel that they should implement the Commission's recommendations* and undertook to prepare proposals themselves.

4. The Secretary of State for Wales set up in 1965 an Inter-Departmental Working Party† to help him to examine the functions and boundaries of all classes of local authorities in Wales. He was anxious that this review should not proceed in isolation from local authority opinion and arrangements were made for the Working Party to consult informally a number of people whose names were suggested by the local authority associations for their knowledge and experience of local government in Wales. In the views expressed by these informal advisers the Working Party distinguished three broad lines of thought:

(a) that the existing structure should be retained, but with substantially fewer and stronger authorities;

(b) that the existing structure should be replaced by a single tier of all-purpose authorities; and

(c) that some kind of regional or sub-regional local authority should be formed.

The Working Party examined (a) and (b) by constructing two hypothetical models and they also tentatively sketched possible functions and constitution for an all-Wales council. This work was conveyed to the informal advisers in an interim memorandum and they were asked, in confidence, for their views on the alternatives put forward and for suggestions for improvements. A majority

* The Commission's recommendations for the county boroughs of Cardiff, Newport and Swansea were, however, examined and inquiries were held into objections to them. The Secretary of State announced his decisions in May, 1965, and orders have since been made bringing into effect boundary changes for Newport and Cardiff.

† The Working Party comprised senior officers from the Welsh Office, Welsh Board of Health, Ministry of Health, Education Office for Wales of the Department of Education and Science, Home Office and Ministry of Housing and Local Government together with Professor Ivor Gowan of the Department of Political Science at the University College of Wales, Aberystwyth.

favoured (*a*), a substantial minority favoured (*b*), and opinion was about equally divided on the suggestions for a possible regional authority. The carefully reasoned and detailed criticisms made by the advisers and their suggestions for improvements greatly helped in the preparation of the present proposals. . . .

63. The proposals put forward are:

County boroughs

(1) Merthyr Tydfil should cease to be a county borough. Cardiff, Newport and Swansea should retain this status with the revised boundaries already approved by the Secretary of State . . .

Counties

(2) The following five new administrative counties should replace the present 13:

Gwynedd – an amalgamation of Anglesey, Caernarvonshire, Denbighshire, Flintshire and Merioneth;

Powys – an amalgamation of Montgomeryshire, Radnorshire and Breconshire;

Dyfed – an amalgamation of Cardiganshire, Carmarthenshire and Pembrokeshire;

Glamorgan – the existing county except for the Rhymney Valley;

Gwent – the existing county and the Rhymney Valley . . .

Districts

(3) 36 new districts, preserving where possible the identities of existing counties which are to be amalgamated, should be created in place of the present 164 non-county boroughs, urban districts and rural districts and the county borough of Merthyr Tydfil . . .

A new Welsh Council

(18) As an evolution of the Welsh Economic Council and of certain organisations peculiar to Wales (particularly the previous Council for Wales, the Welsh Arts Council, the Development Corporation for Wales and the Wales Tourist Board) early action should be taken to set up a new Welsh Council which would initially have the following advisory and promotional functions:

To provide a forum for the interchange of views and information on developments in the economic and cultural fields and to advise on the implications for Wales of national policies.

To formulate development proposals for Wales having regard to the best use of its resources and to advise the Secretary of State for Wales on major land use and economic planning matters.

To advise the Minister of Transport and the Secretary of State on transport policy and planning in Wales.

To give advice on the national parks and countryside.

To advise on the arts in Wales particularly where arrangements need to be made on an all-Wales basis.

To keep under review and help to promote the publicity and similar work for encouraging industrial and tourist development in Wales done by the Development Corporation, the Tourist Board and other bodies.

To encourage co-operation between the local authorities, through schemes which would first require the approval of the appropriate Ministers. . . .

2 London Government

2.1 From the 'Report of the Commissioners appointed to inquire into the existing state of the Corporation of the City of London, and to collect information respecting its constitution, order and Government', *HCP* (1854), Vol. XXIX, pp. xv, xxxiv-xxxvi.

This was the second inquiry into the City of London, the first by the Royal Commission on Municipal Corporations twenty years earlier. It was this second enquiry which marked the beginning of the movement for the reform of London government.

The City of London has no governing charter; in which respect it differs from many of the English Corporations. It is true that the great Inspeximus Charter of Charles II recites and includes almost all the former ones, but it gives no explanation of them; it collects them, but does nothing towards their interpretation. There is no authoritative exposition of the multifarious rights and privileges, many of which are said to be founded on the language of these charters. Hence arises considerable uncertainty as to the meaning of the charters themselves. . . . There is also the further question as to the alteration effected in the authority of the customs and charters of the City by general Acts of Parliament in which the City is not specially named. The customs of the City having been solemnly confirmed by Act of Parliament have themselves the force of an Act of Parliament, and we have been told in evidence by witnesses peculiarly conversant with the subject, that the highest legal authorities are divided as to the effect of general Acts of Parliament within the City, when they conflict with the City customs and do not repeal them by express enactment. . . .

We stated in a former part of our Report that, if the entire system of the Municipal Corporations Act were applied to the Corporation of London, it would be necessary to advance its boundaries until they comprehended the entire metropolis. We attempted, at the same time, to show that such an extension of the City boundaries would entirely alter the character of the Corporation of London, and would create a municipal body of unmanageable dimensions; we therefore advised that this course should not be adopted, and we reserved the mode of dealing with this part of the subject for separate consideration.

With the single exception of London, the local government of every considerable town in the United Kingdom is vested in a municipal corporation. This government is not confined to a portion of the town, but, since the recent statutory reforms, comprehends its entire circuit. In London, however, as we have already seen, the municipal government extends over only a small portion of the entire town, whether measured by area or by population. If it were held that municipal institutions were not suited to a metropolitan city, no reason could be found, except its antiquity and existence, for maintaining the Corporation of London, even with its present limited area. It appears to us, however, that a metropolitan city requires, for its own local purposes, municipal institutions not less than other towns. We believe, indeed, that the utility of municipal institutions is greater, and their want more felt, in a large, populous, opulent, and crowded metropolis, than in a country town of less size, population, and wealth. Those functions of local government, moreover, which in other towns are performed by the municipal authorities, are, in the metropolis, actually discharged by parochial functionaries, or by boards created by local acts, though they may be discharged in a less uniform and efficient manner. In some cases, indeed, in the parishes on the outskirts of the metropolis, they may, from a want of powers in the general law, be left for a time altogether unprovided for, to the serious inconvenience of the inhabitants, and to the permanent injury of the owners of property within the district. We may refer to the evidence of a deputation of the vestry of St Pancras, appended to our Report, as illustrating the evils which now arise in large parishes where new building is in progress on a large scale, from the absence of an efficient municipal organisation, applicable to new portions of the town as they successively spring into existence. . . .

. . . we suggest the creation of a Metropolitan Board of Works, to be composed of a very limited number of members deputed to it from the council of each metropolitan municipal body, including the Corporations of the City. We propose that the management of public works, in which the metropolis has a common interest, should be conducted by this body. At present works of this sort can only be undertaken either by the Corporation of London from its own peculiar funds, or under powers created for the purpose by special legislation, or by the executive government out of Parliamentary grants. The only fund arising from metropolitan taxation is the coal tax, a large part of which is, as we have already seen, devoted to metropolitan improvements, under the control either of the Commissioners of Works, or the Corporation of London. . . .

We propose further that the metropolitan board of works should be empowered to levy a rate upon the entire metropolis, for any improvement of general utility, within a certain poundage, to be fixed by Act of Parliament. The present poor-rate assessment of the metropolis (according to the limits of the Registrar General), is nearly 10,000,000*l.*; and a penny rate upon this amount would produce 41,666*l.* Looking to the unequal incidence of the coal tax, and to the dissatisfaction which it creates in the district over which it is levied, we strongly incline to the opinion that, even if it should not be thought expedient to disturb the existing arrangement before 1862, yet that it will be held advisable to abolish it from that period, and to substitute for it a rate levied upon the whole metropolis, and payable either by the owner or the occupier, or by both in some fixed proportion. If it should not then be thought expedient to renew the coal tax, as we think probable, we assume that the 4*d.* duty now levied on behalf of the City would cease at the same time.

2.2 From *The Times* (23 January and 1 February 1889).

These extracts from leading articles in *The Times* show how the party alignments were emerging from the birth of the London County Council.

The County Council of London will meet tomorrow week for the first time. On that occasion the chairman will be chosen, and then, or at an adjourned meeting, the nineteen aldermen are to be elected. The chair will be taken provisionally, it is to be hoped, by some person of recognised position and ability, who will not only be able to maintain order, but who may induce the inexperienced and undisciplined to defer to his authority in the conduct of business. Sir John Lubbock, who stood at the head of the poll in the City of London and who had a larger number of votes recorded in his favour than any other elected member of the Council, seems marked out for this position. The future of the Council will largely depend on the choice of a permanent chairman, who will be elected at the second meeting, and since the majority, now that the election is over, appear desirous of throwing off the non-political mask and of proclaiming their adhesion to the Radical party, they would naturally be expected to support Lord Rosebery, one of the most distinguished of their own leaders and the only statesman of Cabinet rank who has sought to take a share in the local govern- ment of London. Lord Rosebery, at the same time, has expressly disclaimed any sympathy with the movement for turning the machinery of the County Council to the purposes, not of adminis- trative work, but of political agitation, and it remains to be seen whether, on this ground, the so-called 'Progressists' of the Council will refuse to stand by him. Of even greater importance, perhaps, is the election of the aldermen. We have already strongly urged the elected members of the County Councils, in the provinces as well as in London, to exercise with great care and with a serious sense of responsibility the right confided to them of co-opting a certain proportion of the whole body either from within or without. In this, still more than in the original contests, the political element ought to be excluded, for the elected members hold in reference to the choice of aldermen a strictly fiduciary position. It is the plain and direct duty of the elected members of every County Council to choose the aldermen, not for the sake of reinforcing this or that party, but on the ground of their fitness for the discharge of municipal duties as prescribed by law. We trust that this will be done in the great majority of cases in which politics have been, on the whole, excluded from the primary elections, in spite of bad examples, bad advice, and provocative challenges. . . .

We have held all along that the Council would best consult its own dignity and the interests of those it represents by discarding party prepossessions altogether, and selecting the aldermen with a sole regard for their fitness to strengthen and sustain its own reputation, authority, and capacity. Two lists of names have been put forth, one by those members who are styled 'progressive', the other by those who prefer to call themselves 'moderate'. There are excellent names in both lists. We are as indifferent as Mr Firth says he is himself to the views held by any candidate on Imperial or party politics, provided only he is likely to bring to the County Council some quality, whether of personal distinction, of special acquaintance with some of the matters with which the Council will have to deal, of known and approved good sense, or of tried aptitude for public business, which will strengthen the Council and enhance its general efficiency. For this reason we should be glad to see a selection made from both lists, and we should not be sorry if before Tuesday some other well-known names were added. Now that the initial danger of what is known in America as a 'strict party vote' has been averted by the proceedings of yesterday, we have every hope that all parties, if there are any parties, and all members of the Council, if there are really no parties, will proceed to the election of aldermen in the spirit contemplated by the Act and required by the importance of the occasion. We augur well of the new Council from the results of its proceedings of yesterday. It has shown that it knows how to act with dignity, discretion, and deliberation, and we trust that it will show in its selection of aldermen that it is equal to the responsibilities imposed on it.

2.3 From Sidney Webb, *The London Programme* (London 1892), Chap. III, pp. 17-27.

After the creation of the London County Council to replace the Metropolitan Board of Works, the vestries and the district boards vied with the City Corporation as the most inadequate institutions of metropolitan government. Sidney Webb and his fellow Fabians, notably Bernard Shaw who was a member of the St Pancras vestry, saw that reform of the vestries was likely to be the more successful object to tackle and of benefit to the greater number of citizens.

THE ABOLITION OF VESTRYDOM

Perhaps the most pressing of all questions of the London Programme is the Abolition of Vestrydom. The County Council is all very well as far as it goes, but, as we have already seen, most of the functions of administration in the metropolis are, at present, beyond its scope, and free from its control.

Much of the ordinary work of a municipality, including the paving, lighting, watering and cleansing of the streets, the abatement of nuisances, the enforcement of the sanitary laws, the removal of dust, the construction and maintenance of local sewers, still remains in the hands of a congeries of obscure local boards, the 5,000 members of which, though nominally elected, are practically unknown, unchecked, unsupervised and unaudited. How they have done their work every Londoner knows only too well. The duties neglected by these vestries and district boards are more important than those they attempt to perform. For instance, under the Labouring Classes Dwelling Houses Acts (14 and 15 Vic. cap. 34, and subsequent Acts) they long had power (now transferred to the County Council) to acquire land and to build or hire tenement or lodging houses for the poor. They still have power (under the Sanitary Acts, especially 29 and 30 Vic. c. 90) to condemn and close insanitary dwellings, and (under the Torrens Act, 31 and 32 Vic. c. 130, and others) to acquire and pull down condemned houses. They have power to make and enforce stringent rules for all houses let in lodgings or tenements, providing for their systematic registration, inspection, and sanitation; enforcing proper accommodation; providing against overcrowding, and for the separation of the sexes. They have power (18 and 19 Vic. c. 120, sec. 118) to organise a regular corps of crossing-sweepers – if need be, from the unemployed – and so to put a stop to the present evil system of licensed mendicity. They have power in every parish to do what has been done only in a few – to provide public libraries, baths and wash-houses, mortuaries, open spaces, seats for the weary, and other conveniences for common use.

But these Acts are not compulsory. The vestry has power to do all these things; but it also has power not to do them until the citizens wake up to their responsibilities and compel it to take action. Unfortunately, those who suffer most from parochial neglect are not influential. There has been no really democratic control: consequently the vestries have almost uniformly neglected their most important public functions, and largely mismanaged those which they have undertaken. . . .

The vestrymen are elected by persons whose names have been on the rate-book of the parish for one year prior to the election, which takes place annually, but only one-third of the vestrymen retire each year.

No person is qualified for election unless he is the occupier of premises rated at 40l. per annum. The Local Government Board has, however, power to reduce this qualification to 25l. in districts where five-sixths of the houses are rated at less than 40l. But either qualification is sufficient to exclude nearly all the artisans and labourers, and metropolitan vestrymen are mainly taken from the class of small shopkeepers, or from among the owners of small house property, eager to escape the sanitary laws. The number of each vestry is usually much too great; the larger parishes have to elect 120 representatives, to whom are added the incumbent of the parish church and the churchwardens as ex-officio members. Such unwieldy Boards, formed out of such unpromising material, have, not unnaturally, proved anything but satisfactory.

The arrangements for elections are primitive. A meeting of rate-payers is held on a day in May, the hour being usually fixed in the morning, when few persons can be present. No prior nomination of candidates is required, and the election takes place by a show of hands at the meeting. If a poll is demanded, it must be taken on the very next day. No register of voters is available, and, indeed, any person entitled to have his name on the rate-book is entitled to vote, even if he is not, in fact, rated. The election is not subject to the provisions of either the Parliamentary or the Municipal Corrupt Practices Act, and the Ballot Act does not apply to it. No notice is taken of it by the leading newspapers; the very slightest public interest is aroused; and practically the 5,000 members of the seventy-eight vestries elect each other.

London's first requisite in local municipal administration is a new start. The mere breaking loose from the old vestry traditions will be one of the most important advantages of the establishment of District Councils. These District Councils, to enlist the public interest, must, from the outset, be given important and independent powers; they must be popularly elected for districts forming natural administrative units; and the arrangements connected with them must be systematic and easy of comprehension by the plain man and average citizen. . . .

The first question for decision is that of the number of District Councils and their areas. At present only four districts in the metropolis have one and the same set of boundaries for Parliamentary, Municipal and Poor Law purposes. . . .

This metropolitan chaos cannot be set right all at once, but the establishment of District Councils must, at any rate, not increase the confusion. The least apathetic element in London's collective life is undoubtedly that which has the Parliamentary constituency as its unit. This has already been adopted for the purposes of the County Council. No other division has any kind of popular organisation; no other electoral area is so much aware of itself as a corporate whole. There is, accordingly, much to be said for the adoption of this area as that of the new District Council. . . .

The next question is that of the composition of the new Councils. There is, however, now little left for discussion. The District Councils must, of course, be wholly elected by popular vote, on whatever register of electors is, for the time being, in force. The number of members should never exceed fifty, even in the largest council, and might therefore be fixed at one for every 10,000 inhabitants, within a minimum of twenty members for the smallest council. Except, possibly, the County Councillors for the district, no ex-officio or nominated members can be allowed, and there appears to be no reason for placing any restriction on the choice of the electors. As for the London School Board, 'any person' should be eligible for election, without residential, rating, property or other qualification, and without distinction of sex. The franchise for electors can hardly be other than that for the time being in force for the County Council elections, extensive simplification of the registration arrangements being obviously near at hand. The elections should, it is suggested, take place once a year, the members of the Council being elected for two years, one half retiring each year. . . .

The most important point is, however, the relation which the District Councils should bear to the County Council, and the manner in which the municipal functions of the metropolis should be divided between them. It is urged, on the one hand, that the advantages to be gained by unity of administration, and freedom from local corruption, make it desirable that the County Council should decide all matters of principle, and have power to see that its decisions are carried out. The District Councils would, on this plan, be little more than local administrative committees, carrying out a general scheme of municipal polity imposed on them from above. On the other hand, it is contended that the examples of the Boards of Guardians and Board School Committees of Local Managers show that these advantages can be purchased only at the expense of destroying all vitality in the local bodies, and of rendering it difficult to induce men of ability to serve on them.

There can be little doubt that the latter view, aided by the forces of all the existing local authorities, is destined to prevail. The District Councils will undoubtedly be bodies of independent authority, having power to raise their own rates, expend their own funds, and settle their own questions in their own way. They will take over the existing powers of the vestries and District Boards, including, therefore, the paving, cleansing and lighting of the streets, the control of local sewers; and they will no doubt be given all ordinary functions of a Municipal Corporation except those reserved to the County Council.

The work of the existing multitude of obscure local authorities (such as Burial Boards, Commissioners of Baths and Wash-houses, Commissioners of Free Libraries, and others) will doubtless also be transferred to them.

One apparently minor reform, of far-reaching importance, cannot be too strongly insisted upon. A large part of the inefficiency, stupidity and jobbery of the smaller London vestries has been caused or permitted by the absurd custom of allowing the vestry clerkship to be an appanage of some old-fashioned and busy firm of solicitors. The clerk to the District Council should in all cases be an independent officer, paid to give his whole time to his municipal duties.

2.4 From Beatrice Webb, *Our Partnership*, ed. B. Drake and M. I. Cole (London 1948), pp. 59-61, 68 and 282-3.

These extracts show the Webbs' involvement in London government in the closing years of the nineteenth century. The first is a comment on the emergence of party politics in the early years of the London County Council, and the other two are Beatrice Webb's diary entries on electoral prospects.

The first election, in January 1889, was, from the standpoint of the experienced politician, an unorganised scramble. Neither the Liberal nor the Conservative Party used the party electoral machinery. Candidates spontaneously offered themselves to the electors, mainly as advocates of 'good government'. There were no deliberately formulated party programmes among which the voters could choose. Almost the only lead as to policy was given by what was then an obscure body of young men and women, the Fabian Society, which, by what was then an original device, caused all the candidates to be importuned by showers of printed lists of questions, sent by electors demanding answers to every issue of what ought to be 'municipal politics'. These were accompanied by pamphlets explaining in detail the policy afterwards known as municipal Socialism. In the absence of any contrary policy, a large proportion of the candidates, who had thought only of 'good government', found themselves subscribing to this programme.

The first three years' term of the London County Council was chiefly occupied in framing the elaborate constitution required for so great an administration, and with tentative efforts towards increased efficiency and avoidance of waste. When the second election approached (that of 1892 at which the Other One became a candidate for a seat held by a Conservative), party organisation on both sides became definite and powerful. The Conservative Party saw the importance of controlling so influential a local authority as the London County Council had become. Opposing the Conservatives were those councillors who called themselves the Progressives, with a view to uniting for municipal purposes, along with the Liberals (largely Nonconformists), also the Conservative and Liberal Unionist sympathisers with an active policy in London administration; the churchmen and Roman Catholic philanthropists who wanted the slums and the mean streets reformed; and the trade unionist workmen who sought to insist on fairer conditions of employment. This heterogeneous host was marshalled by a professedly non-political body (the London Reform Union), and was supplied with a programme – the Other One says by the Fabian Society – a programme which, somehow or other, found its way into six months' issues of *The Speaker*, then the weekly organ of intellectual Liberalism. . . .

December 1894. – Crushing defeat at Westminster vestry elections; only 5 Progressives out of 96! We had persuaded ourselves that we should at least carry St John's II solid, and make some show in St John's I and III – the St Margaret's Ward we recognised as hopeless. But, apparently, the slums of Westminster are as completely Tory as the palaces. I do not think there has been any lack of energy or even of skill in engineering such forces as we had. But it is obvious that our attempt to collar the constituency with three weeks' work – mostly amateur – was a fiasco, which we ought to have expected. Against us we had a perfect organisation with a permanent staff, a local paper and unlimited money, we had all the wealthy residents, nearly all the employers of labour, and the whole liquor interest – no fewer than ten publicans and five other persons connected with the Trade, running as Conservative candidates. . . .

February 27th. – Sidney and [Robert] Phillimore returned unopposed for Deptford – a somewhat striking comment on the threats of last summer that 'he shall lose his seat'. He is now turning his attention to getting G. B. S. in for St Pancras. What effect G. B. S.'s brilliant slashing to the right and the left among his own nominal supporters will have, remains to be seen – the party organisers have long ago given up the seat as lost. Sidney has written to every clergyman in the St Pancras constituency (about 21), sending them a copy of his book and imploring them to go hard for Shaw; he has even got the Bishop of Stepney's blessing sent to the Rural Dean. He has now taken charge of two-thirds of the constituency, installed the Spencers [our own secretaries] in a committee room, and called up the whole of the Fabian Society on Shaw's behalf. Whether this effort will win what would be a forlorn hope to any other Progressive candidate, and will counteract the enemies G. B. S. makes in our own ranks, we cannot tell. The Shaws have been good friends to us, and we would not like them to have a humiliating defeat. What that erratic genius will do, if he gets on the L.C.C., heaven will know some day – but I am inclined to think that in the main he will back up Sidney. And he will become the *enfant terrible* of the Progressive Party, and make Sidney look wisely conventional. In the Fabian Society, they have certainly managed to supplement each other in a curiously effective way – let us hope it will be the same on the L.C.C. But he is not likely to get in!

2.5 From *The Times* (30 June 1897).
This extract is from a report of the proceedings of the London County Council and gives details of the attempts of Westminster and Kensington to seek incorporation as boroughs.

PROPOSED INCORPORATION OF KENSINGTON
The Local Government and Taxation Committee reported that they had had under consideration a letter from the honorary secretary of the committee of inhabitant householders of the parish of Kensington forwarding a copy of a petition which had been presented to the Queen in Council praying her Majesty to grant a charter of incorporation to the parish of Kensington. The petitioners said they fully recognised that there were certain matters common to the metropolis as a whole which must be exercised by a central authority, but they submitted that the functions of the central authority should be confined to such matters and that no duties should be thrown upon the central authority which could be

equally well performed by the local authority. At the present time there was overlapping of jurisdiction and there were anomalies of administration between the central authority and the local authority of Kensington which it was desirable should be remedied and adjusted. On February 9 last the committee reported that notice had been received of a petition having been presented to the Privy Council, asking for a charter of incorporation for Westminster, and on February 16 the County Council passed the following resolution:

'That, while the Council does not object to a charter being granted for the incorporation of any suitable area in London for the purposes merely of the change of the corporate name, and the substitution of the name of the mayor or council for the existing name of a vestry or district board, provided that this can legally be done in the manner proposed, the Council will strenuously oppose any transfer of powers by any such machinery, or any such transfer by any other machinery, to a particular area, without the simultaneous consideration of the whole subject of powers and areas in London.'

A copy of this resolution was forwarded to the Privy Council. The committee now recommended that a similar resolution should be passed on the subject of the petition for the incorporation of Kensington and forwarded to the Privy Council.

Mr R. A. Robinson protested against the action of the committee being adopted by the Council. The petition was signed by 9,000 educated and competent householders of Kensington, and it should receive due consideration. Some of his Progressive friends thought this was a selfish movement on the part of the parish concerned. It was nothing of the kind. The reason it had been started was that it had been found that a number of the residents in the parish did not take an interest in local matters because they did not like the term vestry. To set that right they simply desired to give their local body a more dignified title. The parish desired by this action in no way to get out of any of its obligations.

Sir Arthur Arnold said that he was an inhabitant of Kensington and had signed the memorial. But, while heartily in favour of the incorporation of Kensington as proposed, he should earnestly vote in favour of the recommendation of the committee. He thought it was essentially part of the duty of the Council that London should be treated as a whole in regard to this matter and not in a sectional manner.

After further discussion the recommendation of the committee was agreed to.

2.6 From the *London Government Act* (1899), Sections 1, 2(1) and 4(1).
The abolition of the vestries and district boards, and their replacement by the metropolitan borough councils was achieved by this Act. The simple provisions needed to do this, which are given here, give no indication of the immense effort needed to bring about the changes.

ESTABLISHMENT OF METROPOLITAN BOROUGHS

1. The whole of the administrative county of London, exclusive of the City of London, shall be divided into metropolitan boroughs (in this Act referred to as boroughs), and for that purpose it shall be lawful for Her Majesty by Order in Council, subject to and in accordance with this Act, to form each of the areas mentioned in the First Schedule to this Act into a separate borough, subject, nevertheless, to such alteration of area as may be required to give effect to the provisions of this Act, and subject also to such adjustment of boundaries as may appear to Her Majesty in Council expedient for simplification or convenience of administration, and to establish and incorporate a council for each of the boroughs so formed.

2. (1) The council of each borough shall consist of a mayor, aldermen, and councillors. Provided that no woman shall be eligible for any such office. . . .

POWERS OF BOROUGH COUNCILS

4. (1) On the appointed day every elective vestry and district board in the county of London shall cease to exist, and, subject to the provisions of this Act and of any scheme made thereunder, their powers and duties, including those under any local Act, shall, as from the appointed day, be transferred to the council for the borough comprising the area within which those powers are exercised, and their property and liabilities shall be transferred to that council, and that council shall be their successors, and the clerk of the council shall be called the town clerk, and shall be the town clerk within the meaning of the Acts relating to the registration of electors.

2.7 From the *Report of the Royal Commission on London Government* (1923), Cmd. 1830, pp. 69-70.

These extracts show how the Royal Commission dealt with the somewhat conflicting claims regarding the extension of the area of London government and the unification of various services under a single authority.

258. The dual system of government for the county of London, begun in 1855 and definitely constituted in 1899, was adopted as in the circumstances the best suited to the enormous area and its populations. Its chief merit is that, while it provides a central government for the administration of certain services in which there is a common interest, it leaves a substantial residue of functions in the hands of local bodies specially elected by the local ratepayers. Though not autonomous, these bodies have a representative government, the inhabitants are in close touch with the Council and officers who administer the local services, and local sentiment is thus maintained and nourished.

259. On the other hand, the evidence before us discloses many difficulties and questions as to the proper allocation of powers and duties between the County Council and the Boroughs. (1) The Boroughs contend that some services, which must admittedly be divided, ought to be more in their hands, and that others ought to be wholly assigned to them. (2) In some cases, when the County Council have sought from Parliament new powers, the Boroughs have claimed the administration of them. (3) Where the administration is given to the Boroughs and the County Council contribute a subvention, the Boroughs complain that the County Council impose conditions which in effect usurp the Borough Councils' powers; while paying, it may be, only a fourth of the piper's fee, they proceed to settle the greater part of the programme. (4) In some quarters, regardless of the fact that all London is represented on the County Council, the Borough Councils are apt to regard the County Council as an alien authority.

All these difficulties and questions would arise, perhaps in accentuated form, if the dual system were extended to Greater London. The larger the area, the more would the sense of remoteness from the Central Authority prevail. . . .

CONCLUSION AS TO THE EXTENSION OF THE DUAL SYSTEM OF LONDON GOVERNMENT

261. There is undoubtedly a sense of community of interest

between the various parts of London, extending in some matters to places outside. This is strongest in relation to transport. In regard to most services and general executive government, the inhabitants of one place do not concern themselves with the internal affairs of an area remote from their own, regarding them as proper to be dealt with by the Local Authority.

262. The extension of the dual system to the communities of Greater London outside the county would necessarily entail a considerable curtailment of the autonomy of the three County Boroughs and the eight Municipal Boroughs, which would meet with their strenuous opposition. Similar resistance would be offered by the large majority of other Authorities to a scheme which would substitute a London Central Authority for the County Councils now over them, thereby changing their local law, and indeed their whole system of local government. Even if the dual system of London had greater merits and fewer difficulties than it has, we view its extension as being impracticable in face of the opposition it would encounter. We may quote here Mr Lloyd George's warning to the deputation from the London County Council which waited upon him on the 9th December, 1920: 'A Report that would get 128 Local Authorities up in arms against you is not a Report that any Government would face with equanimity.'

263. We therefore recommend that the London County Council should retain their present area of administration, and that the systems of local government now prevailing, on the one hand within the administrative county of London, and on the other hand in the other areas covered by our inquiry, should not be altered on the lines proposed by the Council.

2.8 From the *Report of the Royal Commission on Local Government in Greater London, 1957-60* (3 October 1960), Cmnd. 1164, pp. 18 and 192-3.

The first extract sums up the reasons for the creation of this Royal Commission, and may be compared with the extracts from the Royal Commission of 1923. The second extract gives the summary of the Royal Commission's recommendations, which, with some amendments, became the basis for the London Government Act, 1963.

70. It is natural that after reviewing the history of inquiries into

local government in the Review Area we should speculate on the causes of the setting up of our Commission. These seem to us to be as follows, and we do not set them out in any order of merit.

(1) The spread of Greater London across the existing administrative boundaries and the creation thereby of new problems of local government. This is the continuation of a historic process.

(2) The wide discrepancy in size and resources of the authorities in the Review Area. This is, of course, not confined to the Review Area but is very marked in it.

(3) The influence of the history of local government in the Review Area, which has led in particular to two different systems, i.e. that within the Administrative County of London and that pertaining outside. The difference lies in the distribution of powers and in the existence of concurrent powers in important functions within the Administrative County.

(4) The demand by large boroughs and districts outside the Administrative County for county borough status and the consequent effect on county government. This has been present certainly for sixty years and is still strong. It is not of course confined to the Review Area, but the special circumstances of Greater London make it in a sense a different and particularly acute problem.

(5) The unsettling effect of the situation which has prevailed, with varying degrees of intensity, since 1945. The need for reorganisation has been in the air throughout this period. . . .

743. Our general conclusions are as follows:

(1) The primary unit of local government in the Greater London Area should be the borough, and the borough should perform all local authority functions except those which can only be effectively performed over the wider area of Greater London or which could be better performed over that wider area.

(2) The boroughs should have the style and title of 'Greater London Boroughs'.

(3) An authority covering the wider area of Greater London should be established with the style and title of 'the Council for Greater London'.

(4) The functions to be performed by each type of authority

should be as far as possible self-contained without over-lapping or duplication and without the necessity for delegation from one to another.

(5) The conception of an upper and lower tier of authorities should be replaced by the conception of the Greater London Borough as the primary unit of local government, performing all functions which can be performed within its own limited area, and of the Council for Greater London as a unit of local government performing functions which can only be or can be better performed over a wider area.

(6) The major functions of local government discussed in preceding chapters should be distributed between the Council for Greater London and the Greater London Boroughs in the manner recommended in Chapter XIV.

(7) The remaining functions of local government should be distributed between the Council for Greater London and the Greater London Boroughs in the manner recommended in Chapter XV.

(8) The Council for Greater London should be elected by direct election on the basis of one member for each Parliamentary division and the voting should be in single member constituencies on the normal system. We can see no special circumstances in London which would justify us in recommending any special form of voting.

(9) The area to be under the jurisdiction of the Council for Greater London should be delimited as proposed in Chapter XVI.

(10) Some of the existing boroughs and county districts are not adequate in areas or financial resources to be primary units of local government carrying the full range of local government services.

(11) The appropriate range of population for a Greater London Borough should be between 100,000 and 250,000 and in constructing such Boroughs the following factors should be taken into account:

    (*a*) As far as possible existing boroughs and county districts should be retained or amalgamated without change of boundaries.

    (*b*) In shaping a new Borough, lines of communication should be taken into account.

    (*c*) Regard should be had to the existing service centres.

(*d*) There should not be too many Boroughs.

(*e*) There is room for a little elasticity at each end of the population scale.

(*f*) There should be no county boroughs in the Review Area.

(12) The Greater London Boroughs should be delimited on the basis recommended in Chapter XVII.

(13) The area of south-west Hertfordshire, which we propose should be excluded from the area of the Council for Greater London, should be dealt with in the manner recommended in Chapter XIX.

3 Rates and Rating

3.1 *The Poor Rate Exemption Act* (1840).

One of the landmarks in the history of rating. This Act finally brought to an end the controversy about the rating of stock-in-trade, and henceforth rates were levied on the beneficial occupation of fixed property only.

CAP. LXXXIX

An Act to exempt, until the Thirty-first Day of *December* One thousand eight hundred and forty-one, Inhabitants of Parishes, Townships, and Villages from Liability to be rated as such, in respect of Stock in Trade or other Property, to the Relief of the Poor. [10th *August* 1840.]

'Whereas by an Act passed in the Forty-third Year of the Reign of Queen *Elizabeth*, intituled *An Act for the Relief of the Poor*, it was amongst other things provided, that the Overseers of every Parish should raise, by Taxation of every Inhabitant, Parson, Vicar, and other, and of every Occupier of Lands, Houses, Tithes Impropriate, Propriations of Tithes, Coal Mines, or saleable Underwoods, in the said Parish, in such competent Sum and Sums of Money as they shall think fit, a convenient Stock of necessary Ware and Stuff to set the Poor on Work, and also competent Sums of Money for and towards the Relief of the Poor not able to work, and also for the putting out of poor Children to be Apprentices, to be gathered out of the same Parish according to the Ability of the same: And whereas by another Act passed in the Session of Parliament holden in the Thirteenth and Fourteenth Years of the Reign of King *Charles* the Second, intituled *An Act for the better Relief of the Poor of this Kingdom*, the Provisions of the said Act of *Elizabeth* were extended to certain Townships and Villages: And whereas, by reason of the Provisions of the said Acts, it has been held that Inhabitants of Parishes, Townships, and Villages, as such

Inhabitants, are liable, in respect of their Ability derived from the Profits of Stock in Trade and of other Property, to be taxed for and towards the Relief the Poor, and it is expedient to repeal the Liability of Inhabitants, as such, to be so taxed:' Be it therefore enacted by the Queen's most Excellent Majesty, by and with the Advice and Consent of the Lords Spiritual and Temporal, and Commons, in this present Parliament assembled, and by the Authority of the same, That from and after the passing of this Act it shall not be lawful for the Overseers of any Parish, Township, or Village to tax any Inhabitant thereof, as such Inhabitant, in respect of his Ability derived from the Profits of Stock in Trade or any other Property, for or towards the Relief of the Poor: Provided always, that nothing in this Act contained shall in anywise affect the Liability of any Parson or Vicar, or of any Occupier of Lands, Houses, Tithes Impropriate, Propriations of Tithes, Coal Mines, or saleable Underwoods, to be taxed under the Provisions of the said Acts for and towards the Relief of the Poor.

II. And be it enacted, That this Act shall be in force till the Thirty-first Day of *December* in the Year of our Lord One thousand eight hundred and forty-one, and that from the said Thirty-first Day of *December* this Act, and all the Provisions herein-before contained, shall absolutely cease and be of no effect.

3.2 From *Hansard*, 3rd Series, Vol. 205 (3 April 1871), Cols 1118-19.
This extract from Mr Goschen's speech introducing two bills to reform the system of sanitary authorities and to consolidate the complex mass of rates and rating authorities into a single unified system, shows clearly the problem he was trying to tackle. The Rating Bill met too much opposition and was abandoned.

I believe, Sir, that in treating of this question, I may assume that the House is acquainted with the vastness of the matter of which we are treating, and I need only repeat that the amount of the rates levied in England and Wales is £16,500,000, and if to that you add the amount raised by indirect taxation, such as tolls, dues, and fees, and if you further add the subventions made by the Government, the receipts derived from the sale of property and from rents and miscellaneous sources, and likewise the receipts derived from loans, you will get a total of £30,000,000 sterling administered by local authorities. . . . Then, as regards the number of bodies administering these rates: in a Report circulated among hon. Members this morning there is an enumeration of the various classes of local authorities. They amount to about 20; but some of these are what may be called maritime authorities – managing harbours, ports, and bridges; and therefore if you deduct these there will remain really 16 different classes of local authorities, elected, as I have stated, generally upon different principles, proceeding in an entirely different manner, and standing in very little relation to one another. . . . The Government propose, in the first instance, that, instead of the present system of various authorities being entitled to levy separate rates, only one rate should be levied; and that every authority now entitled to raise funds should obtain those funds by a requisition upon the parochial authorities. We propose, for example, that the Boards of Guardians, the highway boards, the county justices, the local boards, the town councils, and all the bodies who will have a claim on a particular parish, should each on a particular day in the year send in an estimate of the particular amounts which they will require in the course of that year. The parish officers will add all these together, and will accordingly be enabled to make an estimate of the total sum that will be required from the parish for the whole of the year. A demand-note will be sent to each ratepayer, specifying all the items of which the rate is composed. It will have to state that so much is collected for the relief of the poor, so much for the purposes of the highways, so much for the county expenditure; but the whole is to be thrown into one and to be collected in one sum.

3.3 From Edwin Cannan, *The History of Local Rates in England*, 2nd ed. (London 1912), pp. 159-60 and 164-72.

This is the classic work on the history of rates, but is now very much in need of revision in the light of twentieth-century developments. (See later extract from Hicks, J. R. and U. K. and Leser, C. E. V. – number 3.4.)

THE EQUITY OF LOCAL RATES

It is clear that two great principles or canons of taxation swayed the minds both of the people who respected custom in the assessment of the old rates and of the politicians and parliamentary draftsmen who created new statutory rates. These principles or canons are:

(i) That every inhabitant of a district should be made to contribute according to his ability; and

(ii) That everyone who receives benefit from the local expenditure should be made to contribute in proportion to the benefit he receives.

Applied to the same rate, the two principles are obviously incompatible. It is difficult to think of any kind of government expenditure which confers benefits upon people approximately in proportion to their ability to contribute. But it happens that in practice the nearest possible approximation to local rating according to ability and the nearest possible approximation to local rating according to benefit are one and the same thing, namely, the rating of persons in respect of fixed property in the district.

Are we to accept this system?

The ultimate object of every system of public finance, so far as the distribution of taxation, or rather the distribution of all kinds of payments drawn by the State from its subjects, is concerned, must be of course to secure the best results on the whole and in the long run. The two great guiding principles for the attainment of this end are Equity and Economy, the latter term being, of course, understood not in the vulgar sense of spending little, irrespective of the return to the expenditure, but in the sense of the best utilisation of available means.

In the application of existing ideas of equity to our system of taxation, local or other, the first thing to do is to recognise that the present distribution of wealth is not by the great majority of people regarded either as equitable or inequitable in its main features. No one seriously claims that the distribution is equitable in itself, so that for example it is actively just and equitable that one infant should be born owning £100,000 a year, and another nothing at all. On the other hand, few persons regard the distribution as actively inequitable as a whole, though many condemn particular features in it with some asperity. The usual attitude is to accept the scheme as a whole in the shape in which it has come down to us, and merely to propose amendments in it here and there, or to oppose amendments proposed by others, grounding opposition not on any alleged perfection of the scheme as it is, but on the undesirability of the particular alterations suggested. . . .

A great many of the most costly services at present rendered by local authorities are of such a kind that there is no doubt that they are, as a whole, worth what they cost, that is to say, the consumers would buy the services voluntarily, if they were not provided by the local authority and could be bought from private persons. We all feel we must have roads and drains, and if the public authority did not provide them, we should be willing to pay somebody to provide them, just as when the public authority does not supply water or gas or electricity, we are willing to pay waterporters to bring us water in buckets or water companies to supply it in pipes, and gas and electric companies to supply gas and electricity through pipes and cables. If the public authority which takes away sewage charged for the service by the gallon, measured by meter, and for the house-refuse removed by its weight and bulk, the questions that might be raised would be of the recondite character familiar in the discussions of electricity managers about flat rates and differential rates of charge. No one would think of discussing the 'incidence' of the payments.

All that the system of local rating does in regard to these charges is to substitute a particular presumption about expense incurred for an actual measurement of quantity of commodity or service taken. To measure the quantity of roads used by particular persons at all accurately is impossible, and to measure it with approximate accuracy is very expensive. To measure sewage or house refuse would be difficult and expensive. No one knows how to measure the street-lighting required by any particular individual. What can be more reasonable than to select some standard which will lump these services and a great many more of the same sort together, and charge according to this standard for the whole lot? . . .

Attacks on the equity of the rating system have almost always related not to the 'beneficial' services but to what have been called the 'onerous' services, of which the relief of the poor and education are the most important and perhaps the purest examples. An 'onerous' local service is one which is regarded as a burden because it is not worth to the local taxpayers what it costs them. The ratepayers of a town demand with menaces that their town council shall spend some more of their money on tarring the roads to keep down motor dust, because they think they will be more comfortable if they secure immunity from dust, although they have to abandon some other good thing in consequence of the expenditure in this direction. But when they spend more money on the poor or on education they do it because it is their rather painful duty, or because the Local Government Board says they must, or because the Board of Education says it will take away their grants if they do not do it. There is no suggestion that these services are paid for by the persons who benefit in proportion to the cost of serving them.

The prevalent ideal of equity in regard to the expenses of such services in the abstract is that people should be taxed according to their ability. If the British parliament were legislating for Mars and Saturn with no knowledge of the present system of taxation in existence there, this is the ideal which would be set up. But in fact we never have to deal with taxation in the abstract, and equity cannot be attained without regard to present circumstances. A system of taxation, when it has once come into operation and remained in operation long enough to become accepted as something on the continuance of which men may depend in making contracts with one another, becomes part and parcel of the general scheme of the distribution of wealth, and it is considered that expectations founded on it are legitimate expectations which it is unjust to disappoint. Hence, when a duty on an imported commodity is taken off, dealers in the commodity are often repaid the amount of duty which has been collected on the unsold stocks in their possession.* Hence too, to give another example, no one troubles about the fact that the old land-tax is not in proportion to ability and has no pretensions to be an integral part of a system which secures taxation according to ability. The ordinary person is prepared to accept the present distribution of the land-tax along with the present distribution of the land itself, and to a landowner who was rash enough to ask for a redistribution of the tax he might reply: 'Let us begin by a redistribution of the land on equitable principles.'

Conflict of opinion arises when it is arguable whether a particular arrangement is sufficiently well established to make it part and parcel of the accepted scheme of the distribution of wealth on which we all base the calculations of everyday life. In this matter of local taxation we find a system of rating immovable property only which has been in operation for several hundred years, but which has been fairly continuously protested against, and which has never yet been quite recognised by permanent legislation. So far as one great service, the relief of the poor, is concerned, the primitive legislation on the subject goes back to the sixteenth century, but the other, education, was only made a local charge in 1870, and

* E.g., the repayments of South African War Corn Duty, under the Finance Act, 1903, sect. 1.

seems then to have been regarded as a trifling matter. Consequently it is easy for those who would benefit by a shifting of some of the charge from immovable property to other sources of income to believe that such a shifting is demanded by equity. On the other hand, it is equally easy for those who have no bias in favour of immovable property to believe that the special burdens upon it have become 'hereditary', to use an expression which has often been employed in the discussion – that is to say, they have become part and parcel of a system of the distribution of wealth which has no pretensions to equity, but is maintained because it is there and nobody can suggest a more desirable scheme or at any rate persuade his fellow men to adopt and work it. Equity, it is said with much force, does not demand that the system of taxation shall be altered merely because different sources of income are not treated equally. Rateable and non-rateable property have been bequeathed and inherited, bought and sold, and have been the subject of innumerable contracts since 1601, and even since 1870, on the assumption that existing arrangements will remain substantially unaltered, and to tamper with these arrangements is consequently something like tampering with the currency.

The same argument may be brought against the claim, often made, though with far less influential backing, by the localities in which 'onerous' rates are heaviest against those in which they are lighter. The ratepayers in the heavier-rated localities are apt to complain that it is 'unfair' that they should have to pay a much higher rate for a 'national service' than some other place of more ability. So far as the mere occupier of other persons' property is concerned, the complaint is clearly an empty one, since about half the occupiers in most rateable areas, and often a larger proportion, have immigrated into the area and voluntarily made themselves subject to its taxation. The high rates of a highly-rated district undoubtedly tend to deter population and business from settling in it, and this means that they will not settle in it unless the owners charge less than they would if the rates were lower. If the rates were reduced, the owners would be able to charge more for their properties. Consequently these high rates are at bottom an owners' grievance, and to any complaint against them on the ground of equity it may be answered, as before, that property has been bequeathed and inherited, bought and sold, and made the subject of innumerable contracts on the assumption that the inequalities of rates existed and would remain in existence. A man who buys property cheap in Stoke Regis because of the high rates there, and then demands that his rates should be made level with those of Pedlington, where he sold property dear because of the low rates, is little better than a thief. If an owner says in answer to this that as a matter of fact he has held the same property since 1869, and has seen the education rate rise from nil to 2s. while somewhere else it is only 3d., he may very probably be met with some such retort as 'And in the meantime your land, which you used to let at £2 an acre, has been covered with working-class houses on small plots, for each of which you get £2. You don't seem to have much cause for complaint.' Very probably this would be more than a mere chance *argumentum ad hominem*: the highest education rates are frequently the result of rapid growth of suburban residence. In any case the holder of property must be prepared to take some risks, and why should not the development of the rate authorised by the legislation of 1870 be one of them?

The conclusion to which we are driven is that the prevalent ideas about equity provide no great guidance in regard to our existing system of local taxation. They only indicate that it may be left alone without inequity.

3.4 From J. R. and U. K. Hicks and C. E. V. Leser, *The Problem of Valuation for Rating* (Cambridge, 1944), pp. 13 and 18-19.

This work is largely concerned with the problems of fixing rateable values and is much narrower in scope than Cannan's *History*.

By the fifteenth century the basis of rating was usually phrased 'according to ability or substance' (*iuxta facultates*). For particular sorts of rates an additional attempt was sometimes made to measure the extent of benefit conferred by the expenditure (for instance according to the nearness or farness of the improvement from the property) – just as today frontagers are normally charged part of the cost of making up a new road, although part is probably paid for out of the rates in general. More usually the extent of benefit was held to be sufficiently measured by the relative values of the properties.

It must be noted that in a society in which large incomes not derived from property hardly existed, ability and substance were practically synonymous, both depending on the value of property. Liability to rates was thus most conveniently measured by rents. . . .

In 1815 the traditional basis of the distribution of the county rate was abolished in favour of a 'full fair annual value of . . . the hereditaments rateable to the relief of the poor'. Rateable value thus became the measure of inter-parish, as it was of inter-personal, liability to rates. There is no evidence to show how far competitive undervaluation was ever responsible for pushing down valuations. Our investigations into modern practice when the motive for competitive undervaluation had been very much strengthened by the incidence of differential grants, makes us somewhat sceptical on the matter. Much more probably the infrequent and spasmodic occurrence of revaluations was the main cause of differences in the level of assessment between different areas. But the discussion of this question must be deferred to a later stage. Until the last quarter of the nineteenth century the county rate was so small that it can hardly have been worth evading. . . .

Whatever the respective importance of the various factors tending to depress valuations below rents, there is no doubt that it has always been characteristic in England for the basis of rating assessment to sag well below actual rents, although the extent of the divergence has varied greatly from place to place, and no doubt from time to time. The existence of such divergencies between law and practice was well recognised by administrators. To take a couple of early examples, the Poor Law Commissioners reporting in 1834 drew express attention to the lack of uniformity in the making of poor law assessments. Again Sir George Cornewall Lewis, appearing before a House of Lords Committee in 1850 in support of a bill on Rating Reform which he had just been compelled to withdraw, asserted that 'there is a constant struggle to keep the assessment of property below its full value, partly with reference to other classes of property in the same parish, partly with reference to the County Rate'.

After the re-introduction of the Income Tax, the Inland Revenue, whose own Schedule A valuation was based on actual rents, set themselves to screw up rate valuations, with a view to making them both more in accordance with the law, and less mutually divergent. In this task they were by no means unsuccessful. If we compare rating and Schedule A valuations, county by county, it appears that in 1892 the rateable value of the median county was 75 per cent of its Schedule A value, the lower decile was 66 per cent and the upper decile 85 per cent. By 1868 the median county had reached 84 per cent of its Schedule A value, the lower decile was 79 per cent and the upper decile 95 per cent. Finally, by 1910–11 the median had risen to 91.6 per cent of its Schedule A value, the lower decile was 84.2 per cent and the upper decile 105.2 per cent. While not very much weight can be put on these figures, they do suggest that, even without reforming legislation, a fair degree of accuracy and uniformity had been imported into rating valuations. That this is true of the period immediately preceding the last war appears to be the opinion of valuers today. But even assuming that Schedule A valuations had no area variations parallel to those of rating valuations, the degree of accuracy was only fair, and it was by no means secure. It depended on the one hand on administrative pressure, and on the other on the absence of disturbances. The pre-1914 period was an exceptionally quiet one for rating. The output of new building was very moderate, and rents were stable. Rates were rising, but only slowly.

No one imagined that administrative pressure alone would be sufficient to bring rating valuations fully into line. From 1850 onwards administrators repeatedly attempted to get the law of rating tightened up. The campaign was carried out on three fronts, aiming respectively at securing rate consolidation, regular revaluations and uniform practice in respect of deductions. Let us see what success attended their efforts.

3.5 From the *Memorandum on Classification and Incidence of Imperial and Local Taxes* (1899), by E. W. Hamilton, Cd. 9528, pp. 52-4.
This extract from the memorandum by the Financial Secretary to the Treasury to the Royal Commission on Local Taxation summarises the complaints prevalent at the end of the nineteenth century about the burdens of ratepayers, complaints which are still being made about the rating system!

It is not infrequently alleged, that, whatever their real incidence may be, the payment of rates, of which taxation raised for local purposes principally consists, is more sensibly felt than the payment of any other tax in our financial system; and the allegation is probably not ill-founded. . . .

The ratepayer is perpetually complaining that rates (to use an historic formula) 'have increased, are increasing, and ought to be diminished'. The rounds of the rate-collector are viewed with real apprehension, foreboding, as his approach generally does, some increased demand. The most popular platform on which a candidate for a vacancy on a County Council, or on a Board of Guardians, can take his stand, is an undertaking that he will use his utmost efforts to reduce the rates, or at any rate to prevent a rise in them. It is the immensity of the expenditure of local authorities, not of the central authority, which comes home to the people of this country, and which mainly gave rise to the appointment of our Commission. The ratepayers are always demanding to be relieved at the expense of the taxpayers, though in part they are one and the same body; and this of itself may show that it is not Imperial, but local taxation, from which the pinch comes, or at any rate where it is felt. . . .

I will now briefly sum up what seem to be the principal conclusions to be drawn from the remarks with which I have troubled my colleagues on the Local Taxation Commission; they are these:

(1) That a mere classification of taxes does not and cannot represent even their primary incidence, and still less their ultimate incidence.

(2) That, owing to the difficulties inherent to establishing the incidence of taxation, there is much misconception about the sources from which it is raised, and especially so with regard to rates; in other words, that, as a large part of the rates falls on occupiers of dwelling-houses, rates to that extent constitute a tax in respect of a commodity which is a necessary of life, and that consequently local expenditure is not met nearly as much as is commonly supposed by the 'taxation and re-taxation of land'.

(3) That the rates have largely risen throughout the country as a whole; that the rise has been greater in urban districts than in rural districts; but that, as the rise has been mainly in respect of 'beneficial rates', and as 'beneficial rates' are mostly levied in urban districts, it is in those districts that the ratepayers have got most direct return out of the increased expenditure incurred by local authorities.

(4) That the favourite remedy for relief of rates is further assistance from the common purse; and that such assistance, whether it takes the form of Parliamentary grants-in-aid, or of assigned revenues, must really be rendered by the community at large, and be contributed by persons in the proportions in which they contribute to Imperial taxation generally.

(5) That, notwithstanding the recent trend of fiscal policy, the largest share of Imperial and Local taxation combined still consists, on reasonable hypotheses, of taxes of which the most are levied on the community at large, without regard to the means of taxpayers, and thus irrespectively of their ability to pay. . . .

In attempting to solve these difficult problems we must take care not to redress any present inequalities by creating fresh inequalities; and, if we propose any alterations in our existing financial system, we shall do well to bear in mind that there is great force in the old saying that 'an old tax is no tax'. Somehow or other, taxation, if undisturbed, sooner or later finds (so to speak) its own level.

It may be presumptuous and venturesome on my part to have touched ground on which the highest economic authorities have 'feared to tread'; but I hope it will not be thought that I have laid myself open to the charge of dogmatising, and I must beg that my remarks may only be considered as signposts on the road of our inquiry.

28th March 1897   E. W. Hamilton

3.6 From the *Final Report of the Royal Commission on Local Taxation* (1901). Cd. 638, pp. 11-14.

This extract deals with the proposals of the Royal Commission for defining the *principles* on which local government services should be financed, and it introduces the distinction between services which might be described as national and those regarded as local.

We have therefore come to the conclusion that we shall best serve the purpose for which we were appointed, if we start from the existing system, and inquire in what respects it has been or may be held to be unfair or oppressive in practice. Though we do not think, for the reasons above stated, that the grievances of ratepayers can be accurately or usefully expressed by any precise formulae or statistics contrasting the contributions of realty and personalty, we by no means assert that those grievances are imaginary: and we think that the real charges which underlie the current criticisms of our rating system can best be summarised as follows:

(1) Complaint is made on behalf of *ratepayers in general* that

there is thrown on the rates too much of the cost of certain National services which the State requires to be undertaken, and the burden of which, it is alleged, ought consequently to be borne on the broader back of the taxpayer.

(2) Complaint is made on behalf of *ratepayers in certain districts*, that the burden of these services is heavier than in other districts.

(3) Complaint is made that local expenditure is met in too large a measure by what is in effect a tax levied in respect of the occupation of rateable property, or, in other words, that sufficient variety has not been given to the means by which the revenue required by Local Authorities is raised.

(4) Complaint is made that those who possess and enjoy property not rateable are placed in too favourable a position as compared with the owners and occupiers of rateable property.

(5) Complaint is made on behalf of *special classes of ratepayers* (e.g., those interested in agriculture and in certain industries and trades) that, inasmuch as they require for their business an amount of rateable property very large in proportion to their general ability, an undue share of local burdens is imposed upon them, as compared with persons who neither own nor occupy any rateable property except their own residence. It is felt especially strongly that the increase of an onerous rate falls with great inequality.

(6) Complaint is made by *urban ratepayers* and ratepayers other than agricultural in agricultural districts that, relief having been given under the Agricultural Rates Act to agricultural ratepayers, no corresponding relief has been given to urban ratepayers, or to ratepayers other than agricultural in agricultural districts.

(7) Complaint is made on behalf of *urban ratepayers* that all the rates are paid by the occupiers and none by the owners of land (at least directly), although the owners of land benefit largely by the development of towns and by expenditure from the rates on improvements.

WHAT SERVICES ARE NATIONAL AND ONEROUS

In dealing with these difficulties, we believe that the only method which can secure fair play all round is consistent adherence to a principle which has often been put forward in discussion, but to which insufficient regard has frequently been paid in practice. That principle is the distinction between services which are preponderantly National in character and generally onerous to the ratepayers, and services which are preponderantly Local in character and confer upon ratepayers a direct and peculiar benefit more or less commensurate with the burden. The distinction cannot, it is true, be drawn with absolute logical precision. In many cases it is plain enough, e.g., just as water rates are held to be payments for service rendered rather than taxes, so also it is clear that drainage works are a local benefit of a similar kind. But in other cases the two elements are combined in different degrees, since almost all useful local expenditure is indirectly advantageous to the country at large. But a service may be called properly local when a preponderant share of the benefit can be directly traced to persons interested in the locality. On the other hand, universality and uniformity of administration is generally a mark of a national service, because such administration does not confer special benefit on special places. Again, the presumption is that a service is national when the State insists on its being carried out, and on a certain standard of efficiency being reached. . . .

HOW NATIONAL SERVICES SHOULD BE PAID FOR

Since we have described the four services of Poor Relief, Police, Education, and Main Roads as *National*, it may appear to follow that they should be wholly paid for from National Funds, just as the Army and Navy are. We admit that there would be force in this argument, but there are contrary considerations of irresistible weight.

The administration of some of these services is, it is true, already controlled, to a large extent, by the Central Government. But the idea of transferring to that Government the whole responsibility must, we think, be dismissed as impracticable. If so, local self-government carries with it, in bare common sense, the consequence of local self-taxation. Thus there is no possibility of a complete solution of the financial problem on these lines.

There remains, of course, the question of the expediency of partial steps in this direction, for which the successful transfer of the Prison Service in 1877 affords a precedent. We have accordingly considered whether any other service could be so transferred, and we admit that the transfer of Lunatic Asylums is plausible enough to merit full consideration. But we are much impressed by the views expressed by the Lunacy Commissioners against such a change, and, on the whole, we think the administrative risks and disadvantages outweigh the slight advantage of this partial financial adjustment.

Concluding, then, that these services must remain under the control of Local Authorities (subject, of course, to supervision by the Central Government), we next consider in what way the disadvantages of the present system of local taxation, as compared with national taxation, can be mitigated.

The difficulty, stated generally, is that rates fall very much less exactly than taxes in accordance with ability to pay. Taxation according to the taxpayer's ability has long been recognised as a primary aim of national finance. 'Ability' is indeed a rather vague expression, but, in any sense of the word, taxes do approach this ideal more nearly than rates.

Various methods have been proposed for remedying this defect. The most obvious suggestion is a local income tax, and our remarks on this subject will also mostly apply to the often repeated proposal (which is similar in tendency, but less complete and intelligible) for the re-introduction of the 'rating of personalty'. Further, we shall have something to say on the proposal to charge a special rate upon residential property.

The Elizabethan Poor Rate was perhaps originally intended to be something like a local income tax, and the practice of rating on 'means and substance', which continued in some parts of Scotland down to our time, was very similar. It is, however, clear on reflection that a local income tax – i.e., an income tax imposed and levied by Local Authorities within their own district – tends more and more to be incompatible with modern social and political arrangements. The very conception is indeed obscure, for to what locality does an income belong? To the place or places from which it is derived? Or to the place or places where it is enjoyed, i.e., where the recipient more or less permanently resides? . . .

One method of attaining results similar to those desired by the advocates of a local income tax is the imposition of a special local rate on Inhabited Houses.

This suggestion is explained in the paper by Mr R. McKenna, M.P., which we have included in our fourth volume of evidence. The value of the residence which a man occupies bears as a rule some rough proportion to his income, and consequently an inhabited house tax is, in default of a regular income tax, the nearest approximation to taxation according to ability. But there are very serious difficulties and objections.

In the first place, it is open to one of the chief objections which can be brought against a local income tax, that it yields most where least is needed, and *vice versa*. . . .

There is, moreover, another practical difficulty of some importance, viz., the question whether a rate on inhabited houses ought not in some way to be graduated. The case for graduation is much stronger here than in the case of an income tax, because, as a general rule, the smaller a man's income is, the larger is the proportion of it which he is obliged to spend on house accommodation. And, as regards working-class dwellings, either exemption, or at least large abatements, would be necessary, if the existing evils of dear, bad, and insufficient house accommodation are not to be aggravated. We greatly doubt the expediency of introducing the principles of graduation and exemption into local taxation; and in particular, the need for different scales in town and country would be a serious additional complication.

Lastly, a rate on dwelling houses would fall rather unfairly on a householder with a family for which ample accommodation is required, as compared with unmarried persons in receipt of a similar income.

Summing up the various considerations to which we have adverted in this chapter, we conclude that in general the funds for national services ought to be raised in accordance with the principle of *ability*. This principle might be secured to a great extent by transferring them wholly to the Central Government; but such a solution of the problem is out of the question on practical grounds. On the other hand, no mere readjustment of burden within each locality would meet the demands of equity. We are therefore driven to the conclusion that the grievances which we have set forth cannot be remedied without either a direct contribution from the Exchequer or the extension and development of the system of assigned revenues which has been in existence since 1889.

3.7 From the *Final Report of the Royal Commission on Local Taxation*, Appendix (1902), Cd. 1221, pp. 70-1.
Following Hamilton's memorandum (see extract 3.5), it is of interest to read the conclusions of the Royal Commission about the burdens of the ratepayers.

(1) Since 1891 the amount raised by rates has increased more rapidly than at any previous period, the increase having averaged more than 1½ millions per annum.

(2) Sanitary Authorities in Urban areas were responsible for at least one-third of the increase, and now raise more than one-third of the total rates.

(3) The valuation has not kept pace with the rates, and the total average rate in the £ levied has, therefore, increased from 3s. 8d. to 4s. 10d.

(4) The average rate in the £ raised by each class of Local Authorities has increased since 1891, but the average rates in the £ raised by extra-Metropolitan Urban Authorities have, generally speaking, grown more rapidly than those raised by other classes of Local Authorities.

(5) The services imposing the largest burdens upon the rates may be classed under five heads, viz.:

    (a) Poor Relief (including Lunatics and Lunatic Asylums);

    (b) Elementary Education;

    (c) Police;

    (d) Roads, Streets, and Bridges (including Lighting and Scavenging);

    (e) Sewerage. . . .

(15) The rateable value of agricultural land has decreased by about 160,000l., or 0.7 per cent, per annum between 1896 and 1900, but the rateable value of buildings (including houses, shops, warehouses, mills, factories, docks, wharves, etc.) and railways (including stations and depots) is increasing rapidly.

3.8 From the *Final Report of the Departmental Committee on Local Taxation* (1914), Cd. 7315, pp. 86-8.

This Report from the so-called Kempe Committee is the only *general* review of the rating system in the twentieth century. One of its major recommendations, that for the transfer of rating valuation to the inland revenue, was not achieved until 1950 – and only then because it was essential for the operation of the new Exchequer Equalisation Grant, not because of a belated acceptance by the Government of the Kempe Committee's recommendation.

316. Lastly, mention should be made of the important bearing on

the question of valuation for rating purposes of the establishment of a Government Valuation Department under the Finance (1909–10) Act, 1910, subject to the control of the Board of Inland Revenue. . . . .

For the purposes of valuation the country is divided into divisions, each under the charge of a superintending valuer, and these into districts each under a district valuer. Each valuation district in its turn is informally divided into smaller areas for convenience of working. . . .

PROPOSALS FOR THE REFORM OF THE EXISTING SYSTEM OF VALUATION

317. The constitution of this Government valuation staff working on uniform lines all over the country and gradually amassing information with regard to the value of all kinds of real property, naturally raises the question whether it might not be used to obtain a better system of valuation for rating purposes. The evidence that we have received on this subject has been of a very conflicting nature. The representatives of the Rating Surveyors' Association were strongly opposed to the Government valuation staff being associated in any way with valuation for rating purposes.

318. They contended, on the following grounds, that it was unnecessary to make any radical alteration in the present system:

  (i) that for the purposes of obtaining an equitable distribution of county burdens over the several parishes, or for the purposes of Government grants based upon valuation, all that is required is a correct total valuation of each parish, and that this can easily be provided by means of the county rate basis.

 (ii) that as regards the equitable distribution of the burden of local taxation between the ratepayers of each parish a sufficient remedy is provided for any aggrieved party under the present system. . . .

321. Thus, whether we consider the valuation question from the inter-communal aspect or from that of the relations between individuals, we are led to the conclusion that the line of reform would appear to lie in the direction of strengthening the expert element.

322. The question immediately arises as to the manner in which this should be done, and in regard to this there would appear to be three courses possible:

(i) The extension of the present system of employing professional valuers from time to time.

(ii) The appointment of whole-time officers specially for the purpose.

(iii) The employment of the Government Land Valuation staff.

Of these three courses we have no hesitation in recommending the third. We proceed to give our reasons.

(*a*) Valuation of property for rating purposes can be most economically carried out continuously, and for work that can be spread over the year in this way it is cheaper to appoint a whole-time officer than to engage an outside firm from time to time.

(*b*) If a property has to be valued for rating purposes and also for the purposes of the Finance Act, it is obviously better for the same man to do both. We are quite aware that one valuation is on a capital basis and the other is on an annual basis, but we understand that, in regard to some properties, valuation proceeds from annual to capital value, and in regard to others from capital to annual value. Thus, whether the properties in a district were being valued for rating purposes or for the purposes of the Finance Act, there would be considerable duplication of work if the two valuations were carried out separately.

(*c*) As we have already pointed out, an immense amount of information in regard to properties is being accumulated by the Land Valuation staff, the value of which for rating purposes must be considerable.

(*d*) The Land Valuation staff are working on uniform lines in all parts of Great Britain. The uniformity of the valuation that would be produced by the employment of the staff would be far greater than could be obtained by any system of appeals by a Government officer against a valuation by local authorities separately.

(*e*) The independent position of the Government valuers will from the outset enable them to place all properties impartially on a fair and uniform basis without the risk of local friction to which overseers are often subject.

(*f*) The constitution and organisation of the staff are both well adapted for rating valuations, which present problems of every degree of difficulty, e.g., a special staff already exists for the valuation of licensed premises.

(g) As the staff operates over the whole of Great Britain it would be able to value special properties extending into several areas as a whole.

(h) The valuation list prepared by the valuation staff would provide a good basis for all Imperial taxation of real property levied on the basis of annual value.

(i) It would provide a basis for the payment of Government contributions in lieu of rates comparable with that on which rates are paid by private individuals, so removing a grievance of local authorities.

The intervention of the Government valuation staff in local valuation may meet with some opposition, but it will be seen from the detailed recommendations submitted below that the assessment committees will continue to sit in convenient centres, and bring their valuable local experience to bear on the cases submitted for their decision, and the local control thus assured ought to allay any fears of unfair treatment. A further line of objection would be met if the Valuation Office ceased to be under the control of the Board of Inland Revenue.

3.9 From the *Rating and Valuation Act* (1925), ss 1-2.
This Act shows the comparatively short provisions which were needed to create single rating authorities and a consolidated rate – over fifty years after Goschen's first unsuccessful attempt to achieve this.

RATING

1. (1) The council of every county borough and the council of every urban and rural district shall be the rating authority for the borough or for the county district, and from and after the appointed day no authority or person other than the council shall have power to make or levy any rate within the borough or district.

(2) As from the appointed day all powers and duties of the overseers of the poor in relation to the making, levying, and collection of rates, and of any other person who by virtue of any local Act has powers in that behalf, shall in every rating area be exercised and performed by the rating authority. . . .

2. (1) As from the date of the first new valuation, the rating authority of each urban rating area, in lieu of the poor rate and any other rate which they have power to make, shall make and levy for their area a consolidated rate which shall be termed 'the general rate'.

(2) As from the appointed day the rating authority of each rural rating area shall, in lieu of making a poor rate for each parish, make and levy a general rate for the whole of the district.

3.10 From the *Local Government Act* (1929), sections 67 and 68.

This extract gives the provisions of the Act which gave total exemption from rates to agricultural land and buildings and also relieved industrial and freight transport properties from rates on three-quarters of their former value.

RATING AND VALUATION
Relief from Rates

67. (1) No person shall, in respect of any period beginning on or after the appointed day, be liable to pay rates in respect of any agricultural land or agricultural buildings or be deemed to be in occupation thereof for rating purposes, and notwithstanding anything in the principal Act, or in the Rating and Valuation (Apportionment) Act, 1928, no such land or buildings shall be included in any rate made in respect of a period beginning on or after that date.

(2) For the purposes of valuation lists in force at the appointed day, agricultural land and agricultural buildings shall be deemed to have no rateable value, and, notwithstanding anything in the enactments hereinbefore in this section mentioned, no particulars with respect to such land or buildings shall be included in any subsequent valuation list.

68. (1) The rateable value of industrial hereditaments and freight transport hereditaments shall, for the purposes of valuation lists in force at the appointed day as from that day, and for the purposes of subsequent valuation lists, be ascertained as follows:

(*a*) in the case of an industrial hereditament or of a freight transport hereditament shown in a valuation list as being occupied and used wholly for industrial purposes or wholly for transport purposes, as the case may be, the rateable value of the hereditament shall, subject as hereinafter provided, be taken to be one-quarter of the net annual value thereof:

(*b*) in the case of an industrial hereditament or of a freight transport hereditament shown in a valuation list as being occupied and used partly for industrial purposes or partly for transport purposes, as the case may be, the rateable value of the hereditament shall, subject as hereinafter provided, be taken to be an amount equal to one-quarter of the net annual value shown in the list as apportioned to the occupation and user of the hereditament for industrial purposes or for transport purposes, as the case may be, together with the whole of the net annual value so shown as apportioned to the occupation and user of the hereditament for other purposes.

3.11 From the *Report of the Committee of Enquiry on the Rating of Site Values* (1952), pp. 6, 8, 73-6.

The taxation of the increment of land values arising from social developments has provided reformers and economists with a point of attack against both national taxation and local rates over a very long period of time. The consequences of the full-blooded system of town and country planning created in 1947 gave rise to further clamour for the taxation of the 'social increment', especially in view of the unsatisfactory nature of the Development Charge introduced as part of that system. These extracts provide a review of this form of taxation.

5. Our terms of reference are concerned with a rate on site values as a means of raising revenue for local purposes. As the total revenue to be raised must for our purpose be regarded as fixed, the raising of part of it by a rate on site values implies a corresponding reduction in the amount to be raised by the existing method of rating. Hence the questions to be answered are: (1) is it practicable to raise part of local revenues by a rate on site value, and (2) if so, is this desirable?

The idea of raising some part of public revenue from the economic rent* of land is by no means new. It was a principal proposal of the first 'economists', the Physiocrats, whose attention was largely directed to agricultural uses of land. Adam Smith shifted the emphasis to sites of buildings and other non-agricultural land, saying that 'ground rents, and the ordinary rent of land, are, therefore, perhaps the species of revenue which can best bear to have a peculiar tax imposed upon them. Ground rents seem, in this respect, a more proper subject of peculiar taxation than even the ordinary rent of land.' Professor Marshall in his answers to the

---

* 'Economic rent' in this context is used in the sense understood by economists as outlined in the subsequent paragraphs.

questionnaire of the Royal Commission on Local Taxation (C.9528, 1899) proposed a rate on 'the public value of agricultural land, that is, of its value as it stands after deducting for any buildings on it, and any distinct improvements made in it during, say, the preceding twenty years'. This rate he thought should be 'considerable', and a 'rather heavier' rate should be imposed on the site value of urban land.

The case for taxation of economic rent rests upon propositions (*a*) that it is an unearned income, brought into existence not by anything which the owner, as such, has done but by the activities of the community generally; (*b*) that a tax on it does not curtail the supply of goods and services and raise their price as many other taxes do; and (*c*) in particular that it is a means of relieving the burden imposed by rates as at present levied upon dwelling-houses, shops, and other buildings and improvements made to land.

There may, therefore, be a *prima facie* case for a tax on economic rent* as a source of local revenue. . . .

13. Again, in urban valuation it is particularly difficult to distinguish between those elements in site value which are due and those which are not due to the enterprise of the owner. Historically probably the most popular argument in favour of land value taxation has been that as the value of land rises, due to the expansion of demand in a country which is growing in wealth and population, the taxation of site values will transfer to the community the growing economic rent, which from the point of view of the landlord is 'unearned income' since it is due to the growth of the community, not to his own efforts. This was the aspect which seized the imagination of Henry George living in California at the time of its dramatic opening up. This aspect also seemed to some of great importance in Victorian England. On the other hand, it is clear from the history of the development of communities that the

* The idea of rent has by analogy been extended to things other than land. Professor Marshall for example talks of the quasi-rents of machinery and other man-made instruments of production. In a short period during which it is impossible to alter sufficiently the supply of a certain class of such things, it is evident that they may earn more than normal profits if the demand for the goods they are instrumental in making increases substantially, or less than normal profits if the demand falls off. Thus, a quasi-rent may be positive or negative, and has no relation to the matter under our investigation. The emergence of a quasi-rent is the economic incentive which induces producers either to install more capital, if demand is rising, or not to replace worn out capital if demand is falling. It is the motive power of a competitive society. A tax on quasi-rent would, therefore, have exactly the opposite effects to a tax on economic rent of land.

enterprise of landowners, individually or collectively, has played a significant part in directing development towards certain land. . . .

199. Out of thirty-eight bodies or individuals in England and fifteen in Scotland who submitted written or oral evidence, only three in England and two in Scotland gave unqualified support to the introduction of site value rating and they differed among themselves as to the form in which it should be operated. . . .

204. In our view, the desirability of a site value rate can be judged only after consideration of the probable effects of such a rate. We have, therefore, as a preliminary to our consideration of the desirability of such a rate, set out to describe what kind of a rate might be levied in present circumstances, (assuming that it were decided to do so). Our terms of reference require us to have regard to the provisions of the Town and Country Planning Act, 1947, and other relevant factors. In our review of the background, we have drawn attention to the effects of that Act upon the owner-ship of interests in land. That part of the value of land and build-ings that could formerly have been realised by development has been taken away from owners except in so far as values may increase within the narrow confines of the 'restricted use' exempted from development charge (para. 71). Under these circumstances, any site value rate payable by an owner or occupier should be based upon the restricted value.

205. It has been suggested that a rate on the difference between the restricted and the unrestricted value of land might be levied on the Central Land Board (para. 84). Apart from technical difficulties in the assessment of such a rate (paras. 89 and 93), we consider it would, in effect, be merely a national subvention in aid of local rates, since the Central Land Board would have to draw on the Exchequer for payments of the rate, and it would moreover be a subvention distributed on a basis unrelated to the relevant needs of local authorities (para. 95). We have accordingly concluded that any such proposal to rate the Central Land Board is impracticable and undesirable (paras. 96 and 97).

206. While any site value rate on owners or occupiers would be based upon the restricted value, we consider that to adopt such a value as the basis would produce assessments which would lack that uniformity which has always been an essential principle of rating (para. 98). A formula based on Section 80 of the Local Government Act, 1948, would not provide a method of assessment which would be easy to work and it would also provide endless

opportunities for controversy (para. 99). We were accordingly forced to conclude that the only basis for a site value rate left for examination in circumstances set by existing legislation would be existing use value in its literal meaning (para. 100).

207. If such a rate were imposed, we consider that it would most conveniently be levied on the annual site value (para. 104) and its imposition should be obligatory for all rating authorities (para. 105). We think also that the most practicable and equitable way of fixing the amount of such a rate would be for Parliament to prescribe a uniform poundage for the country (para. 106). We feel most strongly on grounds of principle that, if such a rate were introduced, existing contracts should be respected and we see no convincing grounds for over-ruling a contract, under which the occupier has agreed to pay the rates, so as to transfer this liability to the owner; legislation could, of course, provide against conditions of this kind being inserted in future contracts (para. 107). . . .

212. An estimate of the total yield of a site value rate is an important factor in the consideration of the desirability of such a rate. We have, however, been able to arrive at no figure of the total site value of the country even on the basis of existing use, on which an estimate of the yield could be based (para. 124), nor do we consider that assistance of any importance could be gained from calculations by any such analogy as the ratio of site to total value in other countries (para. 126). We have examined the figures of annual value used for income tax and rating purposes and have assumed increases to cover the possibility of considerable present under-assessment; if it is assumed that the proportion of the total value of the total property attributable to the site would be somewhere between 20 per cent and 50 per cent it seems that the site value assessment for England and Wales could not exceed £300m. and might very well be no more than a third of this figure. Assuming a site value rate of 2s. in the pound – the figure most frequently quoted and which was inserted in the London County Council Bill of 1938–39 (para. 128) – the product of a site value rate could provide only a small part of the total expenditure on rate fund revenue account of local authorities in England and Wales which, for the year ending 31st March, 1949, was £675m., £271m. being borne by the rates. We have interpreted our terms of reference as requiring us to consider a site value rate which would not in itself meet an increase in the total sum to be raised in rates.

Its main effect, therefore, must be to bring about a redistribution in the share of rates borne by the present ratepayers. Since the redistribution of incidence between properties would vary according to the ratio of site value to rateable value, there would tend to be a shift of liability from the outskirts of towns and from residential properties to central areas and to commercial properties, and from properties with a low proportion of site value to those with a high proportion of site value (such as sports grounds) (para. 148). Any assessment of the product of a site value rate or of the redistribution in rate liability which might occur can be made only in the light of a comprehensive test valuation and we emphasise our conviction that it would be essential to carry out such a test before any decision to introduce a site value rate were made (para. 129). . . .

214. Hence we conclude that the only effect of a site value rate on existing use value would be a shift of burden as between individuals and classes of property. The evidence at our disposal tends to indicate only very broadly the classes which would be favourably or adversely affected, but we have had no evidence that there would be either advantage or equity in altering the relative amount of rates borne by those classes of property or persons.

215. We may summarise our findings by saying that in so far as we have been impressed by the historical case for the rating of site values, we are nevertheless of opinion that this historical case and the evidence from overseas is not relevant to the conditions in Great Britain today.

3.12 From the Rating and Valuation Association, *Rating of Site Values – Report on a Pilot Survey at Whitstable* (February 1964), pp. 4, 6, 12, and 36-7.

One of the difficulties about the arguments for site value rating has been that they have generally been conducted on the level of assertion. The Pilot Survey at Whitstable gave the first real estimate of the effects of this form of taxation. These extracts show, (*a*) that site value taxation is not likely to produce a source of revenue of a sufficient magnitude to *replace* the existing rating system by a larger source of revenue, and (*b*) that the different incidence of site value taxation is likely to lead to considerable opposition from those adversely affected by it compared with the present system.

THE EXERCISE

The object of the exercise was to create a valuation list on site valuation methods which could be put side by side with what might be called the orthodox valuation list, which was produced by the Board of Inland Revenue, and which came into force on 1st April 1963. The project, therefore, had to be carried through in a short period of time so that its results could be laid against the 1963 revaluation before the 1963 revaluation became itself out of date. . . .

Two main aspects had now to be considered:

(1) It is inherent in any system of site value rating that it shall be the owner and not the occupier who shall be liable for the rates. There will clearly be some definition of owner and occupier, with particular reference to long leasehold property.

(2) Fundamentally, it would appear that the value to be rated could be a capital value or a yearly value. In certain countries, at least, where the method is invoked, a capital value is used as the basis of assessment. It is understood, however, that there are economic arguments arising from the fundamental concept of the tax which lead to the conclusion that the value to be assessed should be a yearly one. In any event, the definition with which I was presented required me to find a yearly value.

I was, therefore, faced with two problems:

(a) to identify the units of ownership; and

(b) to find the yearly site value as defined. . . .

GENERAL COMMENT

It is not for me to comment on the political, social or other repercussions of any movement of burden. Nor is it for me to comment on the effects on existing contractual relationships of landlord and tenant, the Rent Restriction Acts, the Landlord and Tenant Acts, etc.

It is clear that valuation of site values is little more than valuation on the town planning, permitted, optimum user. In effect this means that the town planner will, in the final analysis, dictate the amount of rates an owner pays. This may, or may not, be true of the present system today, to the same or lesser extent. . . .

TABLE A

Summary of Total Rateable Values (all totals to the nearest £50).
Official Valuation List now in force in Whitstable

	£
Total rateable value..	702,300
G.P.O., Water Company, Gas, Electricity, etc...	19,650
British Railways	2,150
	£724,100

Site Value Valuation List

	£	£	
Agricultural Land	14,500		
Church Land	3,400		
General	604,300	622,200	
G.P.O., Water Company, Gas, Electricity, etc...		18,050	(estimate: see above less parts valued separately)
British Railways		2,000	
		£642,250	

TABLE B

Property or Land Group	Rateable Value		
	Present	Site Value Method	Net Reduction
	£	£	£
Houses	342,850	180,200	162,650
Bungalows	179,050	90,200	88,850
Flats and Maisonettes	14,200	5,100	9,100
Shops, Hotels, Public Houses, Banks, Cinemas and Offices	75,300	55,400	19,900
Factories, Workshops, Filling Stations and Garages	48,800	22,500	26,300
Schools and Playing Fields.. ..	13,300	12,700	600
Hospitals and Homes	2,150	1,650	500
	£675,650	£367,750	£307,900

TABLE C

Property or Land Group	Rateable Value		Net Increase
	Present	Site Value Method	
	£	£	£
Scheduled Land			
Future Schools	—	10,900	10,900
Future Industry	—	6,550	6,550
Future Residential Development (including all small vacant plots)	500	81,150	80,650
Public Open Spaces (including beach huts)	1,950	26,550	24,600
Churches, Church Halls, Cemetery, Land earmarked for church, Clubs and Institutes	3,300	10,800	7,500
Allotments, Nurseries, Orchards ..	—	6,700	6,700
Caravan Sites and Holiday Camps..	13,800	41,000	27,200
Golf Courses..	500	39,300	38,800
Public Shelters, Tennis Courts, Sewage Works, Lavatories, Sports Ground, Car Parks, Library, Employment Exchange, Police Station, Ambulance Station, Fire Station, Public Baths	6,100	15,600	9,500
Post Office, Electric Sub-stations (not included in public utilities adjustment)	500	1,400	900
Agricultural Land	—	14,500	14,500
	£26,650	£254,450	£227,800

NOTES

The total rateable values in the present valuation list and the site value valuation list for Whitstable are as follows:

	£
Present	724,100
Site value	642,250

3.13 From the Royal Institute of Public Administration, *New Sources of Local Revenue* (London 1956), Chap. XII, 'Recommendations', pp. 127-9.

This extract from the report of a study group set up by the Royal Institute of Public Administration gives the proposals made for new sources of revenue for local authorities made by the group after an exhaustive inquiry.

The taxes we have reviewed as potentially suitable for local adoption in this country fall into two groups:

(i) Taxes suitable for transfer by the central government to local authorities. Perhaps a better way of expressing this would be to say that the government would vacate certain fields of taxation in favour of local authorities.

(ii) Taxes suitable for imposition by local authorities independently of national taxation.

Clearly the first group would give rise to the least opposition on the part of the taxpayer and would present the fewest administrative problems. To the natural reluctance of the central government to surrender some of its own taxation there is the answer that it would probably have to find the money anyway – if not by concession of taxing powers then by grants to local authorities. The outstanding example is the Entertainments Duty and we would regard this as our first choice in this group if local authorities are to be given additional taxing powers. Driving licence fees are also suitable for transfer to local authorities, although the yield is too small to be of major importance. Because of the difficulties presented by large transport fleets, we would not regard the motor licence duties as a first choice. None of these taxes is of primary importance from the economic point of view, and their transfer to local authorities would not diminish the government's control over economic affairs.

In the second group, the outstanding example is the local income tax. We do not minimise the difficulties to which this would give rise and, indeed, we feel that it could only be operated successfully if it were confined to personal incomes. If on grounds of equity it were felt essential that company undistributed profits should be brought in, we are convinced that this could only be done by some special device, e.g., by central assessment and payment of the tax into a Municipal Fund which would then be divided up among the local authorities; or by empowering local authorities to levy an additional rate poundage or other charge on companies. Nevertheless, the yield of a local income tax would be very substantial, even if imposed at a modest rate and on personal incomes only – possibly for the country as a whole £150 million on a 3d. rate – and this is the only measure which on its own offers a prospect of a long-term solution of local authorities' revenue problems.

When the time comes, as we are sure it will, to broaden the base of local authority revenues, we recommend the following as practicable sources of additional revenue. We have arranged them in the order of our preference, and we think that the case is stronger for the first two than for the last one.

   (i) Local authorities should be given power to impose a local income tax. We think as a matter of administrative practicability that this would have to be confined to personal incomes and that undistributed company profits would probably have to be excluded, but in that event we recommend that steps be taken to impose an equivalent charge on companies. The Act should provide for a maximum rate of tax of 3d. in the £.

   (ii) Local authorities should be given powers to levy an entertainments tax subject to the central government providing by statute (a) for the maximum rate of duty to be chargeable, and (b) for the relationship between the scales of duty applicable to different classes of entertainment. This new local tax would replace the duty at present levied by the central government.

   (iii) Motor vehicle duties and driving licence fees should be transferred to local authorities and the present duties withdrawn. We have considered the possibility of a local tax on motor fuel, and, while we do not consider it impracticable, we make no specific recommendation on the subject.

4 Exchequer Grants

4.1 From *Hansard*, 3rd Series, Vol. 140 (5 February 1856), Cols 234-6.
This extract is taken from the speech of Sir George Grey, the Home Secretary, on the motion to bring in the Police (Counties and Boroughs) Bill of 1856. This eventually became law; its importance in the history of local government is that it introduces the notion of Exchequer grants tied to efficiency. Sir George Grey explains how he came to make this proposal – which was subsequently extended to almost all other forms of Exchequer grant in aid of local authority services.

The Commission of 1839 also recommended that, in the event of their system being adopted, one-fourth of the expense should be defrayed from the Consolidated Fund, while the other three-fourths should be derived from county rates and other local sources. In addition to the arguments urged by the Committee in favour of this suggestion, circumstances have since occurred which give to it additional weight and authority. I allude to the important alteration that was made in the same year by the abolition, in the majority of criminal cases, of the punishment of transportation, and the substitution of a system of penal servitude, by which a large number of offenders formerly sent abroad, and who never returned to this country, are retained here, either on the expiration of their sentences, or with revocable licences entitling the persons holding them to regain their liberty after they had served an allotted period of their sentence. Under the former system a very large expenditure was incurred by this country in Australia under the heads of police and gaols. Since the abolition of transportation that charge has been in process of diminution, and it is to be hoped will eventually disappear. A portion of it, however, has been transferred to this country, and there is, therefore, the greater reason why a portion of the cost of maintaining the police should

F*

be borne by the general revenue of the nation. I do not propose to fix any particular sum to be paid out of the public Revenue on account of the police establishment in every county and borough; but what I propose is in effect this – that upon a certificate of the Secretary of State, founded on the report of the inspectors, attesting the efficiency in numbers and discipline during the preceding year of the police of any county or borough, it shall be competent for the Treasury to pay out of moneys to be provided by Parliament a sum not exceeding one-fourth of the expense incurred for the pay and clothing of such police. The money thus granted will not constitute a fixed charge upon the Consolidated Fund, but will be voted annually, so that it will be every year in the power of Parliament to satisfy itself that the Government has exercised the authority confided to it in a judicious and impartial manner. If this discretionary power be given to the Government it will relieve me from the necessity of doing what at one time I had thought might be necessary – namely, to propose that, with a view to prevent the spirit of the law being evaded, while the letter was complied with, there should be reserved the power of compelling the county and borough authorities by an Order in Council to increase the number of police to an efficient standard. On mature consideration, however, I felt that serious objections might be urged against the adoption of such a course. I have no doubt that those in whose hands is vested the management of the police would be disposed to treat the Order in Council with all becoming respect; but still there might be an inclination to dispute the grounds on which that Order had been issued, and it might be no easy matter to compel a reluctant body of magistrates to do what might be necessary in order to place the police establishment upon a satisfactory footing. On the whole, I therefore thought it better not to ask Parliament to place any such power in the hands of the Government; and another reason which has influenced me is, that if it were granted it would be necessary to establish a maximum of sufficiency universal in its application – a matter of extreme difficulty, since what would be a sufficient maximum for one part of the country might be altogether inadequate to the requirements of another district differently circumstanced, while the maximum fixed in the Act might probably be taken as the general standard, though a very insufficient one. A discretionary power in the Treasury to issue a grant will stimulate magistrates and watch committees to keep up their police in a state of efficiency.

4.2 From *Hansard*, 3rd Series, Vol. 205 (3 April 1871), Cols 1137-9.

In his speech introducing the Rating Bill, Mr Goschen acknowledged the increased burden of rates on houses, and proposed that some relief should be given by transferring the proceeds of the inhabited house duty from the national exchequer to the local authorities. The bill was lost and the proposals were not put into effect, but they were the forerunner to the assigned revenues of 1889–90. These extracts show the manner of Goschen's thought in 1871.

If the burdens on land have not increased, the burdens on houses have most undoubtedly increased to a very considerable extent. It is therefore necessary to consider how far relief should be given. It is conceivable that relief might be given either by a local income tax, or by transferring local charges to Imperial funds, or by inventing new taxes, or by the transfer of Imperial taxes to local funds. As regards the first method, it appears to be impossible to devise an equitable local income tax, for you cannot localise income. . . . With respect to the second alternative, that of charging certain local charges upon the Consolidated Fund, the Government entertain the gravest objections to it. I am sure that the House would take such a step as the transference of many of the branches of local to Imperial administration with great reluctance. . . . After looking through the list of Imperial taxes and consulting with the Chancellor of the Exchequer, who met me in the most liberal spirit, I have come to the conclusion that, as the increase of rates has mainly fallen upon house property, the relief ought to be given in that direction. It is, therefore, the intention of the Government, at a certain date, not mentioned in the Bill, but to be hereafter fixed by an Order in Council, to hand over the present house tax amounting to about £1,200,000, in relief of local rates, which would then be payable, not to Her Majesty, but to the local authorities.

4.3 From *The Economist* (19 April 1890), p. 483.

The Economist attacked Mr Goschen's proposed duties on spirits by reference to the comparative contributions and benefits of the three countries of the United Kingdom; no reference was made to the proposal to use part of the proceeds in aid of technical education.

Thus far we have been dealing with what may be called the Imperial portion of Mr Goschen's Budget. That, however, is supplemented by a series of proposals in regard to local finance which are certain to meet with very determined opposition, and which we regard as altogether indefensible. Mr Goschen proposes to add 6d. a gallon to the duty on spirits, to reimpose the additional duty of 3d. a barrel on beer which in his Imperial Budget he professes to take off, and to hand over the proceeds of this additional taxation to the local authorities. And to this proposal there is the preliminary objection that it increases the existing inequality of the incidence of the drink duties in the three divisions of the United Kingdom. As it is, the alcohol in spirits, which constitute the favourite beverage of Scotland and Ireland, is taxed at eight times the rate of the alcohol in beer, which is the beverage that England most affects. If, then, additional taxation is to be imposed – and the drink traffic we think may very well be made to yield a larger revenue than it does – it is surely unfair to increase this inequality by adding most to the taxation of the already most heavily taxed liquor.

What is still more unfair, however, is, that if Mr Goschen's proposal is accepted, the people of Scotland and Ireland will be specially taxed for the benefit of English local bodies. . . . Now let us see how Mr Goschen wishes to dispose of this additional taxation. His proposal is, that it should be allocated in the same way as the probate duty, 80 per cent going to England, 11 per cent to Scotland, and 9 per cent to Ireland, and if this proposal were acted upon, the amount which each division would receive would compare with the amount they each contribute, thus:

	Amount Paid in Duty £	Amount Returned as Contributed to Local Expenditure £	More or Less Returned than Paid
England	414,000	543,000	+129,000
Scotland	152,000	75,000	−77,000
Ireland	113,000	61,000	−52,000
	679,000	679,000	—

. . . Before concluding, however, we would point out how clearly such proposals as are now put forward indicate the confusion that exists in our system of so-called local finance. We are, in fact, getting back rapidly to an aggravated form of the old and utterly discredited system of grants in aid, which the Local Government

Act was intended to supersede; and it is no wonder, therefore, that instead of local burdens being lightened, they have been very considerably increased. The sooner there is a complete separation between local and Imperial finance the better.

4.4 From *Local Taxation (Customs and Excise) Act* (1890), S.1.
This Act applies the yield of the duties on spirits to various purposes, the most important of which was the aid to technical education. This extract gives the provisions with regard to England.

CHAPTER 60
An Act for the Distribution and Application of certain Duties of Customs and Excise; and for other purposes connected therewith.   [18th August 1890]

Whereas certain local taxation (customs and excise) duties have by an Act of the present session been directed to be paid to the same local taxation accounts as the local taxation probate duty, and it is expedient to provide for the distribution and application of the duties so paid:
Be it therefore enacted by the Queen's most Excellent Majesty, by and with the advice and consent of the Lords Spiritual and Temporal, and Commons, in this present Parliament assembled, and by the authority of the same, as follows:
1 (1) Out of the English share of the local taxation (customs and excise) duties paid to the local taxation account on account of any financial year:
   (*a*) The sum of three hundred thousand pounds shall be applied for such purposes of police superannuation in England as herein-after mentioned;
   (*b*) The residue shall, unless Parliament otherwise determines, be distributed between county and county borough funds, and carried to the Exchequer contribution accounts of those funds respectively, and applied under the Local Government Act, 1888, as if it were part of the English share of the local taxation probate duty, and shall be the subject of an adjustment between counties and county boroughs, according to section thirty-two of the said Act, by the Commissioners under that Act.
(2) The council of any such county or county borough may contribute any sum received by such council in respect of the residue

under this section, or any part of that sum, for the purposes of technical education within the meaning of the Technical Instruction Act, 1889, and may make that contribution over and above any sum that may be raised by rate under that Act.

(3) A county council may make any such contribution by giving the amount of the contribution or any part of that amount to any town council or other urban sanitary authority in their county for the purpose of the same being applied by such council or authority under the Technical Instruction Act, 1889, over and above any sum which can be raised under that Act by rate by such council or authority.

4.5 From *The Economist* (11 October 1890), pp. 1286-7.
This extract reviews the first year of operation of the assigned revenues, and exhibits continued disenchantment on the part of *The Economist* with the scheme.

A considerable portion of the report of the Local Government Board for the fiscal year 1889–90 is devoted to a record of the financial operations under the Local Government Act, 1888. That Act, it will be remembered, withdrew from the local authorities the grants-in-aid they had formerly been receiving, and substituted for them the proceeds of certain licence duties and one-half of the yield of the probate duty. It was also proposed to raise, for the benefit of the local authorities, a further sum of £700,000, by taxing horses and vehicles, but this portion of the scheme failed to meet with acceptance, and was abandoned. The calculation was, that under the new arrangement the local authorities of England and Wales would receive about £2,200,000 more a year than they would have received as grants-in-aid; but, although the assigned revenues proved rather more productive than was anticipated, the gain to the local authorities last year was not quite so great as was estimated. If no change had been made, they would have been entitled to a payment from the Imperial Treasury of £2,860,000, while under the Act the amount they became entitled to was £4,806,000, made up thus:

	£
Local taxation licences	2,994,000
Probate duty grant	1,812,000
	4,806,000

Out of this total, however, a small portion was retained by the Exchequer to meet the costs of revising barristers, etc., and the amount paid over to the local authorities was £4,793,000, so that as matter of fact they obtained £1,933,000 more than they would have done under the old system.

When the Government introduced their Local Government measure the promise was held out that under it the Imperial Treasury would contribute about £3,000,000 more in aid of local taxation in England than it had done in the form of grants-in-aid. That promise, however, it will be observed, was far from being realised, the actual addition to the local receipts in 1889–90 being, as already stated £1,933,000. This year Mr Goschen has provided a further sum, estimated at £830,000, derived from the new beer and spirit duties, which will bring the total addition to local revenues pretty well up to the £3,000,000 originally intended to be given, but in consideration of the new revenue, new obligations have been imposed upon the local treasuries, so that even now the net gain is considerably less than was originally promised. Confining ourselves, however, to the actual results in 1889–90, what we find is that a net sum of £1,933,000 was made available for the relief of rates, and as the value of rateable property in England and Wales is about £150,000,000, that is equal to an average rate of about threepence in the £. . . .

The report deals at some length with the difficulties experienced in arranging for the transfer to the various local authorities of the assigned revenues. These were largely due to the fact that it necessarily took time to get the new machinery into proper working order; but the system itself seems to stand in need of some revision. The assigned revenues are supposed to be paid into what is called the Local Taxation Account, but it is quite clear that they are not passed into that account as they are received. For instance, the amount of the revenue collected during the past half-year on account of local finance must have exceeded the amount collected during the first half of last year by fully £700,000, because of the imposition of the new beer and spirit taxes, but the amount transferred to the Local Taxation Account was only about £120,000 greater. Thus the Treasury must have been holding on the 30th September a considerable amount of money which did not belong to it. And it is not only that there is some delay in making the transfers into the Local Taxation Account. There is also uncertainty as to when money actually transferred will be paid over to the local authorities. As regards that, the Local Government Board seem to act as they think best, and although they doubtless seek to exercise their discretion with perfect fairness, yet matters of that kind ought not to be left unsettled. If the local authorities do not know exactly when they are to receive the money due to them, they cannot regulate strictly their own financial affairs. What is wanted, therefore, is that the assigned revenues should be separated completely from the Imperial revenues, and that they should be made distributable amongst the local authorities at fixed instead of uncertain dates, as is the case at present.

4.6 From the 'Local Taxation Return', *HCP* No. 168 (1892–3), pp. xliii-xlv.

A favourite device of the nineteenth-century Parliaments to secure information for the benefit of Members was to call for a 'Return'. This extract from such a document shows the development of Exchequer grants up to 1888.

GROWTH OF SUBVENTIONS FROM 1868 TO 1888

49. The first new grant paid to Local Authorities after 1868 was the Grant to School Boards, which was paid for the first time during the year ended the 30th August 1872. For some years from its commencement it was a comparatively small grant, but it subsequently grew with great rapidity, and has now risen to nearly 1,500,000*l.*

In 1873–4 two further grants appeared for the first time in the Appropriation Accounts, one being the additional grant paid to School Boards of poor districts under Section 97 of the Elementary Education Act, 1870, and the other the grant in aid of the Salaries of Medical Officers of Health and Inspectors of Nuisances, appointed by Sanitary Authorities under the regulations of the Local Government Board. . . .

In 1875–6, a further grant was made in aid of the expenses entailed on Boards of Guardians by certain additional remuneration authorised to be paid to Registrars of Births and Deaths under the Births and Deaths Registration Act, 1874.

In 1877, the Prisons Act, 1877, was passed, which transferred to the Secretary of State all prisons vested in local authorities, and provided that for the future all expenses incurred in respect of their maintenance, and that of the prisoners therein should be defrayed out of moneys voted by Parliament.

The next new grant was made in 1882, in respect of the main-tenance of disturnpiked and main roads. It was paid to the High-way Authorities outside Quarter Sessions Boroughs, and was intended to cover one-fourth of the cost of the maintenance of these roads.

In 1887, a further grant was made in respect of these roads. This grant was also intended to cover one-fourth of the cost of the maintenance of the roads; but it was paid to the County Authorities who, under the Highways and Locomotives Amendment Act, 1878, were required to repay one-half of the cost of maintenance to the Highway Authorities.

The practical effect of all these new grants, taken in conjunction with the normal growth in some of the old grants, was to raise to 6,870,206*l.* the subventions which, as I have already mentioned, amounted in 1868 to 1,420,083*l.*

The increase or decrease in each subvention is shown in the following Tables:

PARLIAMENTARY GRANTS IN AID OF LOCAL RATES

GRANT IN AID OF	1867–68 £	1873–74 £	1887–88 £
Teachers in Poor Law Schools ..	34,500	36,098	36,825
Poor Law Medical Officers.. ..	104,500	125,602	149,506
Police, Counties and Boroughs ..	225,000	297,459	864,083
Metropolitan Police..	164,848	229,990	575,141
Criminal Prosecutions	150,000	138,466	133,732
County and Borough Prisons, and Removal of Convicts	109,000*	95,870	—
Metropolitan Fire Brigade	10,000	10,000	10,000
Berwick Bridge	90	90	90
Industrial Schools (Local Authorities)	3,574	8,172	32,212
Elementary Education (School Boards): Annual Grants for Day and Evening Scholars	—	76,734	1,255,938
School Boards in Poor Districts ..	—	208	7,167
Medical Officers of Health and Inspectors of Nuisances	—	14,727	73,910
Pauper Lunatics	—	—	485,169
Registration of Births and Deaths..	—	—	9,500
Disturnpiked and Main Roads ..	—	—	498,797
TOTAL	801,512	1,033,416	4,132,070

* This amount includes Estimated Expenditure in respect of Scotland.

LOCAL CHARGES TRANSFERRED TO, AND OTHER CHARGES OF A
LOCAL NATURE BORNE BY, ANNUAL VOTES OF PARLIAMENT

CHARGE IN RESPECT OF	1867–68 £	1873–74 £	1887–88 £
District Auditors	17,900	18,261	15,246
Clerks of Assize	18,500	20,124	19,602
Compensation to Clerks of the Peace, etc.	6,400*	5,348*	1,806*
Central Criminal Court	—	4,065	5,181
Middlesex Sessions	—	956	819
Public Vaccinators	6,000	8,795	16,468
Elementary Education (Voluntary Schools):			
Annual Grants for Day and Evening Scholars	443,345	973,526	1,927,285
Reformatory Schools .. ⎫		70,160	66,920
Industrial Schools (other than those of Local Authorities) ⎬	99,426†		
⎭		79,833	103,667
Rates on Government Property ..	27,000‡	33,799‡	182,459
County and Borough Prisons, and Removal of Convicts	—	—	398,683
TOTAL	618,571	1,214,867	2,738,136
TOTAL Parliamentary Subventions ..	1,420,183	2,248,283	6,870,206

* These amounts include payments to Irish officers.
† This includes payments in respect of Scotland.
‡ These amounts include payments in respect of Scotland.

INCREASE IN THE SUBVENTIONS BROUGHT ABOUT BY THE
LEGISLATION OF 1888 AND 1890

50. In 1888 the Local Government Act, 1888, was passed, which
transferred to the Councils of Counties and County Boroughs of
England and Wales certain licenses, referred to in the Act as the
Local Taxation Licenses, and two-fifths of the Probate Duty, in
substitution for the Grants formerly paid in respect of the salaries
of Teachers in Poor Law Schools and Poor Law Medical Officers,
the County, Borough, and Metropolitan Police, Public Vaccinators,
Medical Officers of Health and Inspectors of Nuisances, Criminal
Prosecutions, Pauper Lunatics, Registrars of Births and Deaths,
Disturnpiked and Main Roads, and compensation to Clerks of the
Peace. The grants thus discontinued were certified by the Local
Government Board, under Section 22 of the Act, to have amounted,
for the year ended the 31st of March 1888, to 2,860,384*l.* The

revenues ceded to the Local Authorities of England and Wales in lieu of these Grants amounted:

	£
In 1889–90, to	4,805,940
In 1890–91, to	4,968,239
And in 1891–92, to	5,313,278

51. In 1890 the proceeds of certain additional Duties on Beer and Spirits, were allocated to local purposes by the Customs and Inland Revenue Act, 1890.

The following Table shows the gross receipts from these Duties in 1890–91 and 1891–2, and the amounts distributed to the local authorities of England and Wales:

Year	Gross Receipts	Amounts distributed in England and Wales
	£	£
1890-91 – – –	1,300,469	1,040,376
1891-92 – – –	1,394,751	1,115,801

4.7 From the *Local Government Act* (1929), Sections 86 and 88 and 4th Schedule, Part III.

These are the provisions of the Act which introduce the General Exchequer Contribution, whilst the schedule gives the formula for weighting the population of the county boroughs and county councils to take account of their different demands and resources.

General Exchequer Contributions

86. (1) There shall be paid out of moneys provided by Parliament in respect of the year beginning on the appointed day, and each subsequent year, an annual contribution towards local government expenses in counties and county boroughs to be called the 'General Exchequer Contribution'.

(2) The amount of the General Exchequer Contribution shall be periodically revised; the amount first fixed shall be for a period of three years beginning on the appointed day, the amount fixed on the first revision shall be for a period of four years from the expiration of the first period, the amount fixed on any subsequent

revision shall be for a period of five years from the expiration of the previous period, and a period for which the General Exchequer Contribution is so fixed is hereinafter referred to as a 'fixed grant period'.

(3) The amount of the General Exchequer Contribution shall be the sum of the following amounts, that is to say:

(a) an amount equal to the total losses on account of rates of all counties and county boroughs;

(b) an amount equal to the total losses on account of grants of all counties and county boroughs;

(c) in respect of each year in the first fixed grant period, five million pounds, and in respect of each year of every following fixed grant period such amount as Parliament may hereafter determine with respect to the fixed grant period so, however, that the proportion which the General Exchequer Contribution for any fixed grant period bears to the total amount of rate and grant borne expenditure in the penultimate year of the preceding fixed grant period shall never be less than the proportion which the General Exchequer Contribution for the first fixed grant period bore to the total amount of rate and grant borne expenditure in the first year of that fixed grant period. In the foregoing provisions of this paragraph:

(i) 'rate and grant borne expenditure' means the local expenditure which fell to be borne by rates and by grants made under this Part of this Act out of the General Exchequer Contribution; and

(ii) if as respects any fixed grant period the Minister certifies that the amount of rate and grant borne expenditure in the penultimate year of that fixed grant period was abnormally increased by reason of any emergency involving the issue of a proclamation under the Emergency Powers Act, 1920, there shall be deemed to be substituted for the reference to the penultimate year of the preceding fixed grant period a reference to the last year preceding the said penultimate year in which no such abnormal expenditure was incurred. . . .

88. (1) The General Exchequer Contributions shall be apportioned amongst the several counties and county boroughs in manner hereinafter following, that is to say:

(*a*) during the first four fixed grant periods there shall out of the General Exchequer Contribution for each year be apportioned to each county or county borough an amount equal to the appropriate percentage of the losses on account of rates and grants of the county or county borough;

(*b*) during the first four fixed grant periods the residue, and thereafter the whole, of every General Exchequer Contribution, shall each year be apportioned amongst the several counties and county boroughs in proportion to their weighted populations.

(2) The amount apportioned under this section to a county shall be called 'the county apportionment' and the amount so apportioned to a county borough shall be called 'the county borough apportionment'.

PART III

Rules for determining Weighted Population

1. The estimated population of the county or county borough in the appropriate year shall be increased:

(i) if the estimated number of children under five years of age per thousand of the estimated population exceeds fifty, by the percentage represented by the proportion which that excess bears to fifty;

(ii) if, according to the valuation lists in force on the appropriate date, the rateable value per head of the estimated population of the county or county borough is less than ten pounds, by the percentage represented by the proportion which the deficiency bears to ten pounds.

2. There shall be estimated and certified the average numbers during the three calendar years immediately preceding the beginning of each fixed grant period of unemployed insured men and of unemployed insured women resident in each county and county borough, and there shall be ascertained the percentage represented by the proportion which the number of unemployed insured men increased by ten per cent of the number of unemployed insured women bears to the average estimated population of the county or county borough for those three years and if as respects any county or county borough that percentage exceeds one-and-a-half, the estimated population of the county or county borough in the appropriate year as increased in accordance with Rule 1 contained in this Part of this Schedule shall be further increased by a percentage

equal to the amount of such excess multiplied by the appropriate multiple.

3. There shall be ascertained and certified the number of miles of road in every county other than the county of London, and the estimated population of every such county as increased in accordance with Rule 1 contained in this Part of this Schedule shall be further increased:

(a) in the case of a county in which the estimated population per mile of roads is in the appropriate year less than one hundred, by the percentage represented by the proportion which the difference between two hundred and the estimated population per mile of roads bears to two hundred; and

(b) in the case of a county in which the estimated population per mile of roads is in the appropriate year one hundred or more, by the percentage represented by the proportion which fifty bears to the estimated population per mile of roads.

4. The estimated population of the county or county borough as increased in accordance with the provisions of the foregoing rules contained in this Part of this Schedule shall be the weighted population of the county or county borough.

5. For the purposes of this Part of this Schedule:

'The appropriate date' shall, as respects the first fixed grant period, be the first day of October nineteen hundred and twenty-nine, and as respects every other fixed grant period, the first, or in London the sixth, day of April in the last year of the preceding fixed grant period;

'The appropriate multiple' shall, as respects the first and second fixed grant periods, be ten, and as respects any subsequent fixed grant period be a number ascertained in the following manner;

(i) the ratio which the total amount of the General Exchequer Contribution in the fixed grant period in question bears to the part thereof distributed in that fixed grant period under paragraph (b) of subsection (1) of section eighty-eight of this Act shall be ascertained;

(ii) the ratio which the total amount of the General Exchequer Contribution in the first fixed grant period bears to the part thereof distributed in that fixed grant period under the said paragraph shall be ascertained;

(iii) the required number shall be such number as bears to ten the same proportion as the ratio ascertained under paragraph (i) of this rule bears to the ratio ascertained under paragraph (ii) thereof.

4.8 From the Ministry of Health, *Local Government Bill 1947*, Part I, Memorandum on the Financial Relations between the Exchequer and Local Authorities, England and Wales (November, 1947), Cmd. 7253, pp. 2, 4, and 7.

This extract is taken from the White Paper which outlined the details of the Exchequer Equalisation Grant which was enacted in 1948. Also extracted are the summary totals showing the financial consequences of the new grant.

1. The figures in the appended statements, which are given by way of illustration only, have been prepared to show the *approximate* effect on rates levied in Administrative Counties and County Boroughs in 1946/47 if *in that year* the following changes in expenditure and grants had been in operation:

(*a*) the transfer to the Exchequer of responsibility for the cost of hospitals and out-relief;

(*b*) the cessation of contributions by local authorities under Section 16 of the Old Age and Widows' Pensions Act, 1940;

(*c*) the addition to the expenditure of Local Health Authorities of the estimated additional cost of services to be administered by them under Part III of the National Health Service Act, 1946, *less* the estimated additional Exchequer grant payable towards expenditure on services under Part III of the Act, based on a flat 50 per cent of total expenditure;

(*d*) the payment in lieu of the existing Education grants of grants under the revised formula;

(*e*) the withdrawal of the Block Grants under the Local Government Acts, 1929 to 1946; and

(*f*) the payment of the proposed Exchequer Equalisation Grants and Exchequer Transitional Grants.

2. The figures do *not* take account of:

(*a*) the effect on the income and expenditure of local authorities of Parts III to VIII of the Bill;

(*b*) the additional expenditure to be incurred by local authorities under the Fire Services Act, 1947; and

(*c*) the additional expenditure to be incurred by local authorities under the provisions of the National Assistance Bill relating to the care of the aged and infirm. . . .

TABLE I

Statement showing for each County and County Borough in England and Wales for the year 1946/47 particulars of population, rateable value per head of weighted population, estimated expenditure on transferred services (Part II of the National Health Service Act, 1946 and Part II of the National Assistance Bill) and the amount of the block grants under the Local Government Acts, 1929 to 1946.

(1)	Unweighted Population (2)	Weighted Population (3)	Rateable Value per head of Weighted Population (4) £	Estimated Expenditure on Transferred Services (5) £	Block Grants under the Local Government Acts 1929 to 1946 (6) £
SUMMARY					
Administrative Counties (other than London)	24,811,880	30,319,278	5·47	27,291,390	35,219,417
County Boroughs	13,013,520	15,893,740	6·34	22,003,401	17,972,736
London..	3,131,600	3,712,120	14·65	13,218,888	4,833,174
England and Wales	40,957,000	49,925,138	6·43	62,513,679	58,025,327

TABLE II

Statement showing for each County and County Borough in England and Wales for the year 1946/47 particulars of the rate levied, the amounts which it is estimated would have been payable as Exchequer Equalisation Grant and Exchequer Transitional Grant, and the rate which it is estimated would have been required after the changes in expenditure and grants mentioned in paragraph 1 of this paper.

Note: The rates in columns (2) and (7), in the case of an Administrative County, represent averages for the whole County.

(1)	Rate Levied (2)		Exchequer Equalisation Grant		Exchequer Transitional Grant		Rate which it is estimated would have been required after the changes in expenditure and grants referred to in para. 1 of this paper (7)	
			Amount (3) £	Rate (4)	Amount (5) £	Rate (6)		
	s.	d.		s. d.		s. d.	s.	d.
SUMMARY								
Administrative Counties (other than London)	15	9	26,511,186	3 4	525,552	– 1	13	0
County Boroughs	16	5	6,700,935	1 5	361,582	– 1	13	9
London	12	6	—	—	—	—	10	1
England and Wales.. ..	15	5	33,212,121	2 2	887,134	– 1	12	9

4.9 From *Hansard*, Fifth Series, Vol. 444 (18 November 1947), Cols 988-92.

This extract from the speech of the Minister of Health, Aneurin Bevan, moving the Second Reading of the Local Government Bill, explains why the General Exchequer Contribution was no longer appropriate to the circumstances of local government after the 1939-45 War.

When we come to 1929, the most important of all the changes took place by the derating of three-quarters of the industrial hereditaments and the complete abolition of the rating of agricultural land and buildings. Then, of course, also occurred the transfer of the Poor Law and rural highways to the county councils.

All these changes had a profound influence upon the financial relationships between the Treasury and local authorities. It was recognised at that time that it was necessary in providing additional financial assistance that regard should be had to the relative wealth of local authorities, and as an old member of local government and as one who took, I think, a quite considerable interest in the matter at that time, I want to pay my tribute to the architects of the block grant formula. I was never convinced that there was any necessary organic relationship between the derating of industrial hereditaments and the redistribution of central moneys to local authorities in order to deal with relative wealth. The one could easily have been accomplished without the other. It could have been possible for industrial rating to continue and at the same time for the Treasury or the Ministry of Health to accumulate a sum of money and to distribute it in accordance with the weighted population formula quite independently of derating; but that was not done.

Nevertheless, it is quite clear that that formula of distributing money, not merely on a percentage basis but in accordance with the relative needs and wealth of local authorities, was a very important departure in local government, and the devisors of it showed considerable ingenuity. I remember how much we were frustrated and cheated by trying to find a principle which would attract money from the centre to the periphery in some objective and dispassionate fashion. However, that principle is now dated. If we revised the block grant formula in accordance with the old principles, it would produce gross injustices, because the test of relative wealth has been changed by a shift of function. In the first place, the able-bodied unemployed have been transferred to the Assistance Board, and when the Bill which is to be presented shortly becomes law and a further transfer takes place, many of the burdens now carried by local government will be transferred to central funds. There will then have matured a long campaign which has been carried on, particularly by hon. Members on this side of the House, so that central responsibility for certain hardships will be accepted and local responsibility will cease. That, of course, at once undermines the block grant formula.

Furthermore, there will be transferred on 5th July next year local financial responsibility for the hospital system. There will also be a number of other relatively small transfers. When the hospital services are transferred to the central government, it will be found that the consequences of the transfer are especially unequal. The reason is that very many local authorities have never been well off enough to undertake hospital responsibilities. Some local authorities in some better endowed parts of the country have expanded their hospital systems much more than others and so, when the whole is transferred, more relief will be given to some than to others. Therefore, this transfer produces an exceptional degree of inequality, and we could not possibly continue it. . . .

In order to distribute the funds available from the centre, it has been decided to take rateable value per head of the weighted population; that is to say, we have accepted – I think students of local government will agree with this – two factors as being largely responsible for the difference in the distribution of local government burdens; that is, the number of children under 15 years of age producing a whole variety of services which I need not detail at the moment – such as educational and child welfare services – which are well known to everybody, and also the scarcity of population in rural areas. Those two have always been regarded – and I have not heard a single argument to the contrary that is valid – and those two stand as the main causes of the additional weight which falls upon some local authorities. Therefore, we take the weighted population and divide that into the total rateable value, and so discover the average rateable value per head of the population.

At once that gives us something to work upon. Some local authorities will be below the average per head, and some will be above. Those who will be above the average per head will obviously be the more prosperous areas. I would ask hon. Members to bear in mind all the while that what we are trying to accomplish, strictly in accordance with one of the original purposes of the block grant, is to bring about an equitable distribution of central assistance; in other words, we do not want local authorities to attract more money from the centre merely because they can afford to spend more money locally, since that would merely mean the fat ones getting fatter, as, indeed, has occurred over the last 20 and 30 years, and it is one of the reasons why we are struggling in this Parliament, and were struggling before the war, to try to mitigate the most evil consequences of failure to share local government burdens equitably. . . .

Therefore, we take the average rateable value per head of the population, and all those below the average attract a share of the block grant. They attract a share of the block grant in this way, that the Exchequer will step in and become a ratepayer to the extent that the local authority's rateable value is below the average. Thus, the local authorities will precept upon the Exchequer in exactly the same way as upon their own ratepayers. In other words, the Exchequer becomes a ratepayer to the extent of the deficit.

4.10 From the Ministry of Housing and Local Government, *Local Government Finance (England and Wales)* (July 1957), Cmnd. 209, pp. 3-14.

The White Paper from which these extracts are taken explained the Government's attitude to the reform of the finances of local government. The later extracts describe the new system of the General Grant and the summary figures show the financial effects.

3. The Government's main conclusions were announced by the present Minister of Housing and Local Government in the House of Commons on 12th February, 1957, preparatory to detailed discussions with the associations of local authorities and other organisations affected. In brief, the Government do not think it practicable to devise a satisfactory new source of local revenue by authorising the collection of a local income tax or other such impost on top of the national system of taxes; nor do they think it appropriate to earmark for the direct benefit of local authorities, or to hand over to them, the motor duties or any other of the taxes now levied nationally. In their view, improvement of the system of local finance in this country must come from improvement of the system of local taxation which is traditionally the right of local authorities, combined with a radical recasting of the system of grants. The kind of improvement in grants which is needed is one

which secures that a substantially larger part of the grant-aid is in the form of general assistance and is not tied (as is so much of the present Exchequer aid) to specific services and expressed as a percentage of expenditure upon these services. The present system of percentage grants acts as an indiscriminating incentive to further expenditure and also carries with it an aggravating amount of central checking and control of detail. The importance to local government of reducing its dependence on percentage grants has been a major factor in the Government's proposals as outlined in this Paper. . . .

PROPOSALS FOR STRENGTHENING THE RATING SYSTEM
Re-rating

7. At present industry and freight-transport are rated at 25 per cent of their net annual value. They will be re-rated to 50 per cent of net annual value; and corresponding alterations will be made as regards industrial properties occupied by the Crown. . . .

The Burden of Rates

10. One of the difficulties in the rating system is that the rate demand is made half-yearly (although many pay rates with the rent at weekly or monthly intervals). Greater efforts are needed to meet the convenience of the payers in the way of instalment payment etc. for those who are faced with half-yearly demands for rates. Taxes are now accepted by instalments; and rating authorities should consider enlarging and publicising their arrangements for paying rates by instalments in appropriate cases. . . .

REORGANISATION OF THE SYSTEM OF GRANTS
The New General Grant

14. As was explained in the announcement on 12th February, it is proposed to replace as many as practicable of the specific grants (which are mostly on a percentage basis) by a general grant of an amount fixed in advance for a short period of years, though not necessarily at the same level for each year of the period. If it appears that expenditure which previously attracted specific grant is bound to increase materially in the later years of a period, the amount to be distributed by way of general grant will be graduated accordingly. This general grant will be distributed to all county and county borough councils by reference to objective factors (mainly of weighted population) which are readily ascer-

tainable and afford a fair and reasonable measure of the relative needs of each authority.

15. At their present levels, the specific grants to be absorbed into the general grant total nearly £300 millions. Taking into account the equalisation grants, grants-in-aid which are general in character (as distinct from grants tied to specific services) will rise from one-sixth to close on two-thirds of all Exchequer assistance.

16. The grants to be absorbed into the general grant are those for:

education (but not school milk and meals)

agricultural education

health services under the National Health Service Act, 1946

fire

child care

town planning (but not grants for blitz re-development)

road safety

traffic patrols

registration of electors

physical training and recreation

residential and temporary accommodation under the National Assistance Act, 1948

school crossing patrols. . . .

19. The services concerned are not static; and it will be necessary to provide for their further development. In determining the total of the general grant for any period the Government will take into consideration:

(a) the latest available figures of expenditure by local authorities on the relevant services;

(b) such factors beyond the control of local authorities and occurring generally in the country as are expected to affect materially the demands on the local authorities in respect of the relevant services in the period;

(c) the need for development of the services, and at the same time the general state of the economy, as determining the amount of improvement which can properly be secured in the period.

20. The amount of the grant will take into account the levels of remuneration and prices current at the time, together with any foreseeable variations. The Government appreciate, nevertheless, that there may be unforeseen increases during the grant period of such magnitude that they cannot reasonably be carried in full by

the local authorities. In this event the Government will be prepared by way of exception to consider interim revision of the grant.

21. As the general grant is fixed in total, and its distribution is regulated by objective factors without regard for the expenditure of the individual local authority, it will not be necessary, as it is now, to withhold a percentage of the grant until the amount of the expenditure which ranks for grant is known. Having regard to the necessary increase in expenditure, the amount involved when the scheme is in operation may prove to be of the order of £40 millions. The Government propose in due course to pay the full amount of the general grant for each year in that year, reaching this position by stages.

22. The formula for the general grant is set out in Annex C. . . .

ANNEX C
General Grant based on Weighted Population
Details of the Formula

1. The grants will be payable to all county and county borough councils. Each authority will receive a share of the total amount fixed in advance. This will be made up of three elements determined in accordance with the formula, viz.:

(*a*) a basic share;
(*b*) supplementary shares;
(*c*) a rate product deduction.

2. The numerical factors in the formula, as well as the total amount of the grant for each year, will be prescribed by Order for each grant period. The figures accompanying this Paper assume a total of general grants of approximately £291¼ millions. The numerical factors in the formula stated below have been fixed so as to distribute in total that amount of grant, and are subject to revision in the light of changes in grant levels.

3. (*a*) *The basic share* is as follows:

£4.76 per head of the total population of the area; *plus* £0.40 for each child under 15 years of age in the population of the area.

(*b*) *The supplementary shares* are as follows:

(i) *School children.* – An amount per head of total population, of £0.06 multiplied by the amount by which the number of children on the registers of the local authority's maintained and assisted schools per

1,000 total population (to the nearest whole number), exceeds 120.

(ii) *Young children and old people.* – £0.32 for each child under 5, and each person over 65 in the population of the area.

(iii) *High density.* – A percentage of the basic share, the percentage being one half of the amount by which the number of persons per acre in the area exceeds 18.

(iv) *Low density.* – A percentage of the basic share, payable in areas where the number of miles of road per 1,000 population exceeds 2; the percentage being twice times the number of miles of road per 1,000 population, subject to a maximum percentage of 60.

(v) *Declining population.* – A percentage of the basic share, the percentage being half the amount by which the percentage decline in population over the past 20 years exceeds 5 per cent.

(vi) *High costs in Greater London.* – An amount equal to 5 per cent of the basic share, payable to all areas wholly or partly within the Metropolitan Police Area.

(c) *The rate product deduction.* – The product of a rate of 12 pence for the area is subtracted from the sum of the basic and supplementary shares.

4. The total amount of grant to be distributed is arrived at as follows:

	£m.
Estimated total for 1956–57 of the specific grants to be absorbed into the general grant	298
Less Reduction to take account of the product of re-rating – see paragraph 31 of the Paper	6¾
Amount of general grant	291¼

5. Details of the effect of the formula in distributing to each county and county borough a share in a hypothetical total of £291¼ millions are given in Annex E. . . .

ANNEX E

General Grant based on *Weighted Population*

Effect of Formula in Distributing a Hypothetical Total of £291¼ million. (See Annex C.)

Local Authority	Basic share (£,000)	School children (£,000)	Young children and old people (£,000)	Supplementary shares				Rate Product deduction (£,000)	Total (£,000)
				High density (£,000)	Low density (£,000)	Declining population (£,000)	Greater London (£,000)		
(1)	(2)	(3)	(4)	(5)	(6)	(7)	(8)	(9)	(10)
SUMMARY									
Administrative Counties (other than London) ..	134,607·1	45,739·2	1,683·6	—	13,603·2	—	1,867·1	17,278·1	180,222·1
County Boroughs	66,231·5	33,475·1	824·8	877·4	27·6	418·8	128·6	9,315·4	92,668·4
London	15,842·0	3,043·9	200·5	2,114·9	—	1,264·2	792·1	4,817·2	18,440·4
England and Wales	216,680·6	82,258·2	2,708·9	2,992·3	13,630·8	1,683·0	2,787·8	31,410·7	291,330·9

G

5 District Audit

5.1 From Beatrice Webb, *Our Partnership*, ed. B. Drake and M. I. Cole (London 1948), p. 337.
This extract from Beatrice Webb's diary records her impressions of the slapdash manner in which the Poplar Board of Guardians dealt with the business of contracting for supplies. It is of interest to note that one of the most celebrated of all District Audit cases (see the next extract), that of Roberts *v.* Hopwood, involved the Poplar Metropolitan Borough Council, amongst whose members was the same George Lansbury referred to here by Beatrice Webb.

March 19th. – Attended a meeting of the Poplar Board of Guardians, held at 6.30. About 30 were present, a rather low lot of doubtful representatives of Labour, with a sprinkling of builders, publicans, insurance and other agents. The meeting was exclusively engaged in allotting the contracts for the year, which meant up to something between £50,000 and £100,000. I did not ascertain the exact amount. The procedure was utterly reckless. The tenders were opened at the meeting, the names and prices read out; and then, without any kind of report of a committee or by officials, straight away voted on. Usually the same person as heretofore was taken, nearly always a local man – it was not always the lowest tender, and the prices were, in all cases, full, in some cases obviously excessive. Butter at 1s. 2d. a lb., when the contracts ran into thousands of pounds worth, was ridiculous. Milk at 9d. a gallon – the best and most expensive meat, tea at 2s. 8d. 'Give Bow a chance' was one of the relevant considerations urged successfully in favour of a change in the contractor. Will Crooks sat in the chair and did nothing to check the recklessness. Even Lansbury, by constitution a thorough-going sentimentalist, and with no other experience of public affairs, protested, and was clearly ashamed of the procedure.

5.2 From the *Ministry of Housing and Local Government Report for 1958*, Cmnd. 737 (1959), chap. V, 'The Growth and Scope of the District Audit', pp. 36-48.

This extract gives a brief account of the development of the District Audit since its inception, refers to the major judicial decisions about its powers and functions, and describes its method of administration.

The present system of district audit is best dated from the reforms of the 1830s when, through concern at the way in which poor law relief was being administered, the board of Poor Law Commissioners was set up and empowered by the Poor Law Amendment Act, 1834, to direct the overseers and guardians to appoint officers for the 'examining and auditing, allowing or disallowing of accounts'. The Commissioners soon recognised the inherent objections to a system by which the appointment and remuneration of auditors was placed in the hands of the authorities whose accounts were being examined, and these weaknesses were largely removed by the subsequent Poor Law Amendment Acts. The Poor Law Amendment Act, 1844, enabled the Commissioners to combine parishes and unions in England and Wales into districts for the purpose of the audit of accounts. The new office of district auditor was created and the holders were given powers and duties which remain substantially unaltered to the present day. The Poor Law (Audit) Act, 1868, took the process one stage further and district auditors became civil servants; provision was made later in the District Auditors Act, 1879, for their remuneration and expenses to be paid out of moneys provided by Parliament, subject to the recovery of the cost by means of a stamp duty payable by the authorities whose accounts were audited.

In the meanwhile, the duties of the district auditor were extended to other fields. The special sessions of the justices to pass the accounts of highway surveyors, held under the provisions of the Highway Act, 1835, were abolished by the Highways and Locomotives (Amendment) Act, 1878, and their powers transferred to district auditors. The accounts of local boards, the forerunners of public health authorities, were made subject to district audit by the Local Government Act, 1858. Between 1870 and 1899 legislation setting up school boards, county councils, parish councils and meetings, and metropolitan borough councils provided for the accounts of all these bodies to be subject to district audit. The reforms of the latter part of the nineteenth century thus extended the province of the district audit system so that by the end of the century the accounts of the great majority of local authorities in England and Wales were subject to audit by district auditors. The principal exception was that of the municipal corporations. . . .

SCOPE OF DISTRICT AUDIT

The provisions about district audit are found in Part X of the Local Government Act, 1933. Section 219 sets out the accounts subject to audit by a district auditor. They are:

(a) the accounts of county, metropolitan borough, urban district, rural district and parish councils, and of parish meetings;

(b) the accounts of any committee of a council or parish meeting included at (a);

(c) the accounts of any joint committee set up under Part III of the Act (or under any enactment repealed by the Act) if one or more of the constituent authorities is a council included under (a) or a borough council wholly subject to district audit;

(d) any other accounts which are made subject to district audit by virtue of any enactment or statutory order or, in the case of the accounts of a borough council, by virtue of a resolution of the council adopting the system of district audit.

At the present time all 63 county councils, 28 metropolitan boroughs, 564 urban district councils and 473 rural district councils are wholly subject to district audit together with 305 drainage boards and a number of miscellaneous authorities including some 11,000 parish councils and meetings. Of the 83 county borough councils, 11 are wholly subject to district audit, as are 137 of the 319 borough councils. In addition, as already explained, certain sections of the accounts of all boroughs are subject to audit by the district auditor. . . .

APPOINTMENT OF DISTRICT AUDITORS

The statutory provisions about the appointment of district auditors are contained in section 220 of the Act. It is clear from the manner of the appointment of the district auditor that great importance has been attached to his independent status. Since 1868 he has been appointed successively by the Poor Law Board, the Local Government Board, the Minister of Health, the Minister of Local Government and Planning and the Minister of Housing and Local Government. At first the appointment was confined to barristers, solicitors and other persons who had served as assistants to a district auditor, but later appointments were also made of chartered and other accountants. The Minister now makes his appointments from assistant district auditors, who are civil servants recruited through the open competitive examinations held by the Civil Service Commissioners. After a period of training they are required to satisfy the Commissioners of their fitness for the appointment by passing qualifying examinations in accounts and law. The course and method of training for these qualifying examinations have recently come under review and the present system is being replaced by a scheme of training for the examinations conducted by the Institute of Municipal Treasurers and Accountants. Potential assistant district auditors will be required in future to pass the Institute's examinations. The Minister will satisfy himself that the auditors have a thorough knowledge of the specialised field of district audit law and procedure. They are also encouraged to obtain qualifications in law or economics, financial assistance being given towards the cost of tuition and examination fees.

The 15 audit districts into which England and Wales are divided are assigned to district auditors by the Minister. Administratively the work of the service is under the control of the Chief Inspector of Audit, who is also responsible to the Minister for the efficiency and training of the district audit staff; this appointment is made not under the provisions of Part X of the Act, as in the case of district auditors, but under the general power of the Minister to appoint officers to assist him. . . .

POWERS OF DISTRICT AUDITOR

[. . .]

Illegal items

The district auditor's first duty is to disallow every item of account contrary to law. It implies a judicial decision by the district auditor by which he expunges an item, either in whole or in part, from the accounts before him at the audit. The expression 'item of account' is not confined to items of expenditure, but extends to such items as income, charges to funds, closing entries and apportionments. The term has been examined by the Courts in a number of cases and the decisions clearly show how comprehensive is the interpretation given to the expression by them. Some of the decisions by district auditors under this sub-section which have come before the Courts on appeal have led to judicial precedents having a most important bearing upon the powers of local authorities and the duties of their officers. A case of considerable historical interest which occurred at the turn of the century and which had far-reaching consequences in the field of education was the well known Cockerton case. Cockerton, the district auditor, was faced with objections to expenditure incurred by the London School Board on science and art schools and upon adult education. His decision to surcharge the members of the Board on the ground that the expenditure was contrary to law was upheld in the Court of Queens Bench and in the Court of Appeal. This decision focussed attention on the need for a clearer definition of educational powers and played some part in the framing of the great Education Act of 1902.

Of the decided cases involving surcharges which are of continuing significance the following may be cited:

(a) In a case commonly referred to as the 'Poplar wages case'* the district auditor held that rates of wages being paid by the Poplar Metropolitan Borough Council to certain grades of workers were so greatly in excess of the prevailing rates that they were in part not wages but gratuities and as such contrary to law. The authority on the other hand maintained that the statutory provisions in the matter conferred upon them an unfettered and unchallengeable discretion. The case aroused a good deal of public and political interest and the House of Lords, in reversing a decision of the Court of Appeal and upholding the auditor's disallowance and surcharge, held that a discretion conferred upon a council by statute must be exercised reasonably.

(b) A local authority has no power to increase retrospectively the remuneration of officers whose salaries have already been fixed by formal resolution.

(c) If the object of the expenditure is legal and the amount paid is reasonable, having been reached after careful assessment of what is due, then the fact of irrelevant considerations having been brought into the assessment will not render the expenditure illegal in part or in whole.

(d) Where a town clerk appreciates that a report which would probably mean the abandonment of a project before the council has been deliberately withheld and that there has not

* Roberts v. Hopwood, 1925 A.C. 578.

been a full and proper disclosure to the council of the terms of an agreement relating to the project, his remaining passive amounts to negligence and misconduct and it is not open to him to excuse his inaction on the ground that he was acting under duress, for example under threats of dismissal.

Surcharges

The district auditor's second duty is to surcharge the amount of any expenditure disallowed upon those responsible for incurring or authorising the expenditure. The Cockerton case and the Poplar wages case referred to above are examples of surcharges consequent upon a disallowance of expenditure contrary to law. . . .

If a surcharge is made, it creates a personal liability against a specified person; and if several persons are involved that liability becomes joint and several. Under the present code a district auditor directs his efforts against those primarily responsible for incurring the expenditure deemed illegal. . . .

The auditor's third duty is to make a surcharge in respect of sums not duly brought into account. It is not limited to sums received and not brought into account, but may be used in cases where amounts should have been collected and the person concerned has failed in that duty. In 1901 it was held that an Inspector of Weights and Measures was liable to surcharge, under a similar surcharge provision then extant, because he failed to collect certain statutory fees notwithstanding that he had been directed by the council not to charge these fees.*

The fourth duty placed on the district auditor is to surcharge persons for losses arising from their negligence or misconduct. Surcharges for loss are more numerous than surcharges for disallowance of expenditure (in 1958 there were 13 of the former but none of the latter). This is so because in practice most of the district auditor's action under sub-section (1) of section 228 is taken in respect of frauds, especially embezzlement, and of other defaults in duty. . . .

CONCLUSION

This review of the district audit system has been made as a reminder that one of the surest ways of maintaining the financial integrity of governmental bodies is to provide them with independent testimony to the state of their financial health. Parliament itself

* R. *v.* Roberts (1901), 2 K.B. 117.

receives such aid through the office of the Comptroller and Auditor-General, and in the sphere of local government financial affairs the district auditor plays a similar role. Both in their separate ways hold office independently of the bodies whose accounts they audit; both have a duty to report on their audits and in both cases the reports are public documents.

The district auditor's independence in carrying out his duties is not the less real because he is appointed by the Minister. The fact that appeals lie to the Minister against the auditor's decisions has been one of the decisive factors in preserving that independence; for it would clearly be improper for the Minister to instruct or even to attempt to influence the auditor in his decisions and then to hear appeals against them.

Apart from his statutory position, however, the district auditor also plays his part, together with the local officers, in securing and maintaining high standards of accounting and financial control. At his annual audits he acts in collaboration with the internal audit staffs of local authorities and takes full account of the work they have done throughout the year. In practice many councils, especially the smaller ones, turn naturally to the auditor for advice on unusual or complicated problems regardless of whether the annual audit is actually in progress; and for every type of authority the annual audit offers an excellent opportunity for discussing points of difficulty. With his wide experience of differing authorities and systems, it is seldom that the auditor is unable to help.

6 Municipal Trading

6.1 From the *Tramways Act* (1870), s. 43.

This is an example of the ease with which the nineteenth-century legislation provided for local authorities to take over, on highly favourable terms, the operation of public utilities which were in the hands of private operators.

. . . Where the promoters of a tramway in any district are not the local authority, the local authority, if, by resolution passed at a special meeting of the members constituting such local authority, they so decide, may within six months after the expiration of a period of twenty-one years from the time when such promoters were empowered to construct such tramway, and within six months after the expiration of every subsequent period of seven years, or within three months after any order made by the Board of Trade under either of the two next preceding sections, with the approval of the Board of Trade, by notice in writing require such promoters to sell, and thereupon such promoters shall sell to them their undertaking, or so much of the same as is within such district, upon terms of paying the then value (exclusive of any allowance for past or future profits of the undertaking, or any compensation for compulsory sale, or other consideration whatsoever) of the tramway, and all lands, buildings, works, materials, and plant of the promoters suitable to and used by them for the purposes of their undertaking within such district, such value to be in case of difference determined by an engineer or other fit person nominated as referee by the Board of Trade on the application of either party, and the expenses of the reference to be borne and paid as the referee directs.

6.2 From G. Bernard Shaw, *The Commonsense of Municipal Trading*, 1st ed., The Fabian Socialist Series, No. 5 (London 1908), pp. 2-5, 103, and 108-14.

Shaw was an enthusiast for municipal reform and in this tract he elaborates the virtues of municipal trading over private capitalism – yet he was wise enough to perceive the dangers to good management arising from the petty-mindedness of the average elected representative.

At first sight the case in favour of Municipal Trading seems overwhelming. Take the case of a shopkeeper consuming a great deal of gas or electric light for the attractive display of his wares, or a factory owner with hundreds of work benches to illuminate. For all this light he has to pay the cost of production plus interest on capital at the rate necessary to induce private investors to form ordinary commercial gas or electric light companies, which are managed with the object of keeping the rate of interest up instead of down: all improvement in the service and reductions in price (if any) being introduced with the sole aim of making the excess of revenue over cost as large as possible.

Now the shopkeeper in his corporate capacity as citizen-constituent of the local governing body can raise as much capital as he likes at less than four per cent. . . . Municipal expenditure in trading is productive expenditure: its debts are only the capital with which it operates. And that is why it never has any difficulty in raising that capital. Sultans and South American Republics may beg round the world in vain; chancellors may have to issue national stock at a discount; but a Borough Treasurer simply names a figure and gets it at par.

This is the central commercial fact of the whole question. The shopkeeper, by municipal trading, can get his light for the current cost of production plus a rate of interest which includes no insurance against risk of loss, because the security, in spite of all theoretical demonstrations to the contrary, is treated by the investing public and by the law of trusteeship as practically perfect. Any profit that may arise through accidental overcharge returns to the ratepayer in relief of rates or in public service of some kind.

The moment this economic situation is grasped, the successes of municipal trading become intelligible; and the entreaties of commercial joint stock organisation to be protected against the competition of municipal joint stock organisation become as negligible as the plea of the small shopkeeper to be protected against the competition of the Civil Service or Army and Navy

Stores. Shew the most bitterly Moderate ratepayer a municipal lighting bill at sixpence a thousand feet or a penny a unit cheaper than the private company charges him, and he is a converted man as far as gas or electric light is concerned. And until commercial companies can raise capital at lower rates than the City Accountant or the Borough Treasurer, and can find shareholders either offering their dividends to relieve the rates or jealously determining to reduce the price of light to a minimum lest they should be paying a share of their neighbours' rates in their lighting bills, it will always be possible for a municipality of average capacity to underbid a commercial company.

Here, then, is the explanation of the popularity and antiquity of municipal trading. As far as their legal powers have gone, municipalities have always traded, and will always trade, to the utmost limits of the business capacity and public spirit of their members. . . .

OUR MUNICIPAL COUNCILLORS

Whoever has grasped the full scope of the case for Municipal Freedom of Trade will see that the practicability of public enterprise is limited only by the capacity of its organisers and administrators. And this raises the question, where are we to find our municipal statesmen? . . .

It is possible for a councillor to be stupendously ignorant and shamelessly lazy, and yet to be not only popular with his fellow councillors, but – provided he is a tolerably entertaining speaker – with the ratepayers also. He passes for a very busy public man when he is really only a sociable one, by attending all his committees and doing nothing on them.

There is at present no way in which the municipal fainéant can be brought to book, even if a community which does not pay for his services had any right to make the attempt. Payment of directors' fees would not improve matters: the guinea-pig has been tried in private enterprise and found wanting. Still, there is a great deal to be said for payment of members of municipal bodies. It would make the voters much more jealous and exacting as to the personal qualifications and public industry of their representatives, besides producing some sort of consciousness that membership of a local authority really means useful work and not mere ceremonial. Far from substituting selfish motives for public ones, it would relieve municipal work from the reproach that men have no reasons but interested – not to say corrupt – reasons for undertaking it. It

187

would give capable Labor leaders that training in public life without which they are apt to be socially dangerous in direct proportion to their ability and earnestness, and with which they stand so usefully for the whole community as well as for their own class against the sordidness and exclusiveness of the commercial classes and the social ignorance and thoughtlessness of the aristocracy. Labor representatives usually make excellent councillors, because they are much more severely criticised than their middle class colleagues. It is possible for a middle class councillor to sit on a municipality for twenty years in a condition of half-drunken stupor without exposure and defeat at the poll; but Labor councillors receive no such indulgence. As a rule they take their public business very seriously; are free from the social pressure which leads to so much reciprocal toleration of little jobs and venial irregularities among the middle class men of business; have the independence of professional men without their class prejudices; are exceptionally sensitive to the dignity of sobriety and respectable conduct; and, as they usually pay inclusive rents, never deliberately shelve necessary public work because it may mean an extra rate of an eighth of a penny in the pound. Thus, oddly enough, the municipal Labor member generally finds himself in alliance with the councillors who are too rich to be penny-wise and pound-foolish, and with the professional men whose livelihood has always depended on their own personal skill, in opposition to the petty shopkeepers and employers whose cramped horizon and short-sighted anxiety to keep down the rates at all costs are the main stumbling blocks in the way of municipal enterprise.

The tyranny of the petty tradesman is a serious evil in municipal life. The municipal constituency is small – only a ward; and the bigger and more important the city, the fewer votes will secure a seat, because of the difficulty of inducing busy or fashionable people to vote at all: in fact, it is easier to poll a village to the last man than to poll 50 per cent of the electors in a London ward. The squares and the slums have the same reason for not voting, because the city man, the laborer and the artisan are alike in respect of not working at their homes; so that when they return home tired in the evening they will not turn out again in the raw November darkness, and trudge through the mud to the polling station at the request of that enthusiastic pest the canvasser. The result is that the smaller shopkeepers elect one another, since they can vote at any moment of the day by leaving their shops for a few minutes. . . .

Still, there is something to be said for the petty tradesman. He is shrewd and effective enough when he is in his depth; and his local knowledge is indispensable. The policing and sanitation of a city consist largely of a running fight with petty nuisances and abuses to which the gossip of a street is a better guide than the most comprehensive municipal statesmanship. When the absurdity of the present municipal areas forces us to reconstruct our whole scheme of local government, there will still be a place for local committees to deal with the small change of municipal life; and on these local committees the petty shopkeeper will be as useful as he is noxious on bodies whose scope far transcends his homely little outlook.

6.3 From Douglas Knoop, *Principles and Methods of Municipal Trading* (London 1912), chap. IX, 'Summary and Conclusion', pp. 379-86.
One of the few academic works on the general subject of municipal trading. This is probably the 'classic' work on the subject.

8. The unsatisfactory character of municipal trading finance in many towns is one very serious drawback to local authorities engaging in trading enterprises, in this country at least. Another drawback of municipal trading is that it involves the employment by local authorities of large bodies of labour. It is perfectly right that municipalities should be good employers, and that they should give their workpeople adequate wages and fair conditions with regard to hours, holidays, etc., in accordance with the generally accepted standards in the various districts. In skilled occupations, where trade union rates of pay and hours of labour are adopted by private employers, a municipality can employ its labour on the same terms and probably no difficulties will arise. Unfortunately, most workpeople in the employ of municipalities are of the unskilled or semi-skilled type, in connection with whom a recognised standard of wages or of hours of labour seldom exists. As a consequence, unduly favourable terms may be granted to these workpeople at the expense of the general body of ratepayers, and in this way a small privileged class of wage-earners may be created. This may be brought about by the direct agitation of the municipal workpeople or by the advocacy of their claims on the town councils by particular members, who make themselves the spokesmen of the workpeople. A municipality is really a co-operative society, of which all ratepayers are members, yet the councillors sometimes

forget their duties to the ratepayers, and seek to exploit that body in the interests of particular people. . . .

On general principles, the employment of a large body of unskilled labour by a local authority cannot be approved of; in the first place, it fosters a somewhat loose standard of honesty according to which people are prepared to spend ratepayers' money freely, if not extravagantly, in a way in which they would never do if it were their own, instead of acting in the true interests of the present and future ratepayers, for whom they are practically trustees. In the second place, the growth in the number of municipal employees increases the danger of corruption; the temptation to councillors to act in a manner which will please those ratepayers who are municipal employees, instead of in the best interests of the ratepayers in general, becomes greater. In the third place, the existence of a highly favoured and privileged class of municipal employees affords most undesirable opportunities for nepotism and jobbery; wherever a local authority engages its workpeople on the recommendation of the councillors, as is not uncommonly the case, the multiplication of jobs under a council offers dangerous facilities for abuse.

There are other drawbacks to municipal trading in addition to its financial and labour aspects. With the continual increase in the duties imposed upon, or voluntarily undertaken by, the councils of local authorites, there is a serious danger of these bodies being overworked. The list of committees and sub-committees in connection with commercial administrations grows, and council meetings last longer, and have to be held more frequently to deal with the additional business involved by the new functions. One effect of this will tend to be that many able, experienced men, whose knowledge of finance and business organisation render them most suitable to share in the local administration, will find themselves unable to spare the requisite time. Another effect may be that town councils will devote insufficient attention to carrying out some of their functions. A further drawback to municipal trading, which is one that applies to all government trading, is that less initiative and enterprise is likely to be shown by the management than would be the case if the undertakings were managed privately.

9. Taking all the attendant circumstances and conditions into consideration, municipal trading in itself cannot be regarded as a desirable institution; the management of industrial undertakings is not really a suitable sphere of activity for a local authority.

Nevertheless, in certain cases it may offer a reasonable prospect of serving the general public better than private enterprise, and in consequence the municipalisation of particular industries may be justified. These industries are such as have a strong tendency to become local monopolies, which is generally true of tramways and of water, gas, and electricity supply undertakings. As water is an absolute necessary of life, and tramways and gas are used very largely by the general public, a private monopolist could not be left absolutely free to charge what he liked, and to provide such service as he chose. It would hardly be fair, in view of the local monopoly it possesses, to leave an electricity company entirely unrestricted in the matter of the treatment it may give to its actual customers and would-be customers, even though electric current does not partake of the character of a necessity from the point of view of the majority of ratepayers. The need arises to control the private monopolists in some way; the fact that they require the use of the streets for the purpose of conducting their businesses, which is often put forward as a reason for municipalising these undertakings, compels them to seek authorisation from the central or local authorities. This affords an opportunity for imposing restrictions upon the monopolists, but unfortunately experience shows that it is practically impossible to draft a lease or franchise embodying the various conditions, in which, sooner or later, one or more serious defects may not prove to exist. The difficulty of exercising satisfactory control over many monopolistic tramway, water, gas, and electricity undertakings affords the principal justification for their municipalisation. There can be no general rule on the subject, each individual case must be considered on its own merits. If there is a reasonable prospect that a local authority, whilst conducting the undertaking on a self-supporting basis, will be able to provide a better service on more favourable terms than a company, which is already in existence or which is about to be formed, a municipality will probably be justified in managing a tramway, water, gas, or electricity undertaking. In the case of water, and to some extent in the case of tramways* and gas, considerations of the public health and general welfare strengthen the movement in favour of municipalisation. . . .

That the management of municipal trading undertakings lacks

* I do not refer to the granting of assistance to certain classes by means of preferential treatment, to which, as will have been noted previously, I am opposed, but to the arrangement of the fares in such a way as to combat as far as possible the tendency to congestion in the centre of larger towns.

enterprise and initiative is due, of course, to the fact that those who are responsible for the conduct of the management have no direct financial interest in the success of the undertaking; such a direct financial interest is not merely an incentive to people to do their utmost to develop a business, but acts involuntarily as a break upon any inclination towards recklessness and extravagance; it both encourages and restrains men in their business transactions, and enables them to conduct undertakings so that their efforts neither run in grooves nor savour of speculation and rashness. The directors and officials of companies frequently have not enough at stake to call for the best that is in them, however hard they may try, and in the case of a municipal undertaking the committee and manager have practically nothing at stake at all. Under the circumstances, the only course which seems to offer a reasonable chance of introducing a progressive spirit into the management of such undertakings is to pay good salaries to the high officials, so that men of first-rate ability may be attracted into the service. There are undoubtedly many able men in the service of British municipalities at the present time, but the salaries paid to the managers of trading undertakings, by the smaller local authorities in any case, are often absurdly inadequate in view of the responsibility of the positions, if good men are to be attracted and kept. It is a great mistake to think that because an undertaking is not large it is easy to manage; to make a tramway or electricity undertaking self-supporting in a small town calls for very considerable ability in the manager, and it would often pay local authorities to offer better salaries than they do at present.

6.4 From *Local Government Financial Statistics* (1967-8), England and Wales, pp. 8-9.

This Table shows a summary of the transactions of trading undertakings of local authorities in England and Wales. It is interesting to compare the amount of surplus transferred in aid of rates (Col. 5) with the amount transferred from rates to make good deficiencies (Col. 9).

. . . TRADING SERVICES AND CORPORATION ESTATES £000's

| Service (1) | Expenditure | | | | | Revenue Account — Income | | | | |
| | Working expenses (including transfers to special funds and to capital accounts) (2) | Loan charges | | Transfers in aid of rates (5) | Totals (6) | General (7) | Government grants (8) | Receipts towards deficiencies | | Totals (11) |
		Debt redemption and Sinking Fund provision (3)	Interest (4)					Rate fund accounts (9)	Reserve funds (10)	
1 Water supply	69,900	12,595	27,902	169	110,566	101,102	1,586	(a) 7,684	696	111,068
2 Passenger transport	95,627	2,293	1,196	145	99,261	96,829	59	1,399	412	98,699
3 Cemeteries, crematoria	11,919	392	536	24	12,871	5,662	3	(b) 7,153	54	12,872
4 Harbours, docks and piers (e)	49,013	1,877	7,542	272	58,704	54,784	18	207	3,793	58,892
5 Civic restaurants	1,872	14	13	49	1,948	1,908	—	27	24	1,959
6 Markets	6,844	506	993	1,964	10,307	10,189	2	215	63	10,469
7 Slaughterhouses	1 999	346	780	36	3,161	2,032	1	1,033	7	3,072
8 Civic aerodromes	4,860	839	1,076	266	7,041	5,159	1	1,840	—	7,000
9 Industrial estates	684	643	1,331	482	3,140	2,447	—	690	1	3,138
10 Miscellaneous	20,585	973	1,033	788	23,379	20,049	—	3,728	24	23,801
11 Totals for Trading Services	263,303	20,478	42,402	4,195	330,378	300,161	1,669	24,066	5,074	330,970
12 General corporation estates	5,401	1,290	3,363	2,593	12,647	10,539	32	2,053	18	12,642
13 Grand Totals	268,704 (c)	21,768	45,765	6,788	343,025	310,700 (c)	1,701	26,119	5,092	343,612

(a) Item 1—col. 9.—Includes £1,971,000 being County Council contributions to rural water supplies and £1,503,000 payments to River Authorities in respect of water resources functions.

(b) Item 3—col. 9.—Includes £40,000 being precepts levied by Burial Boards.

H

Capital Account — Loan debt at end of year

Service (1)	Loans (12)	Government grants (13)	Transfers from revenue (14)	Transfers from special funds (15)	Other sources (16)	Totals (17)	Expenditure (18)	Capital moneys assigned to repayment of debt (included in col. 18) (19)	Gross debt (20)	Held in sinking funds (21)	Net debt (i.e., col. 20 minus col. 21) (22)
1 Water Supply	42,395	421	3,602	355	2,077	48,850	55,032	5,092	515,243	15,517	499,726
2 Passenger transport	4,752	1	1,984	1,281	236	8,254	8,178	82	21,475	91	21,384
3 Cemeteries, crematoria	678	—	93	154	165	1,090	1,019	122	9,347	10	9,337
4 Harbours, docks and piers (e)	7,176	3,274	1,341	141	275	12,207	20,079	125	180,977	9,355	171,622
5 Civic restaurants	29	—	42	11	22	104	106	30	206	—	206
6 Markets	1,478	311	72	224	47	2,132	2,122	136	16,599	824	15,775
7 Slaughterhouses	692	—	75	8	5	780	1,020	1	13,264	3	13,261
8 Civic aerodromes	2,184	896	321	112	15	3,528	3,903	315	18,576	8	18,568
9 Industrial estates	3,381	129	147	206	1,748	5,611	7,616	759	23,801	32	23,769
10 Miscellaneous	1,791	2	1,078	406	230	3,507	3,584	36	19,354	—	19,354
11 Totals for Trading Services	64,556	5,034	8,755	2,868	4,820	86,063	102,659	6,698	818,842	25,840	793,002
12 General corporation estates	10,385	32	700	1,351	3,259	15,727	14,804	1,330	61,878	24	61,854
13 Grand Totals	74,941	5,066	9,455	4,249	8,079 (d)	101,790	117,463 (d)	8,028	880,720	25,864	854,856

(c) Item 13—cols. 2 and 7.—To avoid duplicate reckoning, sums transferred from one account to another of the same local authority (£5,884,000) and sums received by one local authority from another (£19,263,000) for work done, etc., are omitted from both sides of the revenue account.

Item 13—cols. 16 and 18.—To avoid duplicate reckoning, sums received by one local authority from another (£5,709,000) for work done, etc., are omitted from both sides of the capital account.

(d) Item 4—From 1966 a number of dock and harbour authorities have been adopting the recommendation of the National Ports Council that their accounts be kept on a calendar year basis; consequently entries against this item do not reflect a full year's transactions.

7 *Staff and Organisation*

7.1 From J. Redlich and F. W. Hurst, *Local Government in England* (London 1903), Vol. I, pp. 307, 309, 312-13, 337-40 and 347-52.
These extracts give a good account of the emergence of the body of paid officials, the peculiarities of the post of Town Clerk, and the growth of a large mass of committees.

We now pass to the English solution of the problem. An English Town Council is, as we have seen, a deliberative body, too large and unwieldy for the work of administration. Therefore let it be divided in order that it may govern. Let each of the different branches of administration be presided over by a special body, a section of the Town Council. This is what has actually been done. The Town Council forms itself into Standing Committees, groups of Councillors to manage permanent branches of administration, and into Special Committees for special purposes or temporary undertakings. Until the passing of the Education Act 1902, only one of these Committees, 'the Watch Committee', was 'statutory' – constituted, that is to say, by Act of Parliament and obligatory in all boroughs.* The duties of the Watch Committee in connection with the borough police are also fixed by statute, and it is provided that its members shall not exceed in number one-third of the Council. Otherwise Committees are in no sense obligatory. The Legislature merely enables the Council to appoint them without imposing any restriction as to their purposes or

* M.C.A. 1882, sec. 190. 'The Council shall from time to time appoint, for such time as they think fit, a sufficient number not exceeding one-third of their own body, who with the Mayor shall be the Watch Committee.' Cf., however, the Local Government Act 1888, sec. 39, for the transference of the Watch Committee's powers to the County Council in the case of boroughs of less than 10,000 inhabitants. Cf. also M.C.A., sec. 215, which provides that no charter of incorporation shall grant a separate police force to a town of less than 20,000 inhabitants. For the Education Committee see vol. ii., index.

numbers. In the words of the statute, 'the Council may from time to time appoint out of their own number such and so many Committees, either of a general or special nature, and consisting of such number of persons as they think fit, for any purposes which, in the opinion of the Council, would be better regulated and managed by means of such Committees; but the acts of every such Committee shall be submitted to the Council for their approval.'*

A Town Council appoints its Standing Committees for the year at its opening sitting in the month of November.

The number of Committees depends upon the extent to which administration is differentiated, and also upon the number of local and adoptive statutes under which the town is governed. A Standing Committee is appointed as a rule for each separate branch of municipal work imposed by the Public Health Acts, and other general or local statutes. Thus every borough of any size has building, sanitary, water works, markets, gas, and lighting, property and lands, highways, sewerage, finance and Parliamentary Committees. Of course a multitude of variations are possible in the large towns. Branches of business, like the management of highways or sanitation, or of corporate property, can be divided among two or more Committees. Besides all these, there is in most cases a General Purposes Committee, which arranges business for the montly meeting, initiates or discusses new schemes and enterprises, and generally undertakes any work that does not naturally belong to any of the other Standing Committees.†

But the formation of standing and special committees leaves the organisation of municipal government still imperfect. The idea at the root of the committee system followed out to its logical consequences produces a further subdivision of large committees, both standing and special, into sub-committees. In many of the larger towns the Town Council have gone so far as to institute standing sub-committees, which are regularly appointed at the beginning of each municipal year by the newly constituted committees in accordance with the standing orders, just as the committees are themselves appointed by the newly constituted Council. . . .

The number of committees cannot be said to be even roughly proportioned to the size of a town. Thus in the case of Nottingham

---

* M.C.A. 1882, sec. 22 (2). A Committee cannot delegate its power (*delegatus non potest delegare*). Cf. Cook *v.* Ward (affirmed on appeal), 2 C.P.D. 255.

† Sometimes questions of this kind are referred to the Parliamentary Committee, more often to Special Committees.

with eighteen standing committees, Leeds with fifteen, and Liverpool with eleven, you have committees descending, and populations ascending in numbers. . . .

But in order to understand properly the position of a municipal staff that of its *de facto* chief, the Town Clerk, must be grasped.* The Town Clerk is, as before observed, one of the two officials whom a Town Council is obliged by law to appoint.† It is desirable if not absolutely necessary for a Town Clerk to have had a legal training; and he is generally a qualified solicitor, sometimes a barrister. The municipal code seems to regard him primarily as the legal adviser of the Council, as well as the chief of the staff and keeper of the archives. Any important business with government departments or other authorities goes through his hands. He has also to manage, under the directions of the Parliamentary Committee, the conduct of such local Bills and Provisional Orders as may be required. He has, moreover, to look after not only all the legislation, but also all the litigation of the borough. Under his direction briefs are prepared, and counsel employed, in all cases and prosecutions to which the borough is a party. Another important series of functions is assigned to the Town Clerk in connection with the election and constitution of the Council; he has to revise and sign the burgess-roll, and to see that all the statutory notices are duly published, including the summons to meetings of the Council and of committees. Many other similar duties are imposed upon him by standing orders in the different towns.

In other respects also the Town Clerk is evidently esteemed the chief official of the staff; he is as a rule the best paid official – his salary rising in large towns to upwards of £2,000; in small towns, where his duties are light, his pay is comparatively small, and he is often allowed to increase it (if he is a solicitor) by private practice, which, however, must not be of a kind to conflict with the duties of his office. The office of Town Clerk offers a good social position, although social considerations do not usually enter into his appointment. His tenure is during the pleasure of the Council, which means that he may at any time be asked to quit his post after three months' notice; but, except in very rare cases, his tenure is

* Cf. for the Town Clerk's legal position and statutory functions, the M.C.A. 1882, secs. 17, 20, 21, 28, 43, 45, 48, 49, 54, 60, 66, 75, 88, 99.

† Before the reform of 1835 the office of Town Clerk was in many boroughs a freehold office, tenable for life, with rich perquisites attached. The appointment of a Town Clerk was made obligatory by an amendment introduced into the Bill, and passed by way of concession to the Tory opposition.

practically for life, or at any rate for so long as he is equal to the performance of his duties. Consequently the Town Clerk may be regarded as the most stable and permanent element in English municipal government; for after holding a central position for many years, he is, as it were, the living embodiment of the local traditions of government, and his opinions are naturally regarded by his Council with the greatest respect. He attends all sittings of the Council, and has also the right of audience, though it is not customary for him to speak unless called upon by the Mayor. In the smaller towns he also attends committee meetings with great regularity; in the larger, except in the case of some specially important business, this duty is usually undertaken by the Deputy Town-Clerk, or one of his assistants, of whom there are sometimes as many as five.

All the strings of administration are gathered in the Town Clerk's hands; in his own office he is of course the official chief, although as regards its organisation and the payment of his clerks he is subordinated to the Finance Committee. His influence as the chief of the executive over the general work of the committees depends, of course, very much upon personal considerations; but it is always great. . . . It is his principal duty to keep a close watch and a firm grip on every branch of the administration. He it is who knows best what will be the general effect of any given action of a committee; and, therefore, it is customary for a chairman of a committee to keep in touch with the Town Clerk to avoid friction with other parts of the machinery. The Town Clerk, therefore, is necessarily the confidant of all the committees, and more especially of those to which the more important officials are attached. He helps to define the functions and duties of the permanent officials, and to arrange any difficulties which may arise between them. He is consulted, and often exercises a decisive influence, with regard to appointments, dismissals, and the pensioning of members of the official staff. The regular organ of communication between the different departments, the representative of the whole body of officials before the Council, he brings to a head the hierarchy of officials, and provides the Council with all the information and expert advice which they require. In short, he serves as a link between the Council, the committees, and the official staff. It is a difficult position, which requires much tact, circumspection, loyalty, and business ability.

The position of the official chiefs of particular departments is quite independent of that of the Town Clerk, in so far that they are not in any way subordinated to him by the rules of the service. On the contrary, every permanent head of a department is subordinated only to his committee, and through it to the Council. It is the central position of the Town Clerk, his influence with the committees, his comprehensive knowledge and experience, not any definite or legal superiority, which makes him the head official of the town. He is the adviser-in-chief; and that is the function above all others which makes him a person of such importance in the municipal life of England. . . .

Our picture of the municipal civil service will be completed by some remarks on the method of appointing and paying the officers and servants of a municipality. It will be seen how here too the three organs of administration – Council, Committee, and permanent officials – work together in practice. In this matter it is necessary to look at concrete instances and individual towns, because the municipal code is absolutely silent, the appointment of all officials and organisation of all branches of the service having been, as we have seen, left entirely to the discretion of the Borough Council. But as the needs and the conditions of life in all English towns are remarkably similar and the laws to be administrated – private Bill legislation excepted – are the same, there is comparatively little variety in the organisation of the municipal service. The salaries of the officials naturally rise or fall with the size of the town and the extent of their work. According to an estimate prepared by the Municipal Officers Association* in 1898 the average pay of a municipal official is somewhat more than £100 a year. The salaries of the chief officials are always high and generally rise steadily with length of service. The best Councils are always anxious to attract and keep good servants by good pay. Town clerks, borough surveyors, borough engineers, and first accountants receive in county boroughs of from 50,000 to 100,000 inhabitants, salaries ranging from £400 to £1,000, or even more. In the great cities they rise to double or almost treble the amount. . . .

The respect paid to the higher officials of a municipality and the confidence reposed in them by the committees, the Council, and the citizens at large, are due not to their official position but to their

* As the Town Councils have an association to look after and forward their common interests in Parliament and elsewhere, called 'The Association of Municipal Corporations of the United Kingdom,' so their officials have a 'Municipal Officers Association,' which meets yearly to watch over their interests and ventilate their grievances.

character, their ability, and the importance of their work. It follows that the relations between the Council, its committees, and their staff are untinged by bureaucracy, and are characterised by those mutual feelings of loyalty and courtesy which mark the whole of English public life. An official is rarely, if ever, made the object of party recrimination; and if politics often have something to do with his appointment, and also, though very rarely, with his resignation, the motive is not openly avowed. Loyalty to constantly shifting political chiefs is indeed a characteristic mark of the Civil Service in England. It is understood that the political chief shall get the credit or bear the blame of any action taken by his department, and that he shall defend his subordinates when they are attacked. The influence exercised by the permanent official upon his ministerial chief – who in the case of a municipality is the committee or the Council – is often great; but it always depends upon the confidence reposed in him by the representatives of the people, whether acting in full meeting or in one of the many ramifications thrust out by the parent stem; and it is really this representative body, responsible to the burgesses but owning no other superior, which alone governs and administers the affairs of the town.*

7.2 From *The Local Government Officer* (8 September 1907), pp. 11-12.
This is the first issue of a weekly magazine published by Messrs Hodgetts Ltd of Whitefriars Street, London, under arrangements made by H. E. Blain, Chairman of the first National Executive Council of the National Association of Local Government Officers. It was really the continuation of the firm's former advertising medium, *The Public Health Engineer*, but with the changed name and more extensive editorial matter it effectively became Nalgo's official journal. These extracts provide the best contemporary account of the founding of Nalgo.

On Saturday, 29th July, 1905, a Conference was held at the Inns of Court Hotel, London, of delegates from all the existing Local

* There is properly speaking no disciplinary law for the staff of municipal officials. The standing orders of a Council usually include a few provisions as to the duties of the various officers. An officer is also forbidden, as a rule, to travel to London on any Parliamentary or other legal business unless formally requested by a committee. He is also required to preserve silence with regard to proceedings at committee meetings not open to the public. If an official infringes rules such as these, the Committee or the Council is free to adopt such remedy as may appear suitable. An official may always appeal from a decision of the Committee to the Council (cf. *e.g.* Bournemouth Standing Orders, No. 148). All officials on the staff are given leave of absence for at least fourteen days in each year.

Associations, and the majority of the Professional Associations of Municipal and Local Government Officers in England and Wales, as a result of which a movement was inaugurated which it is probable will be fraught with permanent and far-reaching effects.

ITS HISTORY AND CONSTITUTION

The Conference was convened by the then existing Municipal Officers' Association to discuss the possibility of forming a National Organisation of Officials which would have for its objects the furtherance of the interests of Municipal Officers and the encouragement of the formation and working of district or local associations or guilds.

It may be mentioned here that a previous Conference having a similar aim had been held in London in March, 1904, convened by a joint circular issued by the Municipal Officers' Association and the Liverpool Municipal Officers' Guild, but the recommendations of this Conference, which was presided over by Mr Sidney Ashley, fell through owing to the then Executive Council of the Municipal Officers' Association being unable to agree with the financial proposal made by the Conference. . . .

BIRTH OF THE N.A.L.G.O.

The interest of individual members in different parts of the country was revived, and, when all the details had been carefully completed, the Municipal Officers' Association (the body which had been the cause of the abandonment of the recommendations of the first Conference) convened the 1905 Conference. At this Conference, which was presided over by Mr H. E. Blain, the business was carried through in perfect concord and harmony. Several important resolutions were carried, the chief result being the birth of the National Association of Local Government Officers. The following are the principal resolutions which were adopted:

(1) That this Conference is of opinion that an association of local government officers should be formed, of a national and thoroughly representative character.

(2) That a 'National Association of Local Government Officers' be and is hereby established.

(3) That the objects of the Association shall be to further the interests of Local Government Officers, and to encourage the formation and working of district or local associations or guilds.

(4) That the executive committee of each local association or guild shall be responsible for the work of its own district.

(5) That questions of superannuation, security of tenure, and all matters of national importance to all Local Government Officers shall be dealt with by the National Executive Council.

(6) That the National Executive Council shall, on first election, consist of one representative for each 250 members or portion of 250 members, each local association being entitled to at least one representative, and that the National Executive Council thus constituted shall consider and report on future representative and voting power.

(7) That the National Executive Council shall hold its meetings in different parts of the country as may be from time to time determined.

(8) That the delegates present pledge themselves to endeavour to secure the immediate affiliation to the National Association of Local Government Officers of their local associations or guilds.

The Municipal Officers Association having now successfully formed a National Organisation, a general meeting of its members was held at the Inns of Court Hotel on December 9th, 1905, when the Association was formally dissolved.

7.3 From the Royal Commission on Local Government 1923-9. *Final Report* (November 1929), Cmd. 3436, pp. 115, 118-19, 125, and 130-4, 137.

The Royal Commission gave considerable attention to the problems of staff and organisation, as these extracts show. It is worth noting that forty years later, many of these problems still remain.

369. The appointment of Committees for the discharge of particular functions is, of course, a common feature in local government. Except in cases where the establishment of Committees is required by statute – of which the Local Government Act, 1929, is a notable recent example – their appointment is entirely in the discretion of the Local Authority, and we make no recommendation on the point; but we think it well to refer to the fact that representatives both of Local Authorities and of Local Government Officers expressed the view that there is a tendency on the part of some

Local Authorities to appoint an unnecessary number of Committees. . . .

380. Any proposals as to local government officers, to be of practical value, must have due regard to the fundamental principles on which local government has developed in this country, the conditions under which Local Authorities act, and the possibility, politically and administratively, of modifying those conditions. Thus, for reasons which we shall particularise in the appropriate Sections, the analogy which has been drawn between local government officers and the national Civil Service, and the suggestion that the chief executive official might be an officer analogous to the Town Manager as found in some States of America, are found to break down when they are applied to the structure of English local government. In particular, it is to be observed that the autonomy of Local Authorities with regard to the appointment of their own officers is a jealously guarded privilege; and, within proper limits, this is a valuable element in local government. The recruitment and the conditions of service of these officers should, we think, primarily be the care of the Local Authorities, whose officers they are. On the other hand, to ensure that the service secures the best recruits, and that their appointment and tenure of office should not be prejudicially affected by any circumstances attending changes in the membership of the elected Authorities, we are of opinion that certain general principles should be observed by all Local Authorities. With these considerations in mind, we proceed to review in detail certain questions that have come under our notice. . . .

403. Mr Robson regarded the present situation as unsatisfactory. He suggested that 'hardly anything in the nature of a systematic effort has been made by Local Authorities, either singly or collectively, to secure a high general level of efficiency, administrative ability and trained mental capacity in their officers.' He considered that patronage was widespread, with resultant inefficiency in the service, and deplored the absence of a regular supply of candidates with a University education. In the recruitment of local government officers, there was neither an impartial tribunal nor a minimum standard of qualification. In oral evidence, Mr Robson stated that within his knowledge there were five or six Local Authorities where a large proportion of the staff were relatives or friends of the local Councillors. This was put forward as a random sample in support of the suggestion that widespread patronage

prevailed. He was opposed to the sytem of articled pupils, because it involved the making of private profit in initiating newcomers into the conduct of municipal affairs.

404. Mr Robson's proposals for remedying the present position started with the basic consideration that there were certain grades of officers common to all Local Authorities, though he agreed that in local government the staffs did not constitute a single service like the Civil Service. His proposals included (a) provision for the recruitment of University graduates, particularly in the case of the larger towns and the County Councils; and (b) a series of qualifying competitive examinations for the general grades of clerical and administrative officers to be conducted by local Personnel Commissions for regional areas. . . .

422. The National Association of Local Government Officers suggested that 'successful local government administration can be attained only by complete co-ordination of the various departmental activities', and that one of the problems requiring consideration was the 'position and future of the highly-qualified administrator, irrespective of professional qualifications'. Mr Hill explained that what the Association had in mind was that 'in the new future which probably lies before us in local government, with bigger areas we might find room for the qualified administrator of a type that you have in the Civil Service – an administrator as distinct from a lawyer or an engineer', or 'a sort of composite figure between the American Town Manager and the German Burgomaster'. Such a man would need to have a ready grasp of the financial position of the Authority, and be able to visualise the policy as a whole and dovetail the activities of all the departments. He need not necessarily be a lawyer, but a good knowledge of the law would be essential for him in his co-ordinating work. Mr Johnson, on the other hand, thought that the chief officer of a Local Authority must be a lawyer, in view of the increasing complexities of modern legislation.

423. The Society of Clerks of the Peace of Counties were of opinion that the Clerk of the County Council, whether or not the office was separated from that of Clerk of the Peace, should be a member of one of the branches of the legal profession. . . .

424. Mr Jarratt, on behalf of the Society of Town Clerks, expressed the view that it was almost essential for the Town Clerk of any Borough, whether large or small, to have legal qualifications. The Society were of opinion that it was necessary for one officer

of the Council to be recognised as the head of the administration responsible for co-ordinating the work of all the departments, and that the Town Clerk was 'in a peculiarly favourable position to act as the link, the consultant and the co-ordinator in respect of all' Committees, Chairmen and departmental officers. No officer corresponding to the general manager of a commercial undertaking or to a Burgomaster in Germany or a Town Manager in America would, it was suggested, fit in with the traditions of English local government or be acceptable to English municipalities. . . .

433. The Association of Municipal Corporations were definitely of opinion that any appointment similar to that of a managing director of a large business or a Town Manager would be most undesirable and subversive of the democratic system of local government in this country. They were, however, of opinion that where greater co-ordination between officers is desirable, or indeed required, this should be sought through the Town Clerk, who was already universally recognised as the chief officer of the Corporation. Further, they held the view that a legal training was of distinct advantage to a Town Clerk.

434. Mr Simon said that, as a result of correspondence and discussions, he had found a good deal of agreement with the view that a legal training was not necessarily the best for the position of head official of a Municipality. He suggested that a man trained in the office of head administrator would, even though he had no legal training, necessarily acquire a general knowledge of the law governing municipal administration, and that this should be quite sufficient for his purpose. Mr Simon therefore favoured the appointment of a head official, who might or might not have legal qualifications, but whose duty would be to co-ordinate the work of all the departments of the Council, somewhat on the lines of a City Manager in America or a Burgomaster in Germany. Further, Mr Simon suggested that for certain other departments, e.g., public health and education, there was a great deal to be said for having a layman as the head administrative officer. . . .

441. We may sum up our conclusion by saying that in our opinion the Clerk to the Council must be the principal officer of a Local Authority and responsible for securing co-ordination between the several departments.

442. The success of the Clerk in discharging this function will obviously depend largely on his personality and the relations which he establishes with the other chief officers of the Council. But there

has been considerable discussion on the question whether the Clerk should necessarily have legal qualifications. In the majority of cases Local Authorities select their Clerks from persons so qualified. Many Authorities of moderate size find it necessary to combine the duties of Clerk and legal adviser; and we think that, generally speaking, the balance of convenience points to the selection of a Clerk with legal qualifications. We have come to this conclusion with two reservations. In the first place, we are aware that many Authorities are efficiently served by lay Clerks. Secondly, very large Authorities are able to provide for a qualified legal adviser on their staff other than the Clerk, and therefore need not require that the Clerk should have legal qualifications. In these cases it would, in our view, be regrettable if such a requirement were maintained to the exclusion of candidates who might bring into the service of an Authority administrative abilities of a high order.

7.4 From the *Report by the Departmental Committee on the Qualifications, Recruitment, Training and Promotion of Local Government Officers* (Ministry of Health 1935), pp. 31-3, 37-41 and 48-9.

The Hadow Committee was the great hope of the local government officers in the 1930s, from whose deliberations they anticipated the emergence of a fully-trained service. Their expectations came to nought, however, as the local authorities refused to accept the chief recommendation, that for the appointment of a permanent advisory body.

101. *Proposals.* – We recommend that when selecting their clerks, local authorities should direct their attention primarily to the administrative ability and experience of candidates. Nor is this enough in itself. Authorities must take steps to secure that junior officers have an opportunity of developing the necessary ability. We suggest three methods by which this may be done:

(i) Recruitment should be on a wider basis than at present.

(ii) Local authorities should arrange that promising young officers have practical training in administration and, as far as possible, variety of experience.

(iii) Officers should be encouraged to study the principles of public administration. Already some authorities are assisting selected officers to obtain university degrees or diplomas in public administration and kindred subjects, and we hope that this practice will develop.

(ii) Other Principal Officers

102. *Administrative ability.* – The functions of other principal officers vary, of course, according to their departments; and the functions of corresponding officers vary under different authorities. It is a fair generalisation, however, that in the largest authorities the functions of any chief officer of one of the major departments are mainly administrative. Here again, therefore, it is important to secure that these officers should possess administrative ability, and should have had administrative experience before appointment to the principal positions. The technical qualification is of secondary importance (we are speaking of authorities where assistant technical staff is invariably employed); and it is arguable that here too the larger authorities would be well advised not always to insist on a technical qualification. . . .

The Use of Examinations in Training

(i) An Examination Bar

116. *Existing system.* – At the present time the only officers who receive any definite training are, as a rule, those who study for one of the technical examinations. A few local authorities have attempted to provide for the training of their clerical officers on similar lines by encouraging them to take examinations in the non-technical aspects of local government, but this is exceptional.

117. One or two local authorities are, however, making a systematic use of examinations in the training of officers. As already stated the London County Council divide their clerical staff into a general grade, recruited between sixteen and eighteen years of age, and a major establishment, recruited partly from outside between eighteen and twenty-one years of age, and partly from the general grade; and promotion from the general grade to the major establishment is by competitive examination, after five years' service, in general knowledge, an essay and the history of local government. No doubt the primary object of this examination is to solve the problem of promotion, but the study for the examination possesses training value. In some other authorities promotion beyond a certain point is, in one or two departments, dependent on the passing of an approved examination – particularly in finance departments.

It is for consideration whether local authorities might not as a general rule require junior officers to pass some qualifying examination before they are considered eligible for promotion to positions carrying administrative responsibility. . . .

(ii) Nature of the Examinations

122. Two kinds of qualifying examination for promotion from the general grade are required, technical and administrative; technical for juniors proposing ultimately to become fully qualified professional or technical officers, and administrative for the remainder.

A. Technical Examinations

123. Recognised technical examinations already exist. These as a rule involve a preliminary non-technical examination for which a general examination (either the school certificate or matriculation) is accepted, and either one or two technical parts. Where there is only one later part (as e.g. in the sanitary inspectors examination) that part would ordinarily be the examination appropriate to officers on the general grade; where there are two parts (as e.g. in accountancy and engineering examinations) the first part would be the appropriate examination.

124. Our proposal as far as technical examinations are concerned is that local authorities should utilise more systematically the existing examinations. The full technical qualification is ordinarily required as a condition of promotion to certain of the higher posts, but we would suggest that in proper cases – that is where the officer definitely proposes to become a professional or technical officer – the passing of the first part of the appropriate technical examination should be a condition of promotion from the general grade.

We shall deal with the details of technical examinations, and with the extent to which certain qualifications should be insisted on, in Part VII.

B. Administrative Examinations

125. The chief function of the non-technical examination for officers on the general grade should be to provide a broad and appropriate mental training. It should not be directed to knowledge of departmental work. At the same time, the subjects included in the examination should be related to administration. The study of government, properly undertaken, affords an excellent mental training, and it is clearly desirable that officers should acquire some knowledge of the background of administration.

126. *Existing facilities.* – There are at present no widely recognised examinations on these lines. Examinations do, however, exist:

Diploma of Public Administration

The Universities of London, Manchester, Leeds, Liverpool, Sheffield and Glasgow all give courses in public administration, which are being attended by some of the local government officers within reach. A few local authorities are encouraging their officers to attend the courses by contributing towards the fees, or by allowing time off. . . .

Examinations of the National Association of Local Government Officers

The Association hold examinations expressly designed for local government clerical officers, and several local authorities make a grant to officers passing them. The Association also provide tuition by correspondence. . . .

127. We do not think that either of these examinations is well suited to be made a condition of promotion from the general grade.

The diploma of public administration is of too high a standard for universal application. We should like to see many more local government officers studying for the diplomas – or, where practicable, the degrees – as they seem to us to afford a useful background for public servants. Representatives both of the authorities and of the officers have suggested to us that the universities should be asked to extend the facilities available to non-resident students, and we agree that, if this could be done, it would be valuable to the service. But whether the facilities are extended or not, it would not be reasonable to expect junior officers to take an examination of this standard as a matter of course.

The examinations of the National Association are, we think, too much occupied with day to day office practice to serve the purpose which we have in mind. They are designed more to test clerical efficiency, than to indicate fitness for promotion to responsible administrative positions. The Association have done much to improve the standard of clerical officers throughout the service. They have encouraged them to study and to think for themselves; they have assisted them with scholarships, they have provided lectures and classes; they hold annually an instructive summer school; they have interested officers in the wider problems of local government. But they are not an appropriate examining body for our purpose. And they have themselves asked that their examinations should be taken over by a Board composed of representatives of the local authorities and of their association, in order that the qualifications of clerical officers may command wider recognition.

129. *Proposals.* – It appears that an examination has to be devised. We should like to see for the general clerical grade an examination on the lines of the diplomas of public administration, but of a less advanced standard; a standard more suited to candidates whose school education ended with the school certificate, and who will be mainly, if not entirely, dependent on evening reading. We do not propose to make detailed suggestions for this examination ourselves, as these, we think, must be worked out in discussion between the representatives of local authorities through the suggested central committee. We should, however, make it clear that we contemplate only one stage in this examination. Officers wishing to take a more advanced course should study for one of the existing diplomas or degrees. . . .

. . . A Central Advisory Committee

151. *Need for a committee.* – We have made several recommendations for the future development of the local government service, and we hope that every local authority will proceed at once to experiment, so far as they have not already done so, along the lines we have suggested. A number of our recommendations, however, require the appointment of a permanent advisory body, representative of local authorities, before they can become fully effective, a body able to devote continuous consideration to the recruitment, qualifications, training and promotion of local government officers, and to investigate in greater detail some of the problems which have been before us.

152. Thus, we have recommended that entry to the service should be by competitive examinations, and that neighbouring local authorities should combine for the purpose of holding these examinations. There is no reason why groups of local authorities should not at once begin to carry this recommendation into effect by means of local conferences; but the movement towards regional combination would be much accelerated by practical suggestions for grouping, and a central representative body would render valuable service in this respect. Further, it is desirable that the various regional examinations should be of broadly similar standard, and that local authorities should have the advice of educational bodies in devising them; and a central body, in a position to review what local groups are doing and to co-ordinate discussions with educational bodies, would be of great assistance.

153. A second recommendation which would be made more effective by the existence of a central advisory committee is our proposal that university graduates should be encouraged to enter the service more freely than they do at present. We suggested, when making the recommendation, that in order to attract the best graduates available, local authorities should pool information as to openings for this class of entrant, and should establish a definite method of selecting officers from among the candidates who present themselves; and this can best be done through some central body.

154. Another reason for urging the setting up of an advisory committee is that methods of training may be further investigated. We have recommended that local authorities should set an examination bar between the general grade of clerical officers and higher grades; and an administrative examination of appropriate standard has to be devised for this purpose. We are, too, concerned with more than the immediate future. The results of an examination bar will require to be carefully noted, and adjustments made as they become desirable. And other experiments are being made in the training of public servants, both in this and foreign countries, which should be watched on behalf of local authorities.

7.5 From *The Times* (9 September 1942).

This is *The Times* Law Report of the decision by the House of Lords in the famous 'Bolton' case. This decision is one of the great landmarks in the development of industrial relations machinery for the local government service.

WAGES AND NATIONAL SERVICE: LOCAL AUTHORITY'S OFFICERS
National Association of Local Government Officers v. Bolton Corporation
Before the Lord Chancellor, Lord Atkin, Lord Thankerton, Lord Wright, and Lord Porter.
The House allowed this appeal by the National Association of Local Government Officers (a trade union) from a decision of the Court of Appeal (Lord Justice MacKinnon, Lord Justice du Parcq, and Mr Justice Bennett), which had allowed the appeal of Bolton Corporation from a decision of the Divisional Court (the Lord Chief Justice and Mr Justice Tucker, Mr Justice Atkinson dissenting), refusing the application of the corporation for an order of prohibition directed to the National Arbitration Tribunal

to prohibit the tribunal from adjudicating on a dispute which, in February, 1941, had been referred to it as a 'trade dispute' under article 2 (3) of the Conditions of Employment and National Arbitration Order, 1940, by the Minister of Labour.

The case arose out of, and was limited to, a claim made by the National Association of Local Government Officers on behalf of officers of the Bolton Corporation who were still in the employment of the corporation. The claim was that it should be made a condition of their contracts of service with the corporation that their pay should be made up if they undertook war service. The question for decision was whether or not the claim arose out of a trade dispute within the meaning of the Order of 1940 under which the tribunal derived its jurisdiction. . . .

The Lord Chancellor, in giving judgment, said that the National Arbitration Tribunal was constituted by the Minister of Labour and National Service 'for the purpose of settling trade disputes which cannot otherwise be determined'. The Order of 1940 was made under Defence Regulation 58 AA, which conferred power on the Minister of Labour and National Service to make such an Order 'with a view to preventing work being interrupted by trade disputes'. In the regulation the expression 'trade dispute' had the same meaning as in the Industrial Courts Act, 1919. By section 8 of that Act 'trade dispute' meant:

> any dispute or difference between employers and workmen, or between workmen and workmen, connected with the employment or non-employment, or the terms of the employment or with the conditions of labour of any person.

and the expression 'workman'

> means any person who has entered into or works under a contract with an employer, whether the contract be by way of manual labour, clerical work, or otherwise. . . .

While the definition of 'trade dispute' above quoted was practically the same as in the Trade Disputes Act, 1906, the definition 'workman' was entirely different and much wider than that in the Act of 1906, and the effect was to enlarge correspondingly the conception of 'trade dispute' itself.

His Lordship referred to the terms of the reference and continued: – the respondent corporation contended that that reference was *ultra vires* the Minister to make and was in excess of the jurisdiction of the tribunal to entertain.

First, it was argued that a dispute as to conditions of service of officers of a municipal corporation was not a 'trade dispute' at all.

Secondly, it was contended that, even if it was, a dispute as to payments to be made by the corporation to its officers after they had ceased to serve the corporation, in order to undertake war service, was not a dispute connected with the terms of their employment within the definition of 'trade dispute'.

Thirdly, it was argued that the corporation had no power to determine generally in advance whether it would make up the pay of such of its officers as might undertake war service, but must exercise its statutory discretion to decide this, under section 1 of the Local Government Staffs (War Service) Act, 1939, by considering the individual case when the individual officer ceased to serve the corporation in order to undertake war service.

Having regard to the definition of 'trade dispute' for present purposes, and to the wide definition of 'workman' which had to be read into it to ascertain its ambit, he (his Lordship) thought that the phrase could cover a dispute as to conditions of service of officers of a municipal corporation. Mr Turner strenuously argued that such an interpretation gave no effect to the limiting word 'trade'. The answer was that the definition of 'trade dispute' introduced no such limitation. It was further urged on that point that administrative, professional, and technical officials of the corporation were not 'workmen'. In the ordinary sense they were not, but here again the definition provided the answer. They were, in his opinion, persons who had entered into contracts with the corporation 'whether the contract be by way of manual labour, clerical work, or otherwise'. The definition contained no limit of earnings. The use of the words 'or otherwise' did not bring into play the *ejusdem generis* principle, for 'manual labour' and 'clerical work' did not belong to a single limited *genus*. The only common class to which manual labour and clerical work could be said to belong was the broad class of 'mode of service'. As the derivation of 'otherwise' showed, 'or otherwise' meant 'or in another way'. In his opinion, the first point relied on by the respondents failed.

The second point turned on the language and application of section 1 of the Local Government Staffs (War Service) Act, 1939. [That Act provided that, where an employee of a local authority had ceased to serve it in order to undertake war service, the authority had power, while such a person was so engaged, to pay him a sum which should not exceed the remuneration which he would have received if he had continued to serve in his civil capacity, after deduction of his war service pay.] His Lordship read the first three subsections of section 1, and continued:

Before the Act of 1939 came into force it would have been *ultra vires* the corporation to make payments (apart from pensions or superannuation) to its former officers who had ceased to serve it. The effect of section 1 of the Act of 1939 was to confer on an authority such as the respondent corporation a power to make to its ex-officers while engaged in war service the sort of payments described, and therefore put the juristic entity in this respect in the same position as a natural person. While the corporation could not make such payments except during an ex-officer's war service, it could agree beforehand with an officer that, if he ceased to serve in his civil capacity and undertook war service, it would make such payments, and this thereupon became a contractual term of his employment by the corporation. It was a fallacy to regard the payments authorised by the Act as mere gratuities which could in no circumstances be the subject of contract. The second argument of the respondent corporation also failed.

Lastly, he saw nothing irregular or in excess of the powers of the corporation if it bound itself or was required by the award of the tribunal to bind itself in advance to make the payments.

The other noble and learned Lords delivered judgments agreeing that the appeal should be allowed.

7.6 From T. E. Headrick, *The Town Clerk in English Local Government* (London 1962), pp. 29–30.

The office of town clerk gets a mention in the Bible, but this is the first study of the English Town Clerk. This extract sums up the development of the office.

There are several things which seem to stand out in this very brief look at six to seven centuries of Town Clerks. First of all, the Town Clerk has had a long and close connection with the law. In the early corporations, he was often Steward or Deputy Steward of the Borough Court. A little later he might have been Deputy Recorder, Corporation Solicitor or a Justice of the Peace. Before 1835 it was, and most certainly since then it has been, a fairly general practice to appoint solicitors as Town Clerks. Secondly the Town Clerk, as the name implies, has been a record-keeper, the secretary for the corporation, the recorder of its proceedings. And he has frequently carried his duty beyond its normal bounds and compiled records, preserved documents and written histories. Finally, the Town Clerk has been a type of community leader. He has been the spokesman for his council and his town when disputes have arisen between it and another town, or when it has been necessary to smooth something out with the central government. These three functions – lawyer, secretary, spokesman – are the legacy of the past, and even today they form the fundamental bases for the office of Town Clerk.

But there is more. There have been shifts, or perhaps better, adjustments, in the last century and half century, and even in the last ten years, which have had a profound effect on the office of Town Clerk. The nineteenth century saw a Town Clerk performing his three fundamental functions. But apart from these, there were growing up other functions in local government, public health, municipal engineering; and to carry out each of these there was a tendency to establish a separate organisation, centred around its committee and its department. As functions were added, a new committee and a new department were founded. This may have been adequate to meet the needs of the nineteenth century, but it became apparent to writers early in this century that unless some alteration was effected, many pressing problems in the local government sphere would go unattended.

The call was, therefore, for co-ordination of administration, for someone to be at the centre of things. The Royal Commission on Local Government in 1929 said the Town Clerk should be the co-ordinator. The Hadow Committee in 1934 said the Town Clerk should be co-ordinator, and being such, his qualifications should be primarily those of an administrator, not a lawyer. The Coventry Report in 1953 said the Town Clerk should be styled 'Town Clerk/ Chief Administrative Officer' and should be responsible for the establishment, for the organisation and methods study, for the inter-departmental co-ordination, and for the maintenance of a broad view of the policy-implementation mechanism.

At the same time Parliament has placed additional duties upon the Town Clerk. He is to keep registers of a variety of things for local and national purposes and convenience. In the main, he is entrusted with the organisation and conduct of elections, both local and parliamentary. He is obviously an official who can be entrusted with weighty responsibilities.

At this juncture in history, the office of Town Clerk is an

admixture; for in the office, the traditional functions, the special statutory duties, the response to the need for co-ordination in modern local government are merged. . . .

7.7 From the *Report of the (Mallaby) Committee on the Staffing of Local Government* (Ministry of Housing and Local Government 1967), pp. 76-7, 130-5 and 156-7.

These extracts from the Mallaby Committee's Report give its views on three important questions relating to local government officers: the scope for the general administrative officer, the idea of unifying local government employment into a single service, and the position of the clerk of a local authority.

234. There is at present a reaction against the long tradition in this country that positions of authority are generally occupied by persons with a liberal education but with no professional qualifications. The tradition has long persisted in the civil service but it has not applied in local government. We do not support the creation of a managerial class in the service of local authorities to be filled 'by persons of good education and lively minds who are not necessarily qualified in the law, or, for that matter, in any of the other professions on which local government at present depends' and who would ascend 'a broad ladder leading to the topmost rung of chief manager'. On the other hand we do not support the view that the 'general administrator is fast becoming an anachronism'. Our conclusions are that, although in many departments there is no substitute for professionally qualified principal officers, economies in the use of scarce professional resources can be made by the fullest possible employment of the lay administrative officer. We recommend that the career of the lay administrative officer, subject to the size of an authority and the scope of its responsibilities, should take him to the second or third tier position in a department; the lay administrative officer should be equal in salary and status with his professional colleagues at those levels.

235. If this approach could be generally accepted, it would make it possible to offer a full and satisfying career to lay administrative officers in local government; and the attraction of able men into this career would bring valuable support to professional heads of departments and enable them to spend more time on tasks requiring their professional skills.

236. The Clerk in any authority, whatever its size and responsibilities, spends much time in administration, in the servicing of its committees, in the co-ordination of its many activities where this is necessary to prevent over-lapping or confusion of plans, and in the general provision of management services. These are in fact high administrative tasks requiring distinctive gifts of personality and leadership. Men in any profession, including the profession of administration, may possess these gifts. The lay administrator should have an equal chance with members of other professions to become the Clerk of an authority. We therefore recommend that the Clerkship of an authority, being mainly an administrative post, should be open to all professions including that of the lay administrative officer. . . .

403. The Hadow Committee did not propose a unified service for all local authorities, nor did it recommend any departure from the practice that 'local authorities are in the main independent in the appointment and management of their officers'.

404. Local authorities have jointly set up the Local Authorities' Conditions of Service Advisory Board whose functions are to co-ordinate the activities of the employers' side of local government wages negotiating organisation, to provide a joint secretariat for these bodies, to maintain liaison with other employers, and to obtain and disseminate information on service conditions. Local authorities, as employers, are represented on NJC and negotiating bodies. LGEB as an off-shoot of NJC is responsible for the examination of clerical and administrative officers in the service of authorities. It is primarily in collective bargaining, and hence in pay and conditions of service, that there has been a move towards some form of unity. Local authorities have accepted certain common standards; they have not sacrificed their independence in the appointment and management of staff. . . .

A SINGLE LOCAL GOVERNMENT SERVICE

408. There is a view that there should be one local government service and not the services of 1,450 different local authorities. The implications of a single local government service are that:

(a) local authorities would yield up to a central body of their own making their individual responsibilities for the recruitment and selection (and possibly the employment) of staff;

(b) local government officers would cease to be free to seek employment when and where they pleased and their careers would be in the hands of the central body.

The arrangements might be confined to certain classes of officers, and a central body might itself work through regional organisations. . . .

Conclusions

419. We do not advocate the establishment of a unified local government service, in the sense of one recruiting, appointing and employing body deploying all staff within its scope. Accordingly we do not recommend the establishment of a local government staff commission or of regional staff commissions to administer a local government service. But although selection, appointment and employment of staff should remain with individual local authorities, there is a need for a local government organisation to perform a number of functions for the benefit of local authorities. This organisation might be set up by the local authority Associations. We therefore recommend that the local authority Associations should set up a Central Staffing Organisation to undertake the following duties:

(*a*) To publicise careers and employment in local government on a national basis and to make positive and continuous contact with schools, universities and colleges to supplement the work of the local authorities themselves, youth employment officers, the university appointments boards and the professional associations.

(*b*) To carry out national surveys and periodic reviews of the staffing requirements of local authorities, maintain liaison with statutory bodies, with professional associations, with universities and colleges, and, in particular, maintain contact with the central government, whose policies directly affect local government needs.

(*c*) To maintain an oversight of local government staff training needs and of the facilities which should be developed to meet them and to interpret these needs to those largely responsible for meeting them. . . .

490. More than 30 years have passed since the Hadow Committee reported and in that time the range of local government responsibilities has been so greatly extended that some of the Committee's suggestions about the Clerk's functions now seem unrealistic. We felt therefore that if we could find an acceptable definition of the

Clerk's position and functions in existing circumstances, we should know what sort of man local authorities ought to be looking for and what experience and training he should have had. We should at the same time avoid the overtones, unacceptable in many quarters, of titles like 'City Manager'.For our part we prefer the traditional title 'Clerk'. We recommend that the position and functions of the Clerk should be as follows:

(a) He should be recognised as head of the council's paid service.

(b) He should have authority over all other heads of departments so far as this is necessary for the efficient management and execution of the council's functions except where:
  (i) principal officers are exercising responsibilities imposed on them by statute;
  (ii) the professional discretion or judgment of the principal officers is involved.

(c) It should be his duty to ensure that all matters affecting the council or its committees are brought forward in appropriate form, that the decisions are properly recorded and communicated to those officers and persons responsible for carrying them into effect. He should bring to their notice any apparent neglect or failure to execute the council's decisions and should if necessary report the matter to the council.

(d) In order that issues may be submitted to the council and its committees in appropriate form, he should ensure that, where necessary, they have first received inter-departmental consideration, and that all professional and technical advice is available to the council or committees.

(e) He should be the council's official co-ordinator as far as the major objectives and decisions of the council are concerned. He should also be responsible for ensuring that the objectives and decisions of departments and committees are known to each other and that they are consistent with each other and with those of the council.

(f) His position as head of the council's service should be clearly recognised and principal officers told what his responsibilities are and enjoined to assist him, by continuous co-operation and consultation, to discharge them effectively.

(g) Where the circumstances of a council make it possible, he should be divorced from professional work and other extraneous duties to enable him to concentrate on his duties as the head of the council's service and a separate Legal Department under a Principal Legal Officer established.

7.8 From the *Report of the (Maud) Committee on the Management of Local Government*, Vol. 1 (Ministry of Housing and Local Government 1967), pp. x-xii.

The Maud Committee provided the first review of the internal organisation of local authorities, and this extract gives a summary of its main points.

II. INTERNAL ORGANISATION REFORM

8. Without waiting for any change in the structure of local government, each authority should therefore forthwith review its internal organisation, with the following points in mind:

(i) There should be a clearer division of labour between council-member and officer.

(ii) Council-members must exercise sovereign power within the authority and accept responsibility for everything done in the council's name. But having settled the policy they must delegate to officers the taking of all but the most important decisions.

(iii) Committees should cease to be executive or administrative bodies, save for some exceptional purposes. Their main functions should be deliberative.

(iv) There should be as few committees as possible, perhaps not more than half-a-dozen even in large authorities. Each committee should concern itself with a group of subjects: for example child care, personal health and welfare might be the concern of a single 'social work' committee.

(v) There should be as few sub-committees as possible.

(vi) All but the smallest authorities should appoint a management board, of between 5 and 9 council-members, and delegate wide powers to it.

(vii) This board should be the sole channel through which business done in the committees reaches the council. It would itself formulate and present proposals requiring council approval. It would also propose the establishment and dis-establishment of committees. It would serve as the focal point for management of the authority's affairs and supervise the work of the authority as a whole.

(viii) If the council is organised on party political lines, the minority party should be offered representation on the management board; thus knowledge of council business would be shared, and the experience gained by minority-party members would prove valuable if, after an election, their party secured a majority of council seats.

(ix) A council should be free to pay the members of its management board a part-time salary (say, £1,000 a year in the largest authorities), additional to any allowances payable to ordinary council-members.

9. Each authority should appoint a Clerk as undisputed head of the whole paid service of the council. He should not necessarily be a qualified lawyer but should be chosen for qualities of leadership and managerial ability. He would be chief officer to the management board.

10. The other principal officers should form a team under the Clerk's leadership and report to the council through him.

11. Departments should be grouped under not more than, say, half-a-dozen principal officers.

12. The full council would debate and decide questions put to it by the management board, which would sometimes circulate before debate 'white papers' on important issues of policy. Full opportunity should also be given in council for members to ask questions and table motions for debate.

13. It would be essential for the management board to retain the confidence of at least a majority of council-members. If it lost this confidence it would resign and the council would appoint a new board.

III. REFORMED RELATIONS BETWEEN CENTRAL AND LOCAL GOVERNMENT

14. There must be a fundamental change in the attitude to local government of the national authorities. The trend of recent legislation and the practice of government departments have been steadily reducing the discretion of local authorities and converting them into agents of Ministers and Whitehall. This tendency must be arrested and reversed; otherwise persons of the calibre required for effective local democracy will not offer themselves for election.

15. Authorities must be allowed to determine their own internal organisation. Legislation prescribing the appointment of particular

committees for education, child care, health, welfare, etc., must be repealed.

16. Ministers should play no part in the appointment or dismissal by local authorities of their principal officers.

17. Councils should themselves determine the scale of financial allowances which members can claim, but the appropriate Minister should sanction the scale of part-time salaries payable to members of management boards.

18. Whitehall must continue in the interest of the national economy to control local programmes of capital investment, but this control should no longer be used to prescribe the details of local buildings or expenditure.

19. In order that local authorities may establish their own priorities as part of a co-ordinated plan of development, the Whitehall departments (of housing, education, transport, etc.) must co-ordinate among themselves their dealings with individual authorities.

20. The whole complex of central administrative controls needs to be revised, reduced and simplified.

21. The taxing powers of local authorities must be strengthened and the dependence of local government on central finance reduced.

22. An easier procedure must be devised for increasing the statutory powers of local authorities.

23. In addition to particular statutory powers, local authorities should be given (as in Sweden and other countries) a 'general competence' to do what they think necessary for the good of the people they serve.

24. There is a need for a new organisation to represent and promote the common interests of all types of local authority in relation both to central government and to the public. This local government central office would also serve as a centre of research and information for council-members, officers and the press.

IV. CLOSER RELATIONS BETWEEN COUNCIL AND PUBLIC

25. The gulf at present separating 'them' (the local governors) from 'us' (the public) must be bridged and the intelligibility of local government greatly increased.

26. Elections to all types of local authority should take place every three years and on the same day throughout the country. The present variety of electoral systems is partly responsible for

the fact that half the electorate does not vote at local elections and over half the seats are uncontested.

27. In even the largest authority the council should not consist of more than 75 members. Each ward should be represented by only one member.

28. The office of alderman should be abolished.

29. Seventy should be the maximum age for standing for election.

30. Co-option should be more generally used, as a means of involving in some aspects of local government a larger number of people with special knowledge.

31. Released by the council's better internal organisation from the tyranny of detailed agenda-papers and sub-committee meetings, council-members should spend much more time in personal contact with their constituents.

32. Allies must be made of schools and school teachers, so that coming generations may have more chance of regarding local government as the lively democratic activity of good neighbours, rather than something deadly, dull and irrelevant.

33. The co-operation of press, radio and television is indispensable to the success of local democracy. This calls for deliberate and continuous efforts to enable editors and skilled reporters to understand the mind of the council, even on matters which can be explained only on a confidential basis.

V. FINALLY

34. The proposals outlined above would, we believe, encourage more men and women to offer themselves for service in local government as members or officers. But organisational changes, whether resulting from the Royal Commission or from us, will not of themselves achieve our purpose fully. A general change of attitude is needed most of all. The characteristic *result* of local government action is seen in such material things as schools, homes, traffic signs and refuse-bins. But the *purpose* of such action is invariably *human happiness*. And the action itself is taken by *people*, for *people*. Only as local government comes increasingly to be seen in this light will it attract people 'of the calibre necessary to secure its maximum effectiveness'.

8 The Literature of
Local Government

8.1 From J. Toulmin Smith, *Local Self-Government and Centralization*
(London 1851), pp. 30-2.
  In opposing Chadwick and all that he stood for, Toulmin Smith
began his onslaught with a general statement of the nature of local self-
government. This is one of the earliest attempts to theorise on the
subject.

It is by the independence of thought and conduct to be only
acquired by the habit of being continually called on to express an
opinion upon, and to take an active part in, the management of the
affairs of their own district, that men can alone ever be really fit
to elect representatives either to Parliament or the local Council,
or to form sound and respect-worthy opinions on the conduct of
such representatives. . . .
  Free institutions do not, then, exist, and national independence
can never be ensured, nor individual independence and fore-
thought ever characterise a people, unless true local self-government is fully and freely exercised in every district throughout the
land; unshackled alike by local clique-ism and by central intermeddling. The exercise of that local self-government must be
entirely in the hands of the district as to all matters of general
management, police, public works, taxation, and every class of
administrative arrangement whereon the common welfare of a
local community depends. No interference by any central authority
can be permitted without a necessarily consequent sacrifice of
independence, self-reliance, and efficiency. These truths are
logical necessities; and it is a mark of the empirical mode in which
political subjects are too often now handled, that some men,
professing to see the importance of local self-government, will
gravely argue for a central control over some or other point of local

management. It can never be matter of surprise that men seeking to impose schemes of their own upon the public, should strive to shackle local self-government, and to impose control over this or that special matter. But such a proposition can never be consistently put forth by any disinterested man, or honest government. A man who is unable to take care of his own affairs is deserving only of pity as an imbecile. A town or district which is unable to manage its own local affairs – being unshackled in the exercise of that management – is an impossibility, as imbecility can never affect a whole district. No central authority can ever, by any possible human machinery, know, – as the inhabitants must always do, – the circumstances and conditions of a district, and so know how its affairs may be best managed. To speak of such control being a 'protection' is a contradiction in terms. It can never be other than a shackle only. Where true local self-government exists, it is necessarily self-protective; and that *Self-Protection* is the only sure protection, – but it is unfailing.

'Local jobbing', and the influence of 'local interests', are often held up as bugbears. But each of these, wherever it be found, exists, and only ever can exist, because true Local Self-Government is not there found; because the discussion and management of matters is practically left in the hands of a Local clique or oligarchy, – under the form and name, it may be, of a Town Council or otherwise, but without the practical activity of that other part of the Local Institutions which the spirit, the letter, and the long practice of the common Law and Constitution of England require, namely, the Folk and People themselves meeting in frequent, fixed, regular, and accessible assemblies, as matter of individual right and duty, and discussing, and hearing discussed, the matters which the local body, entrusted to administer in their behalf, has done or is doing. Without this, whatever the name of the Local body having authority may be, its reality will always be a clique, in which individual interests will, of course, be more likely to sway and to prevail than the common good of the whole neighbourhood. But a centralised interference or control can only increase this evil, and the tendency to it. It may, sometimes, change the special direction which it takes; but it can never cut it out, nor tend in any way to lessen it.

The primary fundamental principle, then, of true Free Institutions is, – that *All local affairs, of common interest, shall be administered and controlled by true practical Institutions of Local Self-*

Government; – general affairs, affecting the common good of the several Institutions of Local Self-Government, being those only with the administration of which the General Assembly of representatives for all those Institutions of Local Self-Government has concern.

8.2 From John Stuart Mill, *On Representative Government* (London 1861), chap. XV, 'Of Local Representative Bodies'.

Mill's chapter on local government is generally regarded as the most profound statement of the principles of local government that has been written.

It is but a small portion of the public business of a country which can be well done, or safely attempted, by the central authorities; and even in our own government, the least centralised in Europe, the legislative portion at least of the governing body busies itself far too much with local affairs, employing the supreme power of the State in cutting small knots which there ought to be other and better means of untying. The enormous amount of private business which takes up the time of Parliament, and the thoughts of its individual members, distracting them from the proper occupations of the great council of the nation, is felt by all thinkers and observers as a serious evil, and what is worse, an increasing one. . . .

Not only are separate executive officers required for purely local duties (an amount of separation which exists under all governments), but the popular control over those officers can only be advantageously exerted through a separate organ. Their original appointment, the function of watching and checking them, the duty of providing, or the discretion of withholding, the supplies necessary for their operations, should rest, not with the national Parliament or the national executive, but with the people of the locality. In some of the New England States these functions are still exercised directly by the assembled people; it is said with better results than might be expected; and those highly educated communities are so well satisfied with this primitive mode of local government, that they have no desire to exchange it for the only representative system they are acquainted with, by which all minorities are disfranchised. Such very peculiar circumstances, however, are required to make this arrangement work tolerably in practice, that recourse must generally be had to the plan of representative sub-Parliaments for local affairs. These exist in

England, but very incompletely, and with great irregularity and want of system: in some other countries much less popularly governed their constitution is far more rational. In England there has always been more liberty, but worse organisation, while in other countries there is better organisation, but less liberty. It is necessary, then, that in addition to the national representation there should be municipal and provincial representations: and the two questions which remain to be resolved are, how the local representative bodies should be constituted, and what should be the extent of their functions. . . .

The proper constitution of local representative bodies does not present much difficulty. The principles which apply to it do not differ in any respect from those applicable to the national representation. The same obligation exists, as in the case of the more important function, for making the bodies elective; and the same reasons operate as in that case, but with still greater force, for giving them a widely democratic basis: the dangers being less, and the advantages, in point of popular education and cultivation, in some respects even greater. As the principal duty of the local bodies consists of the imposition and expenditure of local taxation, the electoral franchise should vest in all who contribute to the local rates, to the exclusion of all who do not. I assume that there is no indirect taxation, no *octroi* duties, or that if there are, they are supplementary only; those on whom their burthen falls being also rated to a direct assessment. The representation of minorities should be provided for in the same manner as in the national Parliament, and there are the same strong reasons for plurality of votes. Only, there is not so decisive an objection, in the inferior as in the higher body, to making the plural voting depend (as in some of the local elections of our own country) on a mere money qualification: for the honest and frugal dispensation of money forms so much larger a part of the business of the local than of the national body, that there is more justice as well as policy in allowing a greater proportional influence to those who have a larger money interest at stake. . . .

Another equally important principle is, that in each local circumscription there should be but one elected body for all local business, not different bodies for different parts of it. Division of labour does not mean cutting up every business into minute fractions; it means the union of such operations as are fit to be performed by the same persons, and the separation of such as can be better performed by different persons. The executive duties of the locality do indeed require to be divided into departments, for the same reason as those of the State; because they are of diverse kinds, each requiring knowledge peculiar to itself, and needing, for its due performance, the undivided attention of a specially qualified functionary. But the reasons for sub-division which apply to the execution do not apply to the control. The business of the elective body is not to do the work, but to see that it is properly done, and that nothing necessary is left undone. This function can be fulfilled for all departments by the same superintending body; and by a collective and comprehensive far better than by a minute and microscopic view. It is as absurd in public affairs as it would be in private that every workman should be looked after by a superintendent to himself. The Government of the Crown consists of many departments, and there are many ministers to conduct them, but those ministers have not a Parliament apiece to keep them to their duty. The local, like the national Parliament, has for its proper business to consider the interest of the locality as a whole, composed of parts all of which must be adapted to one another, and attended to in the order and ratio of their importance. There is another very weighty reason for uniting the control of all the business of a locality under one body. The greatest imperfection of popular local institutions, and the chief cause of the failure which so often attends them, is the low calibre of the men by whom they are almost always carried on. That these should be of a very miscellaneous character is, indeed, part of the usefulness of the institution; it is that circumstance chiefly which renders it a school of political capacity and general intelligence. But a school supposes teachers as well as scholars; the utility of the instruction greatly depends on its bringing inferior minds into contact with superior, a contact which in the ordinary course of life is altogether exceptional, and the want of which contributes more than anything else to keep the generality of mankind on one level of contented ignorance. The school, moreover, is worthless, and a school of evil instead of good, if through the want of due surveillance, and of the presence within itself of a higher order of characters, the action of the body is allowed, as it so often is, to degenerate into an equally unscrupulous and stupid pursuit of the self-interest of its members. Now, it is quite hopeless to induce persons of a high class, either socially or intellectually, to take a share of local administration in a corner by piece-meal, as members of a Paving Board or a Drainage

Commission. The entire local business of their town is not more than a sufficient object to induce men whose tastes incline them and whose knowledge qualifies them for national affairs to become members of a mere local body, and devote to it the time and study which are necessary to render their presence anything more than a screen for the jobbing of inferior persons under the shelter of their responsibility. A mere Board of Works, though it comprehend the entire metropolis, is sure to be composed of the same class of persons as the vestries of the London parishes; nor is it practicable, or even desirable, that such should not form the majority; but it is important for every purpose which local bodies are designed to serve, whether it be the enlightened and honest performance of their special duties, or the cultivation of the political intelligence of the nation, that every such body should contain a portion of the very best minds of the locality: who are thus brought into perpetual contact, of the most useful kind, with minds of a lower grade, receiving from them that local or professional knowledge they have to give, and in return inspiring them with a portion of their own more enlarged ideas, and higher and more enlightened purposes. . . .

Besides the controlling Council, or local sub-Parliament, local business has its executive department. With respect to this, the same questions arise as with respect to the executive authorities in the State; and they may, for the most part, be answered in the same manner. The principles applicable to all public trusts are in substance the same. In the first place, each executive officer should be single, and singly responsible for the whole of the duty committed to his charge. In the next place, he should be nominated, not elected. It is ridiculous that a surveyor, or a health officer, or even a collector of rates, should be appointed by popular suffrage. The popular choice usually depends on interest with a few local leaders, who, as they are not supposed to make the appointment, are not responsible for it; or on an appeal to sympathy, founded on having twelve children, and having been a ratepayer in the parish for thirty years. If in cases of this description election by the population is a farce, appointment by the local representative body is little less objectionable. Such bodies have a perpetual tendency to become joint-stock associations for carrying into effect the private jobs of their various members. Appointments should be made on the individual responsibility of the Chairman of the body, let him be called Mayor, Chairman of Quarter Sessions, or by whatever other title. He occupies in the locality a position analogous to that of the prime minister in the State, and under a well-organised system the appointment and watching of the local officers would be the most important part of his duty: he himself being appointed by the Council from its own number, subject either to annual re-election or to removal by a vote of the body.

From the constitution of the local bodies I now pass to the equally important and more difficult subject of their proper attributions. This question divides itself into two parts: what should be their duties, and whether they should have full authority within the sphere of those duties, or should be liable to any, and what, interference on the part of the central government.

It is obvious, to begin with, that all business purely local – all which concerns only a single locality – should devolve upon the local authorities. The paving, lighting, and cleansing of the streets of a town, and in ordinary circumstances the draining of its houses, are of little consequence to any but its inhabitants. The nation at large is interested in them in no other way than that in which it is interested in the private well-being of all its individual citizens. But among the duties classed as local, or performed by local functionaries, there are many which might with equal propriety be termed national, being the share, belonging to the locality, of some branch of the public administration in the efficiency of which the whole nation is alike interested: the gaols, for instance, most of which in this country are under county management; the local police; the local administration of justice, much of which, especially in corporate towns, is performed by officers elected by the locality and paid from local funds. None of these can be said to be matters of local, as distinguished from national, importance. It would not be a matter personally indifferent to the rest of the country if any part of it became a nest of robbers or a focus of demoralisation, owing to the maladministration of its police; or if, through the bad regulations of its gaol, the punishment which the courts of justice intended to inflict on the criminals confined therein (who might have come from, or committed their offences in, any other district) might be doubled in intensity, or lowered to practical impunity. The points, moreover, which constitute good management of these things are the same everywhere; there is no good reason why police, or gaols, or the administration of justice, should be differently managed in one part of the kingdom and in another; while there is great peril that in things so important, and to which the most instructed minds available to the State are not more than adequate, the lower average of capacities which alone can be counted on for the service of the localities might commit errors of such magnitude as to be a serious blot upon the general administration of the country. Security of person and property, and equal justice between individuals, are the first needs of society, and the primary ends of government: if these things can be left to any responsibility below the highest, there is nothing, except war and treaties, which requires a general government at all. Whatever are the best arrangements for securing these primary objects should be made universally obligatory, and, to secure their enforcement, should be placed under central superintendence. It is often useful, and with the institutions of our own country even necessary, from the scarcity in the localities, of officers representing the general government, that the execution of duties imposed by the central authority should be entrusted to functionaries appointed for local purposes by the locality. But experience is daily forcing upon the public a conviction of the necessity of having at least inspectors appointed by the general government to see that the local officers do their duty. If prisons are under local management, the central government appoints inspectors of prisons to take care that the rules laid down by Parliament are observed, and to suggest others if the state of the gaols shows them to be requisite: as there are inspectors of factories, and inspectors of schools, to watch over the observance of the Acts of Parliament relating to the first, and the fulfilment of the conditions on which State assistance is granted to the latter.

But, if the administration of justice, police and gaols included, is both so universal a concern, and so much a matter of general science independent of local peculiarities, that it may be, and ought to be, uniformly regulated throughout the country, and its regulation enforced by more trained and skilful hands than those of purely local authorities – there is also business, such as the administration of the poor laws, sanitary regulation, and others, which, while really interesting to the whole country, cannot consistently with the very purposes of local administration, be managed otherwise than by the localities. In regard to such duties the question arises, how far the local authorities ought to be trusted with discretionary power, free from any superintendence or control of the State.

To decide this question it is essential to consider what is the comparative position of the central and the local authorities as to capacity for the work, and security against negligence or abuse. In the first place, the local representative bodies and their officers are almost certain to be of a much lower grade of intelligence and knowledge than Parliament and the national executive. Secondly, besides being themselves of inferior qualifications, they are watched by, and accountable to, an inferior public opinion. The public under whose eyes they act and by whom they are criticised, is both more limited in extent and generally far less enlightened than that which surrounds and admonishes the highest authorities at the capital; while the comparative smallness of the interests involved causes even that inferior public to direct its thoughts to the subject less intently, and with less solicitude. Far less interference is exercised by the press and by public discussion, and that which is exercised may with much more impunity be disregarded in the proceedings of local than in those of national authorities. Thus far the advantage seems wholly on the side of management by the central government. But, when we look more closely, these motives of preference are found to be balanced by others fully as substantial. If the local authorities and public are inferior to the central ones in knowledge of the principles of administration, they have the compensating advantage of a far more direct interest in the result. . . . I need not dwell on the deficiencies of the central authority in detailed knowledge of local persons and things, and the too great engrossment of its time and thoughts by other concerns, to admit of its acquiring the quantity and quality of local knowledge necessary even for deciding on complaints, and enforcing responsibility from so great a number of local agents. In the details of management therefore, the local bodies will generally have the advantage; but in comprehension of the principles even of purely local management, the superiority of the central government, when rightly constituted, ought to be prodigious: not only by reason of the probably great personal superiority of the individuals composing it, and the multitude of thinkers and writers who are at all times engaged in pressing useful ideas upon their notice, but also because the knowledge and experience of any local authority is but local knowledge and experience, confined to their own part of the country and its modes of management, whereas the central government has the means of knowing all that is to be learnt from the united experience of the whole kingdom, with the addition of easy access to that of foreign countries.

The practical conclusion from these premises is not difficult to draw. The authority which is most conversant with principles should be supreme over principles, while that which is most competent in details should have the details left to it. The principal business of the central authority should be to give instruction, of the local authority to apply it. Power may be localised, but knowledge, to be most useful, must be centralised; there must be somewhere a focus at which all its scattered rays are collected, that the broken and coloured lights which exist elsewhere may find there what is necessary to complete and purify them. To every branch of local administration which affects the general interest there should be a corresponding central organ, either a minister, or some specially appointed functionary under him; even if that functionary does no more than collect information from all quarters, and bring the experience acquired in one locality to the knowledge of another where it is wanted. But there is also something more than this for the central authority to do. It ought to keep open a perpetual communication with the localities: informing itself by their experience, and them by its own; giving advice freely when asked, volunteering it when seen to be required; compelling publicity and recordation of proceedings, and enforcing obedience to every general law which the legislature has laid down on the subject of local management. That some such laws ought to be laid down few are likely to deny. The localities may be allowed to mismanage their own interests, but not to prejudice those of others, nor violate those principles of justice between one person and another of which it is the duty of the State to maintain the rigid observance. If the local majority attempts to oppress the minority, or one class another, the State is bound to interpose. For example, all local rates ought to be voted exclusively by the local representative body; but that body, though elected solely by ratepayers, may raise its revenues by imposts of such a kind, or assess them in such a manner, as to throw an unjust share of the burthen on the poor, the rich, or some particular class of the population: it is the duty, therefore, of the legislature, while leaving the mere amount of the local taxes to the discretion of the local body, to lay down authoritatively the modes of taxation, and rules of assessment, which alone the localities shall be permitted to use. Again, in the administration of public charity the industry and morality of the whole labouring population depend, to a most serious extent, upon adherence to certain fixed principles in awarding relief. Though it belongs essentially to the local functionaries to determine who, according to those principles, is entitled to be relieved, the national Parliament is the proper authority to prescribe the principles themselves; and it would neglect a most important part of its duty if it did not, in a matter of such grave national concern, lay down imperative rules, and make effectual provision that those rules should not be departed from. What power of actual interference with the local administrators it may be necessary to retain, for the due enforcement of the laws, is a question of detail into which it would be useless to enter. The laws themselves will naturally define the penalties, and fix the mode of their enforcement. It may be requisite, to meet extreme cases, that the power of the central authority should extend to dissolving the local representative council, or dismissing the local executive: but not to making new appointments, or suspending the local institutions. Where Parliament has not interfered, neither ought any branch of the executive to interfere with authority; but as an adviser and critic, an enforcer of the laws, and a denouncer to Parliament of the local constituencies of conduct which it deems condemnable, the functions of the executive are of the greatest possible value.

Some may think that however much the central authority surpasses the local in knowledge of the principles of administration, the great object which has been so much insisted on, the social and political education of the citizens, requires that they should be left to manage these matters by their own, however imperfect, lights. To this it might be answered, that the education of the citizens is not the only thing to be considered; government and administration do not exist for that alone, great as its importance is. But the objection shows a very imperfect understanding of the function of popular institutions as a means of political instruction. It is but a poor education that associates ignorance with ignorance, and leaves them, if they care for knowledge, to grope their way to it without help, and to do without it if they do not. What is wanted is, the means of making ignorance aware of itself, and able to profit by knowledge; accustoming minds which know only routine to act upon, and feel the value of, principles: teaching them to compare different modes of action, and learn, by the use of their reason, to distinguish the best. When we desire to have a good school, we do not eliminate the teacher. The old remark, 'as the schoolmaster is, so will be the school,' is as true of the indirect schooling of grown people by public business as of the schooling of youth in academies and colleges. A government which attempts to do everything is aptly compared by M. Charles de Rémusat to a schoolmaster who does all the pupils' tasks for them; he may be very popular with the pupils, but he will teach them little. A government, on the other hand, which neither does anything itself that can possibly be done by any one else, nor shows any one else how to do anything, is like a school in which there is no schoolmaster, but only pupil teachers who have never themselves been taught.

8.3 From G. L. Gomme, *Lectures on the Principles of Local Government* (London 1897), pp. 26-31.

Sir Laurence Gomme was one of the first practitioners – he was Clerk of the London County Council – to attempt to analyse as well as describe our local government system.

Whether the State authority exercises wholly new functions unknown to the Middle Ages, or takes over to itself powers which once belonged to local authorities, and makes them serve national, instead of local, ends; whether it asserts a new direction and control over municipal administration, or whether, instead of replacing local authorities by its own rule, it upholds them with the support of its vast resources and boundless strength, every townsman, every burgher, every shireman feels that the State Government, which he helps to constitute by his vote, is charged with the final sanctions for all government. But there is still a great force, moral if not legal, sentimental if not constitutional, in what may be termed the intermediate sanctions of municipal custom and municipal rule. I am compelled to say municipal here, because in the towns and in the counties the great sanctions of local government have been stifled out, thought not, I hope, for so long a time as to be incapable of being revived by the new life which is now opened out to them. These sanctions are derived from all that is best in our natures – from the love that we bear to our birthplace, to our place of up-bringing, to the familiar scenes of our playing-time and our work-time, of our griefs, misfortunes, and cares, of our successes and good fortune – to our fondness for being classed as Kentish men, as Dorsetshire men, or even as Londoners. They are derived, too, from the demands of science, which have laid bare some of the first necessities of health and of life, particularly in places with crowded populations, and which are found to be necessities only to be met by common action. Finally, these sanctions are derived from economical considerations. Strong and powerful, therefore, as are the sanctions for local government derived from the State law and State police, the sanctions proceeding directly from local government itself are as strong. Because they are put in motion constantly, and because they operate quietly and upon great masses of people, they are not so much in evidence as the State sanctions, which are only put in motion when the municipal sanctions have failed; but, if I mistake not, it is the constant action and wide operation of these sanctions of local government which are the real cause of the new departure in modern legislation relating to local government matters.

Looking back upon the distinction which I have drawn between the two classes of local governments, it will be seen that while in the matter of locality the local governments properly-so-called and the quasi-local governments were not on the same footing, in the matter of representative governing authority they are quite on a par. This, indeed, is the real force which has given quasi-local government its vitality. The election of a representative authority, even if its powers are limited to the administration of certain fixed duties, is a force which tells for good. When that force is combined with the force which is derived from a locality fostered under the influence of common interests of long-continued standing, or of strong, immediate character, the tendency is towards local government of the true type, – county, borough, or parish; and it is to these combined forces that we owe the growth of the modern municipal borough, and, in the case of London, of the modern county – a growth that will compel us to consider a great principle of local government later on: namely, the principle of development. One other point will have become clear to you: namely, that localities properly-so-called have, in a sort of unconscious fashion, served as models for the purpose of extending the machinery of government by authorities subordinate to the State, and hence the *idea* of local government has become a fixed point in the national will. It is from this *idea* that has proceeded so much of the political talk about local government, and so much of the credit allotted to England as the mother-home of local government. But in being satisfied with the idea much of the substance has not been obtained. Indeed, the very looseness with which the models have been copied testifies to the fact that localities have never been allowed to develop their own system of government in a natural way, in the same manner as they developed down to the end of the Middle Ages. Everything is now governed, not by the needs of the locality, but by the cast-iron mould of legislation, which allows no room for even some of the elementary difficulties, and certainly not for the greater difficulties attending the growth and expansion of localities from the condition of a simple parish to that of a borough, or of a group of parishes to that of a county.

If I have succeeded in fixing attention upon the primary elements of local government, and if, further, I have shown that the growing functions of government which must be delegated by the State affect very largely the future of local government, there is still another part of the subject which must be dealt with in this preliminary survey – namely, the position which local government holds in reference to the other subordinate authorities of the State. Let me remind you that local government derives its power from, and is answerable to, the electors – a portion of the whole body of electors who form the representative element of the State government; and that the other subordinate authorities derive their power from, and are answerable directly to, the State government.

Now we have already seen that local government in modern times practically forms two out of three classes of subordinate authorities which it has become necessary for the State to use or to create for the purposes of carrying on the affairs of the country. In order to understand the position of local government in relation to the State, apart from local government itself, it is necessary to give a very short account of that third class of subordinate authorities which are not wholly devoted to local affairs. I am obliged to say 'not wholly devoted', because it will be found that they include one kind of authority which performs functions of strictly local government.

This class of subordinate authorities consists of (1) the judges and other ministers of justice; (2) central departments of State, like the Board of Trade, Local Government Board, Patent Office and other sections of the Civil Service; (3) commissions appointed by the State government, and responsible to the State government. The two first of these subordinate authorities need not concern us more than is sufficient to take note of their constitution in relation to the State. But commissions appointed by the State closely touch the subject of local government. Up to the year 1888 the counties were entirely in the hands of such commissions; there are a few of them left elsewhere who perform functions generally performed by local governments. These were created for some special purposes of drainage, fisheries, docks, river conservancy, and the like, and, in the case of the Home Counties and London, of police. They possess in most cases powers of taxation, direct or indirect, and they are not responsible to the locality which is taxed, but only to the State. Standing in direct contrast to local government, locality is no real or essential element in their constitution or their responsibilities. What they have to do with is a section of the kingdom, not a locality. The duties they have to perform are not for the locality, but for the State. The contrast is, of course, a vital one, though I think it is but little understood.

8.4 From J. Redlich and F. W. Hurst, *Local Government in England* (London 1903), vol. I, pp. 11-14, 22-3, and 214-16.

Redlich, ably assisted by his English translator Hurst, produced one of the most perceptive studies of the development of local government in England. These extracts show the extent to which he was able to comment on the constitutional importance of the developments he recorded.

The double movement of government from and to the centre found its first monumental expression in the provisions of the Magna Charta (1215 A.D.), which require that jurisdiction shall no longer follow the King's court, but shall have a fixed court; that Judges shall travel throughout the country to hold Assizes; and that fines and penalties imposed for offences against the peace shall in all cases be assessed 'by honest men of the neighbourhood sworn to that purpose'.

The whole remaining period in the development of the Anglo-Norman State is occupied by an attempt to bridge over the chasm, which divided the local instincts of the governed from the centralising policy of the Government, by changing the Norman organisation of the kingdom into one more in conformity with the territorial patriotism of the shires or counties. Though it is unnecessary to enter at length into the obscurities which shroud the constitutional history of this period, the permanent consequences of its struggles may, nevertheless, be indicated with precision, for they are to be found in the new system created by the reforming genius of Edward III (1327–77). This system was a compromise between two excesses – the centralising tendencies of the Norman tradition and the obstinate provincialism of the Anglo-Saxon. The main outlines of the compromise are easily discerned. The figure of the Sheriff as a Crown Officer directly responsible to the King for the government of each county retires to make way for the new institution of Justices of the Peace, who are persons appointed by the State to carry out certain of its precepts and generally 'to keep the peace'. From this time forward the preservation of the peace, the punishment of offenders against the laws for its maintenance, and the control of police are all functions pertaining to these magistrates. They are defined as men holding land in the county nominated to that office by the King. . . . The Justices were even entrusted with the carrying out of the statutes of labourers, the first great instance of administrative legislation in mediaeval England. As in all other modern States, so in England public administration, beginning with the bare idea of police, gradually widened and deepened its preventive activities to meet the growing and diversifying requirements of economic and social development. And so the Justices of the Peace, originally instituted solely to superintend police, came to be recognised by the English Crown as the first and only local organs of its executive. Along with this institution were erected three great principles of English administration which still stand.

1. Henceforward the counties and the towns taken out of them by charters of incorporation were recognised by constitutional law as the only territorial divisions of the kingdom. Every attempt to subdivide the country for the administrative purpose of the kingly power and its central departments without reference to this historical classification was regarded from that time forward as an attack upon the constitution.

2. The qualifications for executing public authority in these districts were landed estate in the particular county for a county Justice and for a borough Justice membership of a municipal corporation. Necessary outlay and expenditure might be made good; but practice, confirmed by a statute of the sixteenth century, has refused to attach a salary to an appointment which confers so honourable a distinction. That the office is (as we have said) a compromise appears from two of its incidents. First, a Justice of the Peace must be a man of the county or town. This was a concession to local spirit. Secondly, the appointment is made by the Crown. This secured the central control of the State over local government. Thus it was decided that, for the future, local administration and jurisdiction in England should be entrusted, not to official dele-

gates of the Crown, sent like the Vicecomes from the centre of the State to its circumference, but to landed gentry or enfranchised burgesses living in the locality and only appointed by the central authority.

3. A third point to be noted in this institution is the judicial character of the functionaries to whom local administration was entrusted. That fact was equivalent to a declaration that all local administration is jurisdiction – that is to say, the interpretation and execution of laws. Justices of the Peace were appointed to put an end to the rule of lawlessness by enforcing laws for preserving the peace and by employing their delegated powers for the punishment of offenders; and the institution has been continued in order to ensure the effective maintenance of all the laws and ordinances which form the sphere of a Justice's duties and activities. A Justice of the Peace is appointed by Commission – that is to say, by a mandate from the King conferring jurisdiction. . . .

This tendency to create a strong system of government from above achieved the more importance by virtue of a process of development which took effect in the smallest subdivision of the hierarchy of local government. Besides the deep political and economic consequences which flowed from Henry the Eighth's confiscation of the monasteries and the creation of a State Church, the Reformation also worked directly upon the inner organisation of the State. In England, as on the Continent, the relief of the poor had been the duty of the Church; and although the increasing inefficiency of the Church in the performance of that duty had already necessitated a measure of State intervention, it is yet true that the transition of poor relief from a religious to a civil function was one of the fruits of the Reformation. The problem was undertaken and solved with all the thoroughness and vigour of Elizabethan statesmanship. The care of the poor was treated as a national duty, but as a local burden to be undertaken separately by each local unit; and hence it was that the parish – the smallest local division of the ecclesiastical organisation of the country – made its appearance as a civil unit. The original units of local government (usually called tithings or townships) were merely subdivisions of a 'hundred' and administrative districts of a county, the growth of manorial courts followed by two centuries of magisterial rule having deprived them of their territorial basis and real meaning. And so it came about that village life and its needs had become associated with the Church and the parson; and the functions of each church being bounded by its parish, the ecclesiastical parish emerged as the real unit of local activities and interests, whether it corresponded with the civil township or not. All the inhabitants belonging to the church met in the parish assembly, elected parishioners as churchwardens, and transacted parochial business through the churchwardens and the parson. These were bound duly to collect contributions for defraying the cost of divine service and for the maintenance of the structure of the church – contributions voluntary in their origin, out of which there slowly developed the church rate, the oldest form of local taxation in England. Finding this old organisation ready to hand, our Elizabethan legislators built upon it the new organisation which was required to perform the new task now devolving upon the State. By the famous statute of 1601 the parish was made the unit for poor law purposes, the duty of caring for the poor was attached to the office of churchwarden; special overseers of the poor were appointed in addition, and finally, to cover the cost of maintaining the poor, a local tax entitled the poor rate was instituted. . . .

A new structure has been raised to replace the old system of administration, but it has been raised upon the old foundations of a unified and sovereign law. A full and unrestricted acceptance of the principle of representative democracy has given new life and form to local government. The whole of local administration must be carried out by the constitutionally elected representatives of the inhabitants of each local circumscription. But the new principle of representative democracy has not merely left intact – it has given fresh meaning and value to, that grand old doctrine of the sovereignty of law upon which the English polity is founded.

Several problems of home government have, it is true, been left in suspense. The Poor Laws are in dire need of consolidation and amendment. Primary education is still divided between responsible and irresponsible managers. No satisfactory system of secondary education has been set up. Now that School Boards have been abolished by the Education Act of 1902, the question arises whether any *ad hoc* authorities should be allowed to continue, and whether it would not be better that the poor should be relieved under the direction of the County, the Town and the District Councils.

Again many problems of local taxation, and particularly the relations between rates and taxes, require to be handled in a comprehensive and statesmanlike spirit. The last five years of the nineteenth century were in this, as in some other respects, not merely years of inaction, but years of reaction and retrogression. The bad example set by Mr Goschen was extended. Grants in aid of rates amounting to more than two millions of money were given in relief of agricultural ratepayers. Tithe owners were relieved of half their local burdens; and voluntary schools, whose boards are nominated, received further assistance from the Imperial Exchequer. In none of these cases was any service received or any public control* obtained in return.

But from the standpoint of organisation the tasks and problems of the future are of secondary importance. The grand principle of representative democracy has been fully applied to local government, and securely established by the series of measures which culminated in the Act of 1894. In England, at least, De Tocqueville's prophecy of the triumph of democratic ideas was substantially fulfilled before the close of the nineteenth century.

Parliament, which controls by popular mandate the destiny of the nation and the empire, is itself largely guided by a free press, free combinations, free meetings, and other manifestations which mark the current and direction of public opinion; and thus the course of national policy and the temper of national administration is decided, or at least influenced, by all classes in the community. The stability of the State is secured by the participation of all its citizens in the common life. As with the national Parliament, so with the local councils. They are elected by the people of the locality; they work under the censorship of local opinion. These little parliaments of the county, the town, and the village, like the great Parliament of the nation, employ paid officers to execute their commands. But these paid executives have no authority and (theoretically) no discretionary power of their own. At last class rule, in so far as it rested on law and constitution, has been totally abolished; and England has created for herself 'Self Government' in the true sense of the word, and not in the sense which Gneist has made popular in German literature and politics. She has secured Self Government – that is to say, the right of her people to legislate, to deliberate, and to administer through councils or parliaments elected on the basis of popular suffrage, with a civil service of municipal and imperial officials entirely subordinated to the popular will in law and in fact. The one great (and wholesome)

* Unless we regard the grant to Irish landlords in 1898 as the price of their acquiescence in the establishment of a democratic system of local government in Ireland.

limitation upon the sovereignty of the people, apart from the anomaly of a hereditary chamber, lies in the existence of a pure and independent judiciary which makes it impossible for any person or combination of persons, or even for the Government itself to break the law with impunity. The authorities which have power to make laws and bye-laws have power to change but not to infringe them. The people is law-abiding as well as law-making. And this is the root of the incomparable strength and health of the English Body Politic.

8.5 From G. D. H. Cole, *The Future of Local Government* (London 1921), Chap. XIV, 'General versus Ad Hoc Authorities', pp. 126-35.
Cole was a socialist with a strong adherence to the ideas of Guild Socialism. Another unique tendency was his preparedness to consider the advantages of the *ad hoc* authority when it was at its nadir of respectability. Yet in the fifty years after Cole wrote these words, the *ad hoc* authority was resuscitated as a remedy for some of the defects of local government.

It is a very old controversy in the sphere of Local Government whether better administration and democratic control are secured, and the greater effective interest of the electors stimulated, by the entrusting of Local Government functions to general or to *ad hoc* authorities. Ought the citizens of a particular place to choose one body to represent them in all concerns of public administration, economic and social alike; or ought they to choose several different bodies each to represent them in a distinct sphere, and each to be entrusted with a part of the work of administering the affairs of the locality? This is not a question of the form of franchise to be adopted; for where the *ad hoc* principle is followed, all the bodies chosen may be elected on a suffrage as direct and universal as where there is only a single *omnibus* local authority. It is a question whether it is better for the will of the citizens to be expressed directly in all matters through a single representative assembly, or whether this will can be more effectively expressed and better administration secured if the work is divided on a basis of *function*.

In this country the modern tendency of Local Government administration hitherto has been towards the *omnibus* authority. The amazing complexities which existed in the experimental stages of Local Government administration a century ago have largely been swept away, and it is no longer usual to find separate boards and commissions existing for all manner of special purposes of local administration. The Boards of Guardians are almost the only *ad hoc* authorities which remain in existence throughout the country, although there are still quite a number of *ad hoc* bodies in particular areas such as ports. Even the separate School Boards have been swept away in favour of the Local Education Authorities, which are committees of the elected Town or County Council. The tendency has been, on the one side, to sweep away the independent and separately elected *ad hoc* authorities, and on the other to increase the complexity of the system of Committees through which nearly all the actual administrative work of Local Government is carried on. There has also been, in conjunction with the spread of this system of committees, an increase in the element of co-option onto them of persons specially concerned in, or possessing an expert knowledge of, a particular branch of Local Government administration.

In face of this general tendency, a good many people are inclined to dismiss out of hand the question of a possible establishment of the *ad hoc* system in Local Government. The *ad hoc* bodies, they say, have been tried and have failed, and it only remains to sweep away the last wide-spread survival of them, the Board of Guardians, and to distribute its functions among the appropriate Committees of the local authorities in town and country. . . .

The principal functions of local authorities at the present time fall into three main groups. First, there is the group of activities, often regarded as the principal function of the local bodies, which has grown up mainly since the time of the Public Health legislation passed in the middle of the last century. . . . The second group of activities may be roughly classified together as 'trading' activities. . . . The third group of activities centres round education in the broadest sense, and includes, not only the ownership and control of the schools devoted to elementary and higher education, but also many related cultural services from libraries to art galleries, municipal theatres, and many other amenities which we may hope to see far more liberally provided or assisted by Local Government authorities in the future. . . .

I believe that in future the interests of the community will be best served by the existence of three separately chosen local authorities in each area, or at least in each area of considerable size, each entrusted with the care of one of these broad groups of functions. This is the proposal for *ad hoc* authorities in the form in which it appears to comply best with modern needs, and to recognise most clearly the conditions imposed by the modern development and widening of the functions of Local Government. It is also the form of organisation which would be most readily adaptable for the great expansion of Local Government services contemplated in this book. . . .

The case for *ad hoc* organisation in this new form seems to me to be three-fold, and to be based upon a consideration, first of the type of representative required, and the demands made upon him by those whom he represents; secondly, of the present confusion of issues in local as well as national public elections, and the possibility of ensuring a greater public control over the elected person by a clarifying of election issues; and, thirdly, of the confused mass of work with which local authorities are already called upon to deal, and the need, especially if this work is to be very much farther extended both in the sphere of health and education and by the adoption of large measures of socialisation, for a distribution of the burden among a larger number of bodies, which would thus be better able to cope with it.

First, then, what is wanted of the elected person who is chosen to represent the citizens of, say, Manchester on their City Council? Would the citizens, if they were given a free range of choice, be likely to choose the same person to represent them in relation to all the widely divergent functions with which the Manchester City Council has to concern itself? They might do this under present conditions; but they would do so only because they owe allegiance to a particular Party, and are giving their votes either for Labour, or for a candidate who is pledged to reduce the rates. If the class differences in society were removed, there would still, no doubt, remain party differences based on divergent ideas of the sphere of Local Government action and the right measures to be adopted; but is it not certain that, whereas now the cleavages in relation to all the various functions of Local Government tend, for economic reasons, to run along the same lines, the position would be widely different if the class divisions in Society no longer existed? There would then be no conceivable reason why all the people who hold a particular view about the control of the local gasworks should also be bound together in support of the same opinion about the latest town-planning scheme, or the extent of the educational provision required in the City schools or the regional University. The cleavages would then run along lines of opinion and not of class differences expressing themselves in party loyalties. Men would, naturally, group themselves very differently according to the particular question under discussion. . . .

This is not a question of government by the expert; for I am not suggesting at all that the type of man it would be desirable to elect to the various local authorities would be a man possessing professional or expert knowledge in the types of administration concerned. It is a question, not of professionalism or government by the expert, but of interest and point of view. Very many men who are in no sense experts in teaching possess the sort of educational interest which would make them good representatives of the public on a body dealing with education, while they are almost entirely devoid of any interest or competence in industrial administration which would make them good representatives on a local trading authority. Such men are to a large extent excluded by the present system of Local Government, or, if they secure election on to a general authority, are compelled to deal with a great mass of work in relation to which they are in no sense fitted to fulfil a representative function. . . .

The second and third reasons which I gave a few pages back in favour of the *ad hoc* as against the general authority can be dealt with far more briefly. I urged that the constitution of *ad hoc* authorities is necessary in order to secure clarity of election issues and an effective control by the electors over their representatives. Not only is it necessary that the elector should be placed in such a position that he is able to choose to represent him the man who is particularly competent in relation to the special purposes with which the representative body in question is constituted in order to deal; it is also necessary that the actual election should be conducted under such conditions as will enable the real issues of policy to be brought effectively to the front, and so make the election itself a fair test of the will of the electors on the more vital and fundamental questions which have to be decided. It hardly needs much argument to show that these conditions are far from being realised under the existing arrangements of Local Government. It is true that the opportunities for the obfuscation of the real issues of government are less manifest and less numerous in the case of local than of national elections; but they are still enough to prevent the citizens from plainly declaring their minds even on the most important issues which are actually decided by those whom they elect. A clear election result cannot be secured when there are involved in the election all the diverse questions with which the present *omnibus* local authorities exist to deal, and, if the present artificial party distinctions, themselves largely the result of artificial class divisions in Society, were removed, the impossibility of achieving such a result on the basis of any single election for an *omnibus* authority would immediately become obvious. . . .

The third reason which I gave related not to elections or to methods of choosing representatives but to the actual administrative work of the bodies concerned. It is literally impossible for any elected body, however efficient it may be, and however much of their time its members may be prepared to devote to its work, to conduct satisfactorily the huge agglomeration of duties which has already been accumulated in the hands of our local authorities, and this task would become far harder if the expansion of Local Government work which is contemplated in this book were actually accomplished. In practice today the growth of Local Government powers and duties means a steady decrease in the amount of effective control which the City Council or similar body is itself able to exercise over its various committees, and an increasing transference of the actual administrative power into the hands of those committees. . . .

This, however, is the case only on one condition; there must be no such splitting up of Local Government functions as will serve to destroy the unity of the whole work done by the public bodies within the area concerned. If we are to return to the *ad hoc* system, we must have such an amount of co-ordination between the various *ad hoc* bodies by which the existing Councils with their functional committees will be replaced, as will ensure an effective co-operation of them all in carrying out the desires of the citizens of the area.

The problem of providing this co-ordination clearly centres round the question of finance. It is not desirable that each functional body should be in a position without limit to levy rates or other forms of taxation upon the citizens; nor on the other hand is it desirable that the amount to be expended upon a particular group of services should be arbitrarily limited by national statute law in the way in which for so many years up to 1918 the expenditure of local authorities on higher education was limited. I am therefore suggesting, not that each functional or *ad hoc* local authority should have an independent power to levy rates or other forms of taxation, but that this power should be exercised only by the various functional bodies acting together and in concert. There should be provision for the bringing together in a single assembly of the members of the three *ad hoc* authorities. There should be a standing Joint Finance Committee of the three bodies, and the sole power to levy rates or taxes should rest with the Joint Assembly as a whole, acting on the advice of the Joint Finance Committee.

8.6 From C. H. Wilson (ed.), *Essays on Local Government* (Blackwell, Oxford 1948), 'The Foundations of Local Government' by C. H. Wilson, pp. 12-21.

This extract is from a twentieth-century attempt to formulate basic ideas about local government, but the author could do little more than repolish the ideas of John Stuart Mill in the light of developments since Mill wrote.

In the light of the brief period of relevant history which we have outlined, two sets of purposes can be distinguished, one political, the other administrative. The political purposes are those involved in the general objective of democracy, expressed in the establishment of central and local representative institutions. The administrative purposes are subordinate to and consequent on the political; they are the canons of working efficiency demanded by democratic political ends. There are, of course, administrative canons of a narrowly technical or economic character – such as division of labour, specialisation of function, minimum cost and the like – but these are universally applicable to all administrative operations and are not the clue to the distinctive character of any particular organisation. That clue can only be found in the wider ends which the organisation serves and in terms of which its real efficiency is measured. In local government administration these ends are political. It will be proper therefore to begin with the discussion of the political purposes of local government. When these are clear the way will be open for the examination of the administrative requirements.

The defence of democracy in local government must in part be the same as the defence of democracy in general, and the general purposes of democracy as a form of national government must in part be operative at the level of local institutions. But it is not self-evident that national democratic institutions *entail* local democracy. It is perfectly possible to conceive, or so it seems at first sight, a system of national self-government administering its local affairs through the agencies of a central departmental civil service.

Indeed it might seem almost a confusion of thought which leads to a conception of citizens as possessing a double political personality – one person an elector of a national government and another elector of a local government – the two personalities not infrequently at war with one another, pursuing separate objectives, subject to separate and sometimes conflicting duties, paying tax to two separate fiscal systems; such systematic employment of the principle of *zwei Seelen in einer Brust* seems to require some explanation. The explanation must lie somewhere in the central doctrines of democracy or in some necessary corollary attached to these. . . .

The central thread of democratic theory is to be found in its doctrines of the person. For it seems clear that the many views of democracy have this in common – that their point of departure is the individual person. From their view of the nature of the person develops their view of the state, and not the other way about. Other political philosophies may establish their systems by the contrary process, they may begin by exploring the nature of kingly power or monarchical state, of sovereignty or *imperium*, of peace or justice, of law or force and then go on to erect a conformable individual whose nature reflects the requirements of these pre-established ends. Democracy on the other hand starts with the man, and with theories about his nature. . . .

Between them these theories of freedom and equality, but especially the two meanings of equality just noticed, combine to establish the characteristic attitude of man to man which distinguishes democratic societies. That attitude is one of tolerance or consideration, expressed negatively in the refusal to impose any but common constraints upon each other, and positively, in the acceptance of the right of each to share in the determination of matters which are of common concern. Matters of common concern are held to be matters of common responsibility. If, sinning against the light, some deny or evade that responsibility the fundamental tolerance of their society will protect them against the retributive censure of their fellows. But every great writer on these questions will be found to maintain that the participation of every citizen of a democracy in his government, at some level of the political process and to the degree of his capacity, is not only a right but also a duty which at some time in his adult life he must discharge.

In terms of political method, this requirement of sharing or participating in government entails a preference for a particular way of taking political decisions – the way of discussion followed by the register of consent. The principle of majority decision which here comes into play represents an empirical and expedient limitation of the abstract idea of universal consent. . . .

If a system of government is to work by discussion and consent, it is still a matter for deliberate choice how often that consent shall be registered and at what levels effective political discussion shall take place. The field here is too vast to be considered in this essay. It is complicated too by the presence of the great assemblage of active political organisations, parties, professional and voluntary propaganda associations whose political activities are an essential element in that process of selecting, contesting and stating issues which is the real meaning of political discussion in the broad sense. These organisations, many of them, operate at the local level (often with distorting effect upon local affairs). As regards political discussion in the narrower sense of debate by responsible representatives, the debates of local councils are, at least in domestic policy, an essential element in national deliberation and decision. Of this something more will be said later.

When we come to the principle of political education, what John Stuart Mill called public education, the case for local representative institutions emerges at its strongest. What is meant by political education? Political education is, in the first place, an education in the possible and the expedient; in the second place, it is an education in the use of power and authority and in the risks of power; in the third place, it is an education in practical ingenuity and versatility.

The first object of a political education is to dispel in the citizen's mind the manifold Utopian notions of man's nature and of the nature of his world with which most persons emerge from the arduous experience of adolescence. He has to learn that men are moved not only by principle but by interest, that their actions are aimed not only at the discharge of duty, but also at the satisfaction of passion, appetite and unreflecting habit. He has to learn that the world in which he acts is a world of scarcity and that all the resources at his disposal are limited, both the material resources of wealth and the immaterial ones of time and political support. He must learn that all these resources have alternative uses between which he must choose and that generally his choice is irrevocable. The world with which he has to deal in fact is a world not of the perfect and desirable but of the possible and the expedient, where the vital data are actual not hypothetical situations and where reflection, though it can provide conceptions of end and purpose, must be informed and qualified by factual knowledge and experience. Such knowledge and experience can, of course, be acquired in a great many other fields of practice beside politics, but in most of those other fields the instruction is limited and partial, whereas in politics, which deals with the relations of all activities and mutually regulates all these relations, experience is at its most comprehensive.

The second object of political education is to teach the citizen the use and the risks of power, and of authority, which is legitimate power. And here the first lesson, conformably with the fundamental view of government which, as has been said, is the view of democracy, is that the power the citizen is concerned with *is* legitimate power, fiduciary power, power held in trust. The use of such power within the terms of the trust is what is meant by responsibility; the risk is irresponsibility or arbitrary use. Properly to grasp and understand this dependence of power upon authorisation, that is, in the democratic case, upon consent, and having understood to know how to enforce it is an indispensable qualification for the citizen, who is both agent and guarantor of the process of delegation. What it means to use power within the terms of a trust and what it means to abuse it can in part be learnt at second-hand and by reflection on the history of politics, but here again nothing teaches the lesson so well as actual contact with men in office and responsibility, nothing so well as acting with them in concrete measures and projects.

These lessons in power and actual possibilities, as well as the lessons of practical ingenuity in the devising of remedies and solutions, are all education in political capacity, which is the sense of what is expedient and possible and within the terms of the trust. Without this capacity men are children in politics, that is, in the organised common life of their society, children or anchorites. To the extent that they fail to develop political capacity they are governed but not self-governing. Nor is this all. In the process of exercising responsibility men fit themselves to what they learn; they grow to be at home in what they know. The world of politics and public affairs becomes intelligible and familiar to them. So they can stand up to strain and to the tides of national fortune with stability and fortitude – they develop a political resilience which is a national asset of supreme importance, absent in rigid autocracies, only present in those constitutions where political capacity is deeply and widely nourished by organs of local self-government.

It is undoubtedly one of the greatest virtues a state can possess that its structure, its operation, its policies should be intelligible to its citizens. To possess that virtue a state must deliberately and systematically associate the citizens in the general working of government at all levels. It must, however, do more than this. It must make its machinery such that it *can be* intelligible, that is, capable of being understood in terms of its principles and underlying conceptions. Any large development of arbitrary, that is, unprincipled, planless confusion in its methods or structure hinders the acquisition of understanding by its citizens. This danger is most liable to develop in democratic societies which are always more complicated and subtle in their working than autocratic societies. In this country, as will be said again later, it is in the field of intermediate government that the danger of unintelligibility is greatest. Unfortunately, this danger is at its greatest just when the need for intelligibility is most urgent, namely when the state is taking a larger part of the nation's life out of the field of private enterprise and putting it into government.

So far, the argument on the value of local representative constitutions has gone to show mainly the advantages which these institutions confer upon the citizen, though it is not really possible to divorce the citizen's advantage from the general national advantage. But there is one specific advantage to central government which arises from local government institutions. That is the contribution of local information. By itself this function of local government is not sufficient to support the whole weight of the defence of local institutions as it is sometimes made to do. Yet it is a function of very great importance. The services which are administered by local government vary from those in which there is absolute uniformity in application as between area and area to those in which there is the maximum diversity. In all the services where uniformity is not essential the recruitment of local knowledge for the purpose of suiting a service to its object and recipient is best done in the locality itself and by, or assisted by, those who live in the locality. Local knowledge can be acquired by persons sent to an area from the central departments to acquire it but the information so acquired is inferior to that which can be provided by those who have not only knowledge but interest, the local residents themselves. This is the intimate and first-hand knowledge which makes administration concrete and relevant. And it is needed not only for the successful administration of the local area itself but by the central government where, assembled, collated and reflected on, it provides the data for national domestic policy.

To sum up the foregoing considerations, local representative institutions are designed to meet the fundamental requirements of participation, discussion and education. They do provide, on the largest scale, an opportunity for the citizens to share in public decision and administration, they do provide the machinery of discussion and vote to elicit his consent, they do provide, in the only possible way, for the political education of the people. It is their additional merit that they also serve the administrative purposes of central government as channels of local intelligence and agents of local executive action. Theoretically speaking, the most important of these effects is that the citizen is given a chance to share in the political process, for that participation is the expression of his fundamental status as a member of his society. But practically speaking, the most important effect is the political education the citizen receives. It is this that makes his society intelligible to him, so that he knows it not only with his theoretical reason but also with his practical reason, that is to say, is able not only to entertain an understanding of it but is able to act in it.

8.7 From the *Report of the Royal Commission on Local Government in Greater London*, 1957-60, Cmnd. 1164 (3 October 1960), Chap. VI, 'Some General Considerations', pp. 61-3.

This chapter, almost a sideline to the main purposes of the reorganisation of London government, is about the only official statement that we have of the nature and purposes of local government set in the modern framework of party politics, paid officials, and complicated services which are increasingly required to conform to minimum national standards.

229. The main purpose of any government (and local government is no exception) is to do for people what a group of persons, elected according to law by a majority of the citizens but on election becoming representative of them all, conceive to be good within the limit of their legal powers. The assumption is that that good is something that can only be done, or can be better done, collectively. We are well aware that we have stated the main purpose of government in extremely summary terms. This subject has been one of the main matters of inquiry in the civilised world by thinkers and writers for at least 3,000 years and probably much longer. It is a very live intellectual and practical issue today. We do not offer

our definition as an original contribution to thought or as an accurate summary of the accumulated knowledge or wisdom of thousands of years of thought and experience. We know that it could easily be torn to pieces as a philosophic assertion. Some of our number have already gone through this process, to the edification of the rest of us. But we feel the need of some stated objective if we are to do justice to our subject, and we feel safe in taking our definition as a very rough and ready practical guide, remembering the modesty of our purpose and its intellectual limitations.

230. This collective good-doing by local authorities can be beneficial, but it can also become oppressive. It consists partially in stopping people from doing things (e.g. throwing slops into the street), partially in forcing people to do things (e.g. sending the children to school), and partially in making people pay for services rendered whether they individually want them or not. Subject, of course, to the control of the Courts, these powers may go far in the restriction of individual freedom. Old people may be removed from home, or children from the care of their parents. It is impossible to carry out the vast range of local government services at the present day without the employment of an army of 'professional' people technically skilled in their respective activities.

231. The actual interfering with people's lives will be done mainly by the professionals; planning of services involves much work by professionals, contacts between citizens and authorities about personal matters will be largely contacts with professionals, and the more impersonal services (e.g. refuse disposal) will be performed entirely by professionals. So good professionals are indispensable; and an important criterion of size and area is the need to attract good professionals. This in practice means that (1) there must be scope for enough of them, organised by function in proper ranks and grades: (2) there must be the possibility of paying adequate remuneration: (3) there must be enough work to give full scope for the use and development of their professional abilities: (4) the 'hierarchy' must be large enough to offer some scope for advancement or promotion, even if promotion at or near the top is usually achieved by moves from one authority to another: and (5) one must not have more posts of such importance as to require exceptional ability than one may hope to fill from the relatively small number of exceptional people upon whose existence one can safely reckon.

232. But to provide scope for a full professional life for officers

is not by itself enough. There must also be proper control of professional activities, since without such control (and the stimulation that comes with it when it is wisely exercised) the view of the expert can become too narrow. Professional enthusiasm can carry the expert beyond the bounds of good judgement, and 'Bumbledom' can be a real danger. Professional zeal on the other hand can run down and need renewing by the stimulus of frequently changing contact with the representatives of the 'consumer'. The desire of the experts (except the very good ones) to get as far away as possible from amateur control, administratively and even physically, is a factor to beware of.

233. The control of the expert by the amateur representing his fellow citizens is the key to the whole of our system of government. It is probably what people have at the back of their minds when they use the words 'democracy' or 'democratic'. It is therefore important that one should find the right sort of councillor, and another criterion of size, scope and area must be 'What is best to attract good councillors'? The best professionals readily agree that they do their best work when they can rely on the informed criticism, stimulation, counsel and support of good councillors. Good professionals and good councillors need one another. Neither is likely to remain good for long without the other. The public need both, working in proper balance, each pulling his full weight in his own sphere and respecting the sphere of the other.

234. The sphere of the councillor includes these activities:

(1) He must know his people, those who have elected him, their needs, desires and fears. He must also remember that he represents not only those of his constituents who have voted for him but also those who have voted against him. Even where, as so often happens, seats are uncontested, a councillor usually represents some who would have voted against him if they had had the chance.

(2) He must be prepared to learn enough to participate effectively in policy decisions carrying out 'compulsory' functions and in policy decisions as to the extent to which 'voluntary' functions should be undertaken.

(3) He must learn how to utilise professional advice in coming to policy decisions without becoming a slave to it.

(4) He must learn to keep away from interference in the administrative execution of policy, leaving case work to the professionals.

(5) He must maintain close enough relations with the officials and their work to enable him to form opinions as to their competence; to be satisfied that policy is being faithfully and competently carried out; and to ensure that matters involving policy are brought at the right time before the appropriate committee.

(6) He must, in the circumstances of today when politics almost universally pervade local government, act as an intelligent link between his party and the council, interpreting the one to the other.

235. It is unlikely that any form of local government will attract as councillors a very large number of people who will perform to perfection the duties mentioned in the foregoing paragraph; but a high standard of intelligence, experience, personality and character should be aimed at and can be legitimately hoped for. Indeed, in the course of our travels we have met many councillors, both men and women, amply qualified by these standards. Genuine devotion to the public good in a disinterested way exists as a motive in many instances and should be fostered. But ambition (often inextricably mixed with disinterested devotion) is a motive which can, and often does, make for efficiency in local government. Power and influence attained by long years of work, and the hope of attaining them, are things that can make both men and government tick, and ambition is not in itself a human motive to be disparaged or despised.

236. If we are to encourage a sufficient supply of councillors of ability, the scope and size of the authority on which they serve must be such that the arena in which their talents are displayed is wide enough to require (and indeed stimulate) their qualities and to satisfy their ambitions; there does seem to be some relationship between the size and scope of the authority and the capacity of the councillor and official attracted. On the other hand it is useless to create too many 'outsize' jobs when one knows there will not be enough 'outsize' people to fill them.

237. While therefore a certain minimum size and scope of authority seems to be needed to attract councillors and officers of the right calibre, to throw them together in the right atmosphere of responsibility and so to achieve a proper balance between the amateur and the expert, an authority of too great size and scope may tend to throw this balance out. This is for the opposite reason to that to be found in the too small authority; the balance may be thrown out if councillors have too little to do and also if they have too much.